MELE ON THE MAUNA

ACTIVIST ENCOUNTERS IN FOLKLORE AND ETHNOMUSICOLOGY
David A. McDonald, editor

MELE ON THE MAUNA

Perpetuating Genealogies of Hawaiian Musical Activism on Maunakea

—⁕—

JOSEPH KEOLA DONAGHY
with
Kaimana Barcarse • Kamanamaikalani Beamer • Richard Bissen •
Pua Case • Isaac Maluhia Castillo • David Aiona Chang •
Sandy Essman • Gerard Gonsalves • Hōkūlani Holt •
kuʻualoha hoʻomanawanui • Kainani Kahaunaele •
Starr Kealaheleokalani Kalāhiki • Lehua Kalima-Alvarez •
Kumu Micah Kamohoaliʻi • Zachary Alakaʻi Lum • Yuki Kaʻea Lyons •
Kalani Makekau-Whittaker • Kenneth Makuakāne •
Jamaica Heolimeleikalani Osorio • Andre Perez • Elizabeth "Bam" Post •
Punahele • Lee Ann Ānuenue Pūnua • Hāwane Rios •
Amy Kuʻuleialoha Stillman • Chad Takatsugi • Josh Tatofi •
Hinaleimoana Wong-Kalu • Noe Noe Wong-Wilson •
Jaz Kaiwikoʻo Yglesias

INDIANA UNIVERSITY PRESS

This book is a publication of

Indiana University Press
Office of Scholarly Publishing
Herman B Wells Library 350
1320 East 10th Street
Bloomington, Indiana 47405 USA

iupress.org

First Printing 2024

Library of Congress Cataloging-in-Publication Data

Names: Donaghy, Keola, author.
Title: Mele on the Mauna : perpetuating genealogies of Hawaiian musical
    activism on Maunakea / Joseph Keola Donaghy.
Other titles: Activist encounters in folklore and ethnomusicology.
Description: Bloomington : Indiana University Press, 2024. | Series:
    Activist encounters in folklore and ethnomusicology | Includes
    bibliographical references and index.
Identifiers: LCCN 2024013131 (print) | LCCN 2024013132 (ebook) | ISBN
    9780253070401 (hardback) | ISBN 9780253070395 (paperback) | ISBN
    9780253070418 (ebook)
Subjects: LCSH: Hawaiians—Hawaii—Music—History and criticism. |
    Music—Political aspects—Hawaii—Mauna Kea—History—21st century. |
    Protest music—Hawaii—Mauna Kea—21st century—History and criticism. |
    Activism—Hawaii—Mauna Kea. | Telescopes—Social aspects—Hawaii—Mauna
    Kea. | Mauna Kea (Hawaii) | BISAC: MUSIC / Ethnomusicology | POLITICAL
    SCIENCE / Political Process / Political Advocacy
Classification: LCC ML3560.H3 D66 2024 (print) | LCC ML3560.H3 (ebook) |
    DDC 781.5/9209691—dc23/eng/20240328
LC record available at https://lccn.loc.gov/2024013131
LC ebook record available at https://lccn.loc.gov/2024013132

This book is dedicated to the memories of my father, Joseph Norman Donaghy, and my sister, Barbara Ann Māpuana Sablas Enovijas, whose love and support of my aspirations knew no bounds.

CONTENTS

ACKNOWLEDGMENTS

I FIRST THANK MY WIFE, Marie Elena, for her love and patience as I embarked on this journey and many previous ones. I also thank my mother, June Donaghy, who encouraged and supported my travels in academia, music, and beyond. To my keiki (children), Francis Keith Palani Donaghy and Denyce Kathryn Mālia Donaghy, my daughter-in-law Sheena Tagalicod Donaghy, and my moʻopuna (grandchildren), Kayden Ryker Kaʻehukilihuneokalihikai Donaghy and Makenna Kamakahaniokamoaniʻalaopuna Anita Donaghy, whose silent presence hovered over me as I wrote, knowing that the outcome of the conflict on Maunakea will have an impact on them, their children, and our future descendants.

This book would not have been possible without the support, encouragement, and aloha of those whom I consider collaborators in, not simply contributors to, this work: Kaimana Barcarse, Kamanamaikalani Beamer, Richard Bissen, Pua Case, Isaac Maluhia Castillo, David Aiona Chang, Sandy Essman, Gerard Gonsalves, Hōkūlani Holt, kuʻualoha hoʻomanawanui, Kainani Kahaunaele, Starr Kealaheleokalani Kalāhiki, Lehua Kalima-Alvarez, Kumu Micah Kamohoaliʻi, Zachary Alakaʻi Lum, Yuki Kaʻea Lyons, Kalani Makekau-Whittaker, Kenneth Makuakāne, Jamaica Heolimeleikalani Osorio, Andre Perez, Elizabeth "Bam" Post, Punahele, Lee Ann Ānuenue Pūnua, Hāwane Rios, Amy Kuʻuleialoha Stillman, Chad Takatsugi, Josh Tatofi, Hinaleimoana Wong-Kalu, Noe Noe Wong-Wilson, and Jaz Kaiwikoʻo Yglesias. I also extend my gratitude to everyone with whom I conversed and corresponded during my research and writing.

I sincerely thank Dan Bendrups and Stephen Fox for their constant support and valuable advice while writing this book. Mahalo nui to Amy Kuʻuleialoha Stillman for having influenced my work since I first encountered her writings over twenty years ago and who has become a treasured friend, mentor, and colleague. Māuruuru to Alexander Mawyer for our conversations, opening my eyes to the place this work could find in broader Pacific contexts, and his detailed feedback on my attempts to achieve this goal. Mahalo piha to Manulani Aluli Meyer for being a mentor and hoa (friend) whose work continues to inspire and to kuʻualoha hoʻomanawanui and Emalani Case for their support, encouragement, and their maka uila (sharp eyes) in reviewing drafts of this work. Go raibh míle maith agat to Sean Williams for her prolific and inspiring writing and for graciously answering a litany of questions as I navigated this project. My endless gratitude to the anonymous reviewers who offered incredibly valuable feedback and enthusiastic support for this book's publication. Finally, my aloha and mahalo to Kenneth Makuakāne and Robin Leihuanani Kealiʻinohomoku, my musical collaborators on mele (songs or Hawaiian poetry) for the kiaʻi (protectors, guardians) and Maunakea. Mahalo for gifting your talents, your hā (breath), and much more.

In 2018, I was invited to participate in a unique gathering of scholars at the School for Advanced Research in Santa Fe, New Mexico. This gathering, which included Indigenous and non-Indigenous scholars from various fields, was organized to discuss and produce a book on indigenizing the field of Sound Studies. Raven Chacon, Robin Gray, Chad Hamill, Kevin Fellezs, Stephen Fox, Candice Hopkins, Sunaina Kale, Jessica Bissett Perea, John-Carlos Perea, Trevor Reed, Amber Ridington, and Renata Yazzie—mahalo piha to you all. While I did not contribute a chapter to this yet-unpublished text, the influence that our conversations at SAR had on the writing of this book is profound, and I will be eternally grateful for our time together.

Finally, to the legions of Aloha ʻĀina (those who embody and practice aloha ʻāina), those who shared their experiences with me and those I could not speak with but who were ka maka o ka ihe (the tip of the spear) at the Ala Kūpuna (path of the elders) and protected Maunakea from further desecration, your efforts are celebrated within the words of countless mele and in this book.

LANGUAGE USE AND PRESENTATION

IN THIS TEXT, I HONOR and use the most commonly accepted spellings for words in ʻōlelo Hawaiʻi (the Hawaiian language) and other Indigenous languages. I am grateful for the technologies that make the presentation of these languages possible in ways unachievable for speakers and language advocates in the recent past. The proper presentation of Indigenous language is essential because "Indigenous authors, editors, and publishers work to create titles that reflect the highest levels of understanding, and authentic meaningful stories, and truth telling" (Younging 2018). Therefore, following the lead of Younging and other scholars working in Indigenous languages, I do not italicize words in ʻōlelo Hawaiʻi and related Polynesian languages as they appear in the text, nor do I italicize any Indigenous language terms presented within except when found in writings I am quoting.

I use the ʻokina (glottal stop) and kahakō (macron) as they appear in the *Hawaiian-English Dictionary*, written by Mary Kawena Pukui and Dr. Samuel Elbert, and the *Māmaka Kaiao Modern Hawaiian Vocabulary Dictionary*, published by the Hale Kuamoʻo at the University of Hawaiʻi at Hilo. The ʻokina is the first character that appears in the word ʻokina—the single, open quotation mark that has been printed as a back tick or sometimes as a straight apostrophe in older texts. The ʻokina is sometimes called a diacritical mark, but it is not. It is a consonant in ʻōlelo Hawaiʻi, as it is heard and appears as consonants in other Polynesian languages. The kahakō is the short, horizontal line that appears over the letter *o* in kahakō. The kahakō is a diacritic mark that indicates increased duration and vocal emphasis of the vowel over which it appears. The presence or absence of either results in different meanings of otherwise similarly spelled words. For example, ahi is the Hawaiian word for "fire," and ʻahi (with ʻokina) is a type of tuna. Other examples are naʻu (the possessive "mine") and nāʻū (a native gardenia). For some words, the addition of the kahakō indicates plurality, such as kanaka/kānaka (person/people), wahine/wāhine (woman/women), and kupuna/kūpuna (elder/elders). These distinctions are important in this text and are reflected in the definitions that follow the first occurrence of Hawaiian words and in the glossary of terms.

I have chosen to minimize my use of "Hawaiian" and "Native Hawaiian" to designate those whose ancestors resided in Hawaiʻi before the arrival of Westerners. I instead use Kanaka ʻŌiwi or Kanaka Maoli when identifying an individual and Kānaka Maoli or Kānaka ʻŌiwi when referring to more than one such person. In addition, I disregard the terms "part-Hawaiian," "part-Native," and any other identifier that potentially diminishes someone's claim to indigeneity, as has been done in the past and continues to be done. Such terms reflect a foreign epistemology using blood quantum to divide Hawaiian and Indigenous communities and rarely, if ever, benefit those communities and their members (Kauanui 2008, Thornton 1997). I embrace Eva Marie Garroutte's (Cherokee) approach she calls "Radical Indigenism," which calls for scholars to "take philosophies of knowledge carried by Indigenous peoples seriously" (2003). Her approach includes individuals with a recognized affiliation within that community, of which blood quantum may be only one consideration.[1]

I do not pluralize Hawaiian words through English conventions, such as adding *s* or *es*. Instead, I have attempted to make meaning clear by carefully choosing words around the word. Perhaps the most common word the reader will encounter impacted by this decision is mele. Here is an example: "Many mele are composed." My use of "many" and "are" clearly indicate that mele is plural without the addition of the letter *s*.

It has become common practice to capitalize some Hawaiian nouns in particular contexts, such as locales and titles. In this text, I use lower-case aloha ʻāina when referring to the conceptualization of this historical and cultural value and capitalize Aloha ʻĀina when referring to those who embody its precepts. For the Ala Kūpuna (path of the ancestors), I capitalize the name of this area on the Maunakea Access Road; it has become the area's de facto place name and should be afforded this respect.

Finally, I provide a list of Hawaiian terms and a definition or explanation of their meanings at the back of this book. I restrict these definitions and explanations to those found in this book and do not include all possible glosses of words.

NOTE

1. Blood quantum is determined by calculating an individual's ancestry based on the number of ancestors of Kanaka ʻŌiwi, Native American, or First Nations ancestry. If an individual has one parent who has only Kanaka ʻŌiwi ancestry, and one parent of another race, they would be considered 50 percent Kanaka ʻŌiwi. The Hawaiʻi state government, the US government, and some tribes still use blood quantum in various ways. Beyond the legal ramifications of blood quantum to determine eligibility for Hawaiian homestead lands, the prevailing attitude in the Hawaiian community—supported by documented older practices—is that if an individual can establish a blood connection to a single Kanaka ʻŌiwi ancestor, they are considered Kanaka ʻŌiwi. This is also the criteria for students applying for admission to the private Kamehameha Schools.

'ŌLELO MUA (PREFACE)

THIS BOOK EXPLORES LOCAL, NATIONAL, and international reactions—political, social, personal, cultural, and musical—to plans to build a massive telescope near the summit of Maunakea (also known as Mauna A Wākea). Maunakea is often referred to as "the mauna" in everyday discourse, a reference I use throughout this book. It is a place of immeasurable spiritual, genealogical, and historical significance to Kānaka 'Ōiwi (the Hawaiian people). This book is the product of discussions and collaboration with—and support from—a group of individuals collectively known as kia'i (protectors) of Maunakea. They have taken numerous actions to protect Maunakea against settler-colonial aspirations and aggression.[1] Aggressors include all three branches of Hawai'i's state government and its many agencies, the administration of the University of Hawai'i (UH) and some of its employees, and an international consortium of private and government entities determined to construct the Thirty Meter Telescope (TMT) on Maunakea. The kia'i encampment at the base of the Maunakea Access Road leading to the summit of Maunakea was not simply the site of physical encounters; it was an ontological, epistemological, methodological, and sonic contact zone where kia'i, their supporters, musicians, law enforcement, the state government, UH administration, and individuals on both sides collided. I use "contact zone" here as defined by Mary Louise Pratt: "social spaces where cultures meet, clash, and grapple with each other, often in contexts of highly asymmetrical relations of power, such as colonialism, slavery, or their aftermaths as they are lived out in many parts of the world today" (1991).

The origins of the issues that led to confrontation on the Maunakea Access Road can be traced to the arrival of Westerners in Hawai'i in the late eighteenth century and the imposition of foreign concepts of land ownership and control in the nineteenth century. Kameʻeleihiwa (Kanaka ʻŌiwi) notes that "the Hawaiian system of Land tenure, which they [foreigners] found so oppressive, had served the Hawaiian people extremely well for centuries" (1992). These foreign concepts were compounded by Western capitalist notions of extracting value from natural resources and disregard for an Indigenous worldview emphasizing Kānaka ʻŌiwi's relationship to and dependence on the ʻāina (land, that which feeds). In 1848, colonizer-manipulated processes began to impose a system of private ownership known as the Māhele (division, to divide), which disproportionately favored non-Hawaiians and led to the mass dispossession of Hawaiian lands.

The ʻāina surrounding Maunakea are some of many lands confiscated following the illegal overthrow of the Kingdom of Hawaiʻi in 1893—an act in which the US military was complicit that violated treaties between the two countries and international law. The Provisional Government, established after the overthrow of the monarchy, claimed lands owned by Hawaiʻi's royals. Included were illicitly acquired lands totaling approximately 1.8 million acres, later ceded to the government of the United States as a condition of its annexation of Hawaiʻi in 1898. This land was turned over to the Territory of Hawaiʻi and eventually to the State of Hawaiʻi. The land was to be held in trust and benefit Kānaka ʻŌiwi, but the state government never adequately fulfilled that obligation.

The State of Hawaiʻi has approved and endorsed the construction of TMT through dubious procedures, decisions, and actions by state government-appointed boards and even more questionable court decisions by judges appointed by former governor David Ige and his predecessors. The University of Hawaiʻi administration has officially supported TMT's construction and sided with members of its astronomy faculty and of the broader science community who support it. They espouse the benefits of potential gains in understanding the history of the universe. The state and university also tout the economic benefits to the state and the island of Hawaiʻi of short-term job gains in construction and peripheral industries. However, both refuse to acknowledge and address legitimate historical claims by the Hawaiian community, which contests the state's control and the university's administration of Kānaka ʻŌiwi lands on Maunakea and elsewhere.

Kānaka ʻŌiwi scholars and legal experts continue to challenge the legality and legitimacy of the annexation of Hawaiʻi and the dispossession of these lands. One of the more contentious and pertinent manifestations of land issues concerning Maunakea centers on the confrontations on the Maunakea Access

Road. The state claims that it transferred the land from the Department of Hawaiian Home Lands (DHHL) to its Department of Transportation. However, research has demonstrated that the state has not fulfilled the requirements and obligations of that transfer, including financial remuneration to DHHL. As a result, questions about the state's authority over the road remain unresolved more than four years after the arrest of kiaʻi.

Much has been written about the encounters on Maunakea (E. Case 2021; Goodyear-Kaʻōpua 2017; Hoomanawanui et al. 2019; Kuwada and Revilla 2020; Kahanamoku et al. 2020; Maile 2021; J. H. Osorio 2021; Silva 2023). This work seeks to complement and extend prior writing by examining how the composing, performing, and recording of mele (Hawaiian language poetry or song) have played into defense of the mauna. This research began shortly after the arrest of kūpuna on July 17, 2019, when these kūpuna assumed defensive positions across the Maunakea Access Road and halted the movement of construction equipment to the TMT construction site near the summit. Research continues even as I prepare this book for publication. Most of its contents are based on recorded conversations with composers, musicians, kiaʻi, kūpuna, kumu (teachers), haumāna (students), scholars, and others who have participated in the efforts to defend Maunakea from desecration. This research also includes conversations with individuals who support the construction of the TMT and others who hold no strong opinions regarding its construction but participated in this research because of their specific expertise, experience, or connection to Maunakea. Most of these conversations occurred from late February through the summer of 2020, when many were isolated due to the COVID-19 pandemic. Additional conversations were held in 2021 and 2022. Due to COVID-19 mitigation protocols, I completed most interviews by phone or Zoom video conferencing. My sources also include the plethora of video evidence recorded on the mauna and shared through traditional and social media before, during, and after the arrests of kūpuna.

While my training in ethnomusicological and anthropological methods, theories, and techniques has informed the research and writing of this book, these influences are subordinate to my education and experiences as an educator in Hawaiian programs, practitioner of haku mele (Hawaiian language composition), musician, and advocate/activist for the perpetuation of ʻōlelo Hawaiʻi (the Hawaiian language). The epistemological underpinnings of this journey have been foundational to my studies, research, compositional practice, and teaching since I enrolled at Maui Community College (now University of Hawaiʻi Maui College or UHMC) in 1992. My contributions to perpetuating the Hawaiian language began after I accepted a kumu kōkua (teacher's assistant) position at the Pūnana Leo o Maui Hawaiian Language Preschool. They continued for the eighteen years I spent at the University of Hawai'i at Hilo as a student, staff member, and eventually faculty at what is now Ka Haka 'Ula O Ke'elikōlani College of Hawaiian Language.

The college's primary goal during my time there was and continues to be preparing individuals to contribute to the perpetuation of the Hawaiian language in many different fields and disciplines and in education, government, and the home, ultimately achieving the normalization of 'ōlelo Hawai'i in all aspects of life. The college's approaches are pragmatic; it seeks to benefit and provide resources for the Hawaiian language schools and community. I brought this approach and practice to UH Maui College when I was hired in 2012 and worked to strengthen the Hawaiian language and cultural knowledge and the Western academic rigor of the program. The philosophies and approaches I learned at UH Hilo and applied in my program at UHMC align with the relatively recent emergence of the subfield of applied ethnomusicology, which puts "ethnomusicological scholarship, knowledge, and understanding to practical use" (Titon 2015). Titon adds that applied ethnomusicology "is music-centered, but above all, the intervention is people-centered, for the understanding that drives it toward reciprocity is based on the collaborative partnerships that arise from ethnomusicological fieldwork" (2015).

The application of knowledge gained through ethnomusicological inquiry has been addressed since the 1960s through the writings of prominent ethnomusicologists like Alan Merriam and Mantle Hood. They acknowledge the benefits, if not the necessity, of applied ethnomusicological work. Loughran observes that some ethnomusicologists ignore applied work and the scholars who produce it and sometimes consider it dangerous or "meddling" (2008). While applied ethnomusicology is still a relatively young field attempting to define itself, its practioners have made valuable contributions to many of the communities in which its theories methodologies and ethics have been used. Timothy Rice has recently observed that "only in the last fifteen years or so have ethnomusicologists fully embraced a new set of themes concerning the relationship of music to the social, political, economic, and ecological crises facing so many people in today's world" (2014). Thankfully, this approach has become more the norm and less an aberration, and I hope this book contributes to the kinds of outcomes of which Rice speaks.

For several years, I chose to set aside many Western ideas and approaches to focus on the writings of Indigenous scholars—primarily Kānaka 'Ōiwi, Native Americans, First Nations, and scholars of other Pacific islands. While I found that focus incredibly valuable, two experiences caused me to reconsider this radical departure from Western writings. The first was revisiting interviews I conducted in 2008–2009 as part of my doctoral research. I came across a quote from Kīhei de Silva (Kanaka 'Ōiwi) about the practice of taking foreign ideas and making them relevant in a Hawaiian context. For example, he discusses John Kameaaloha Almeida's use of the image of a flower vase in his composition "Ka Nani A'o Hilo":

> I enjoy the fact that there are, when you get to the fourth verse, you've got a Western image, the vase, the kī'aha (vase), that there is this Hawaiian ability to draw in objects, whether Western or not, into the Hawaiian framework. It reminds me in a way of the train chants, or of the boat chants, or the horse riding chants, where there's this ability to appropriate something that is more often associated with another world and bring into and make it a part of the Hawaiian expression. To me, that's one element of Hawaiian creativity in composition. It is almost a little act of revenge, in a way. (de Silva quoted in Donaghy 2010)

Like most academic fields, ethnomusicology has been dominated by white male scholars since its beginnings as an academic disciple. I acknowledge and am grateful that female scholars, scholars of color, LGBTQ+ scholars, and others have made significant contributions to our field and contributed to my growth as a scholar. Indeed, there have been many, and their numbers and impact in the discipline are growing. Moreover, I need to acknowledge the impact that the work of many non-Indigenous ethnomusicologists has had on my development. I have sought to privilege the writings of Hawaiian, Pacific, and other Indigenous scholars and in doing so, encountered these impactful thoughts from Teresia Teaiwa (Banaban, I-Kiribati, African American): "Engaging broadly with theory and theorists of all kinds is part of exercising intellectual agency and is a necessary foundation for achieving fuller self-determination for Native and Indigenous, and Pacific peoples in the academy. Sovereign intellectuals have nothing to lose by admitting that some white men, white women, and white people are part of our genealogies of thinking, whether we like it or not. Some white men, white women, and white people, are ancestors we get to choose" (2014).

Because of the diverse ontologies, epistemologies, and methodologies at play in encounters on the mauna (mountain), I apply elements of Kanaka 'Ōiwi and other Indigenous and Western academic lenses to the events described within this book as needed and to the best of my ability. The work of Western academics has been and continues to be used to inflict tremendous epistemic and physical violence against Indigenous people and their lands. For example, in Hawaiʻi, foreign ideas about the authenticity of culture were used against the Kānaka ʻŌiwi community as it fought to end the bombing of the island of Kahoʻolawe by the US military in the 1970s. These encounters are discussed further in chapters 3 and 5.

In a special 2019 issue of the *Journal of the Society for American Music* titled "Music, Indigeneity, and Colonialism in the Americas," editors Jessica Bissett Perea (Denaʼina) and Gabriel Solis build on the work of Opaskwayak Cree Nation scholar Gregory Younging (2018). They provide a framework for music scholars "to grapple with coloniality and engage with moves toward decolonization and decoloniality in the contemporary academy in ways that do not exacerbate current and ongoing erasures of Indigenous Peoples' presence and agency" (Perea and Solis 2019). I have attempted to implement these moves and approaches in this book. Most visibly in alignment with Perea and Solis's recommendation, I indicate the tribal, national, or other affiliation of Indigenous individuals as can best be determined before their name or in parenthesis following it—as I have for Perea here—when their name first appears. I do not note affiliations for every individual mentioned in the text but do for those with whom I held conversations and whose words and thoughts are quoted or paraphrased.

As I am not a Kanaka ʻŌiwi but a settler-ally, my attempts to apply an ʻŌiwi lens are inherently imperfect. While I have moved within, studied, trained, and participated in various degrees in the Kanaka ʻŌiwi community on Maui and Hawaiʻi Island for nearly fifty years, my representations and analysis of events may lack the rigor and depth of someone possessing the eyes and embodied experiences of a Kanaka ʻŌiwi. For this reason, I have shared with and received feedback from each individual whose thoughts appear in this text to ensure the accuracy of quotes and my commentary and analysis. While my thoughts and writing have been scrutinized by many Kānaka ʻŌiwi, Indigenous, and non-Indigenous friends and colleagues, I alone am responsible for any shortcomings or inaccuracies in this book. I hope that they feel their contributions are accurately represented and that the actions of kiaʻi are honored.

Kū Kiaʻi Mauna!

NOTE

1. Mauna means "mountain." However, it became common to say "the mauna" to reference Maunakea or, more specifically, the kiaʻi encampment. "See you on the mauna" became a popular phrase among kiaʻi.

MELE ON THE MAUNA

HO'OLAUNA (INTRODUCTION)

MAUNAKEA IS A DORMANT VOLCANO located on Hawai'i Island, the southernmost, easternmost, and by far largest island in ko Hawai'i pae'āina (the Hawaiian archipelago).[1] The mauna is central to the cosmology of Kānaka 'Ōiwi (Native Hawaiians), the meeting place of Papahānaumoku and Wākea (Hawaiian deities) and the genealogical connection between 'āina (land, that which feeds) and Kānaka 'Ōiwi. Many Kānaka 'Ōiwi who live on the flanks of the mauna and others worldwide have significant genealogical connections to the region through generations of ancestors who lived there. The astronomy industry has coveted its summit region for over fifty years.[2] Some argue that it is the best location on Earth to observe the stars and universe. As a result, thirteen telescopes and their supporting facilities have been built near the summit— some currently in use and others in various states of disuse or disrepair.

The current and most pressing threat to the sanctity of Maunakea is the proposed construction of the Thirty Meter Telescope (TMT). An international consortium of universities and scientific agencies from the United States, Canada, China, and India designed the TMT and proposed its construction on Maunakea. The State of Hawai'i government has supported this endeavor for its economic benefits and potential advances in knowledge. The University of Hawai'i (UH) administration, whose board of regents is appointed by the governor, also supports its construction. If built on Maunakea, the TMT would cause irreparable environmental damage to more than six acres of land and devastate additional acreage for peripheral use in one of the largest remaining pristine environments on the summit. Construction would require digging into the mauna to a depth of at least thirty feet, and the structure housing the telescope would rise more than 180 feet above the summit's surface. The consortium has failed to provide a detailed plan to decommission the telescope once it has outlived its usefulness. Likewise, the state has failed in its responsibility to the mauna by not requiring the consortium to create such a plan.[3] The TMT is not alone among observatories on Maunakea in that respect.

The complicity of the University of Hawaiʻi—my employer—is worthy of significant analysis and critique. The university's administration and some faculty support the construction of TMT, and the university has chosen to disregard the voices of its faculty and staff who stand firm in their defense of Maunakea and oppose any further astronomical development on the mauna. These voices include many Kānaka ʻŌiwi faculty, staff, students, and allies. The university's faculty and other protectors have highlighted the university's history of mismanagement of Maunakea. Former governor David Ige and the university's administration have publicly acknowledged these failures. Sadly, the state and university have consistently prioritized the growth of astronomy on the mauna and the exploitation of its resources over the preservation mandated by its status as a conservation district deserving of the most protection possible. The state and university's leadership have apologized and promised to "do better" for the mountain. However, they have consistently refused to revoke the permits granted to TMT and return control of the mauna to its rightful stewards—Kānaka ʻŌiwi. Better stated, they refuse to give authority to those Kānaka ʻŌiwi willing to oppose the state and university's positions and their commercial and scientific aspirations for the mauna. Instead, the state government and university's leadership seek out and amplify the voices of those supporting their agenda—settlers and Kānaka ʻŌiwi alike. No compromise offered by the state and university has ever contained the only concession acceptable to kiaʻi: that TMT not be built.

To the university's credit, I am aware of no acts of retribution against faculty, staff, or students for their actions as kiaʻi. As Edward Said has written, "no one has ever devised a method for detaching the scholar from the circumstances of life, from the fact of his involvement [conscious or unconscious] with a class, a set of beliefs, a social position, or from the mere activity of being a member of a society" (2014). Ethnomusicologist Svanibor Pettan is even more expansive regarding the responsibilities of music scholars: "I would suggest that this volume does not question whether scholars should break away from a position of contemplative self-sufficiency, the so-called ivory tower of academia. Rather, I argue that they should do so efficiently, employing their knowledge and understanding of music in the broadest sense for the betterment of humanity" (2010). We can only hope that the university continues to resist the temptation to take punitive action against faculty and staff who publicly oppose its policies.[4]

Noe Noe Wong-Wilson after her arrest and the arrests of other kiaʻi, awaiting transportation to be processed by law enforcement on July 17, 2019. Photo credit: Kapulei Flores

On the other hand, it is difficult to overstate the role that Kānaka ʻŌiwi and settler-ally academics, staff, and students at the University of Hawaiʻi have played in the efforts to protect Maunakea. Members of the university community from every UH campus have visited the mauna and contributed to efforts to defend it, as have faculty, staff, and students of institutions of higher learning from around the world. In August 2019, I traveled to Maunakea with a large contingent from the University of Hawaiʻi's Pūkoʻa Council, which represents Hawaiian programs, faculty, students, and staff throughout the UH system. In September 2019, University of Hawaiʻi faculty members were instrumental in establishing Puʻuhuluhulu University—a place of learning created shortly after the arrests of kūpuna on July 17, 2019. It provided kiaʻi and supporters opportunities to continue their quest for knowledge, whether pursuing a degree or simply seeking personal enrichment and development. In addition, Maunakea's kiaʻi leadership called on the university community to extend online class offerings to Puʻuhuluhulu University students. Ultimately, UH faculty identified over two hundred University of Hawaiʻi classes students could attend from Maunakea. These included one of my online Hawaiian music classes and other music studies courses at UHMC. Some UH faculty members also taught classes from the mauna to students at home campuses and elsewhere using distance learning technologies.[5] Their presence and activism on the mauna inspired many who could not physically be there.

An alliance of organizations and individuals with strong ties to the mauna has attempted to prevent the telescope's construction through legal action and protest since the TMT consortium first applied for a permit to build the telescope. The TMT's board submitted a permit application to build TMT in Maunakea's conservation district to the State of Hawai'i Board of Land and Natural Resources (BLNR) in October 2010. In June 2015, law enforcement officers arrested a dozen kia'i for attempting to block access to Maunakea's summit and prevent construction vehicles from beginning their work. In late 2015, the Hawai'i State Supreme Court voided TMT's permit, ruling that the BLNR had acted inappropriately in granting a construction permit while the pending contested case hearing remained unresolved. Hearings and legal actions continued until November 2018, when the Hawai'i Supreme Court voted 4–1 to uphold TMT's permit and remove the final legal hurdle to the construction of TMT. State Supreme Court justice Michael Wilson, former chair of the BLNR, offered a sharp rebuke to his fellow justices in his minority opinion: "The BLNR substitutes a new standard for evaluating the impacts of proposed land uses, a standard that removes the protection to conservation land afforded by Hawai'i Administrative Rules § 13–5-30(c)(4). Using the fact that the resource has already suffered a substantial adverse impact, the BLNR concludes that further land uses could not be the cause of substantial adverse impact. Under this new principle of natural resource law, one of the most sacred resources of the Hawaiian culture loses its protection because it has previously undergone substantial impact from the prior development of telescopes" (Hawai'i State Judiciary 2018).

The State of Hawai'i—its departments, appointed boards, and judiciary—and the University of Hawai'i have deliberately and methodically conspired to weaken laws and administrative rules designed to protect critical, environmentally sensitive, culturally significant sites, often under the guise of public safety. They have controlled administrative processes to claim a legal higher ground of their own manufacture and justify their aspirations for development on Maunakea and other locations. The state judiciary has also facilitated the state's attempts to legitimize TMT's construction and trivialize legitimate legal challenges. David M. Forman, director of the Environmental Law Program at the William S. Richardson School of Law, University of Hawai'i at Mānoa, characterizes court decisions regarding various state agencies' failures to fulfill their duties to protect the environment and Maunakea specifically as both reoccurring cultural insensitivity and abdication of core judicial functions: "Rather than providing the 'badly needed judicial guidance' and 'enforcement by the court of these rights' as specifically called for by delegates to the 1978 constitutional convention, the court's recent decisions in several agency appeals suggest a willingness to abdicate the court's constitutional duties to the detriment of public trust [including natural and cultural] resources" (Forman 2020).

Public discourse regarding the protective actions on Maunakea is often framed around the misconception that Kānaka ʻŌiwi and their allies remained silent during the approval processes for TMT's construction and other astronomical activities on Maunakea. In fact, significant portions of the Hawaiian community and others have openly opposed construction on Maunakea since the first telescope was proposed.[6] TMT supporters have disingenuously claimed that earlier telescope projects proceeded without objection from the Kanaka ʻŌiwi community. In reality, opposition to these projects was grossly underreported, if reported in the media at all. Kumu Micah Kamohoaliʻi (Kanaka ʻŌiwi) is a kumu hula (master hula teacher), kapa maker (maker of kapa/tapa cloth), haku mele (composer of Hawaiian language poetry or song), and fashion designer from Waimea, a community on the northwest slope of Maunakea. He recalls a conversation with his grandfather, who related concerns among community members that there would be retribution if they opposed government plans to develop the first telescopes on Maunakea. However, he also notes that his family and others from the community always appeared at hearings to testify against the proposed expansion of facilities:

> When I was young, my mother used to take us to meetings where they decided to build this big extension to one of the telescopes. They want to build this and that. I was seven years old, chanting in meetings with many people. There were only Waimea families there, and we felt like the minority because we were against many things that had been built. So, I think just naturally when the TMT came we rolled into it because we've always been kiaʻi. We've always been defenders of Maunakea, mainly because we've always been taught that whatever you do to the top of the mountain falls down to us on the bottom of the mountain. That's our resource, that's our grounds, that's where our food and water comes from. (Kamohoaliʻi 2020)

Rhea Rollmann explains that such opposition—when Indigenous communities line up against development on sacred lands—is frequently ignored: "In actual fact, the 'protesters' in many cases have been raising their concerns for years and attempting to use existing structures to bring change. But media tends not to cover these things, and so the public remains unaware of simmer-ing tensions and opposition to projects until they explode, in the final instance, in protests and occupations" (2016). Rollman also notes how colonizer gov-ernments politicize language in their attempts to control the narrative during these conflicts, portraying Indigenous opponents and their allies as "protest-ers" and "activists." Such was the case on Maunakea, where kia'i objected to these terms, self-identifying as "protectors" and "defenders." Likewise, those standing in opposition to the building of the Dakota Access Pipeline (DAPL) referred to themselves as "water protectors." The Office of the Commissioner of Human Rights of the United Nations endorses these labels. It notes that "'human rights defender' is a term used to describe people who, individually or with others, act to promote or protect human rights in a peaceful manner. Human rights defenders are identified above all by what they do" (Office of the High Commissioner United Nations Human Rights n.d.). Maunakea's defenders were regularly referred to in media as protesters and activists by the government and media.[7]

In May 2019, Governor Ige announced that the construction of TMT would resume, and on July 10, 2019, he announced the date construction would re-sume: Monday, July 15, 2019. The state-imposed restrictions were designed to ensure the unimpeded transportation of the equipment necessary for construc-tion to begin. This announcement resulted in the mobilization and arrival of several groups and individuals who had opposed TMT's construction when initially proposed. Unbeknownst to Ige and state officials, a group of kia'i had assembled in Kona earlier to strategize their resistance to TMT's construc-tion. They scouted the area around Pu'uhuluhulu, a small cinder cone south of the Daniel K. Inouye Highway and directly across the highway from the Maunakea Access Road. Approximately thirty kia'i drove to Pu'uhuluhulu in the days before construction vehicles were to ascend the access road and reach the summit. Across the highway from the access road, they established a camp later declared a pu'uhonua (place of refuge) for the kia'i and supporters. Andre Perez (Kanaka 'Ōiwi) describes their preparations:

> We [Perez and Kaho'okahi Kanuha] drove up two weeks in advance, and we scouted. We hiked up to Pu'uhuluhulu, took some photos, and—believe it or not—I saw that camp. When I was on Pu'uhuluhulu, looking down at the empty parking lot two weeks in advance, I envisioned that camp. I looked across, and I could see the old Saddle Road, that remnant where the kūpuna camp was; there was a remnant of the old highway. I could see there's lots of space for parking there. I could look at the corners of Pu'uhuluhulu and see

there's enough space to hold like three hundred people in this camp. We'll be lucky if we get one hundred fifty, but anyway, at the very last moment, one of our friends was pushing us—we gotta have some kind of context to what we were calling for. (2020)

The number of kiaʻi rose for several days before July 15, 2019, as did the number of law enforcement officers from the state's Division of Conservation and Resources Enforcement (DOECARE) and the Hawaiʻi County Police Department. As a result of actions taken by law enforcement on July 15, 2019, several kūpuna (elders) established what became known as the kūpuna line—a row of lawn chairs, beach chairs, and wheelchairs covered by tents that effectively blocked the Maunakea Access Road.[8] Each kūpuna had a younger kiaʻi to see to their needs, as singer and kiaʻi Starr Kealaheleokalani Kalāhiki (Kanaka ʻŌiwi) explains: "I was kākoʻo [support person] to Aunty Maxine Kahaʻulelio. So if you see the videos, I am literally singing lyrics to songs at her back while she's going off because I'm just in prayer for her blood pressure. I got her food. But then, when the switch out happened, from DLNR (Department of Land and Natural Resources) to SWAT, I heard her going off again.[9] My weapon and shield is mele; I'm literally just singing and praying at her back" (2022).[10]

With no other means to transport equipment to the summit, officials attempted to negotiate with the kiaʻi. Ultimately, the state offered no solution that included abandoning the planned construction of TMT—the only solution acceptable to the kiaʻi.

On the morning of Wednesday, July 17, 2020, law enforcement officials approached the kūpuna line and explained that if the kūpuna refused to move, they would be arrested. After the they refused to clear the roadway, officers began to arrest them. While no kūpuna resisted arrest, law enforcement officers carried some kūpuna; others were pushed to vans in their wheelchairs, while some walked to the vans with law enforcement officers. Several kūpuna required medical attention before being transported to an area at a lower elevation, where officers processed their arrests. Thirty-eight kūpuna were arrested until just after noon, when officers suddenly ceased to make arrests and retreated to a location below the kiaʻi encampment.[11] By this time, officers had processed several kūpuna at a location miles below the access road. Some kūpuna were released from custody and returned to the encampment and their places in the kūpuna line. After several tense hours and realizing that the heavy and slow-moving construction vehicles would be unable to reach the summit before sundown, many officers left the encampment area. The kiaʻi and their supporters celebrated the victory with speeches, songs, and dances.

It was not until later that most kiaʻi became aware of the magnitude of their audience. Supporters throughout the state and worldwide had watched the proceedings via the live streams of supporting organizations such as Kākoʻo Haleakalā and Kanaeokana, individuals using cell phones, and representatives of mainstream media outlets. The celebration was shared by thousands via digital devices—devices whose significance would become evident and grow in the coming months. In addition, support for the kiaʻi rolled in from around the world in donations of money, clothing, equipment, food, and supplies. The number of kiaʻi and supporters on the mauna continued to grow, as did tensions when even more law enforcement officers arrived armed with military-grade vehicles, weapons, and other equipment.

Tensions grew and ebbed in the ensuing months. Most of the law enforcement presence withdrew with the arrival of winter weather, and the population of the kiaʻi encampment also diminished. In late March 2020, kiaʻi removed the encampment's facilities. Most withdrew from the site due to concerns over the COVID-19 pandemic. The movement's leaders asked the individual campers who remained to depart for their health and safety, and only a handful of kiaʻi remained on the access road. The kiaʻi who left Maunakea did so with a clear message to the state government and TMT officials: we are leaving, but we will return at any indication that the state is again attempting to move equipment to the summit to begin construction of TMT.

The events described in this chapter provide a brief chronology and description of the events that unfolded and led to confrontations on the Maunakea Access Road. In later chapters, significant events that occurred before, during, and after this time are described in greater detail.

CHAPTER CONTENTS

Chapter 1 identifies and explores four major themes that recur throughout this text: (1) soundscapes, hearing, and listening, (2) musicking, (3) Kānaka ʻŌiwi connections to Pacific and other Indigenous peoples, and (4) haku mele (Hawaiian poetic composition). These ideas' density and frequent appearance throughout this book require that they be discussed in depth to prepare the reader.

Chapter 2 examines the concepts of listening, hearing, sound, and silence and their role in Maunakea's soundscape, including the strategic use of silence by the mauna's protectors. The soundscape of Maunakea included the energy-filled and resounding gathering on August 11, 2019, when thousands of Maunakea supporters assembled on the Ala Kūpuna to perform a medley including

"Kū Haʻaheo e Kuʻu Hawaiʻi" and "All Hawaiʻi Stand Together."[12] In contrast, there were periods of relative silence during the nights and at other times when kiaʻi leadership strategically and effectively invoked silence. I differentiate hearing and listening and their implications, discussing the significance of silence in Hawaiian and Fijian cultures and its strategic use in Indigenous protective actions in Hawaiʻi and Aotearoa.

Chapter 3 examines the significance of genealogical connections between ʻāina and Kānaka ʻŌiwi. This connection was foundational for Kānaka ʻŌiwi as they identified or defined their roles in the movement. Many mele composed for the mauna and kiaʻi are imbued with the concept of aloha ʻāina (love of land/ patriotism), reflecting the Kānaka ʻŌiwi's foundational and genealogical connection to Maunakea and ʻāina more generally. I also examine two frequently heard terms on the mauna—aloha ʻāina and aloha ʻāina ʻoiaʻiʻo—and explore their historical and modern contexts, interpretations, implications, and place in musical composition. I apply a concept coined by Noenoe Silva, moʻokūʻauhau consciousness, and consider how the actions of kiaʻi reflected this conceptualization. Finally, I examine two songs containing expressions of aloha ʻāina: Kainani Kahaunaele's (Kanaka ʻŌiwi) mele entitled "Aloha ʻĀina ʻOiaʻiʻo" and Josh Tatofi's (Tongan) "For the Lāhui."

Chapter 4 examines the term and concept of kapu aloha—one of the most potent expressions associated with the Maunakea movement. Most of the composers of mele written during the confrontations over Maunakea eschewed any display of anger or animosity toward pro-TMT individuals or groups in their lyrics. I have seen few examples of criticisms—and no personal attacks—of TMT supporters or entities in the Hawaiian language compositions I have examined. I argue that the practice of kapu aloha on Maunakea inspired an analog in the compositional practice of haku mele, who adopted the same approach. Their goal was not to antagonize or make enemies of law enforcement and pro-TMT individuals—it was to demonstrate the power of kapu aloha and deliver its message of aloha ʻāina in a musical form. I support this argument by analyzing a mele for Maunakea and its expression of kapu aloha: Ānuenue Pūnua's (Kanaka ʻŌiwi) "Lei Ana Maunakea I Ka ʻOhu."

Chapter 5 examines the historical and modern contexts of conflict and music in Hawaiʻi, particularly on Maunakea, and draws on other examples from the Pacific. First, I discuss the events of July 15, 2019—two days before the arrests of kūpuna. On this day, a group of kiaʻi chained themselves to a cattle guard grate that crosses the Maunakea Access Road, blocking the only access road to the summit of Maunakea. I examine the role of social and traditional media on the mauna and in sharing the music composed, performed, and recorded for the mauna. Finally, I discuss how the state government has imposed its own narrow, self-serving, and ethnocentric view of authenticity and sacredness to deny the historical and genealogical basis for Kānaka ʻŌiwi assertions of the mauna's sacredness.

Chapter 6 discusses the roles that anthems and songs of an anthemic nature play in society, including the four different compositions that have served as anthems for Hawaiʻi. It considers how nations, states, and social movements have created, adapted, changed, and used anthems in Hawaiʻi, French Polynesia, and Aotearoa. This chapter also examines the origins of the mele "Kū Haʻaheo e Kuʻu Hawaiʻi," considering the composer's description of her compositional process, how kiaʻi recontextualized the composition for protective actions, and how it reached an anthemic status. Finally, I examine the most potent and resounding example of musical defiance on the mauna, which occurred on August 11, 2019, at eleven o'clock in the morning. This event, Jam4Maunakea, was live streamed worldwide from the encampment and is still viewable on YouTube.

NOTES

1. All Hawaiian translations and definitions are my own unless otherwise specified.

2. I have observed that those working in the field of astronomy are often referred to or self-identify as the "astronomy community." In fact, they are members of a multi-billion dollar industry that receives significant financial support, legislative favors, preferential judicial treatment, and even logistical support—such as law enforcement on Maunakea—from the government in pursuit of their goals. For these reasons, I choose to refer to it as the "astronomy industry."

3. The failure to maintain and properly dismantle astronomical facilities has been an issue on Maunakea for decades. Several telescopes have fallen into disuse and disrepair with no action taken by the organizations that constructed them, the university, or the state until tensions came to a head because of the proposed construction of TMT.

4. University of Hawaiʻi administrators initially questioned whether or not faculty members would be allowed to teach classes from Puʻuhuluhulu or offer courses online to students on the mauna. They eventually agreed to allow students on the mauna to attend and receive credit for classes provided the terms and outcomes of the course syllabi were achieved (Lovell 2019).

5. At the time of this writing, the list of 237 classes offered to students at Puʻuhuluhulu in fall 2019 is still accessible on Google Docs: https://docs

.google.com/spreadsheets/u/2/d/15MVemAQDq_-qszdrM5lduweDeo4CHV
-69FpOo7yWZLE/htmlview.

6. A collection of these older testimonies was published in ʻŌiwi, volume 3 (2005), and more recent testimony will be published in the forthcoming issue ʻŌiwi, volume 5, "Mana Maunakea."

7. Several individuals with whom I spoke noted, as did I, that the media practice of labeling kiaʻi as "protesters" and "activists" shifted slightly, with some later mainstream media reports noting that the kiaʻi preferred to be identified as "protectors" or "defenders." These terms were used more frequently in media reports as the standoff continued.

8. The kūpuna line subsequently became known as the Ala Kūpuna (the path of the elders).

9. The Deparment of Land and Natural Resources (DLNR) is the state agency that oversees state land. The Board of Land and Natural Resources (BLNR) is comprised of community members appointed by the governor to review submissions made by staff and the general public. The BLNR chair is the executive head of the DLNR.

10. Kalāhiki had explained to me earlier that Kahaʻulelio was the one kūpuna who seemed to be free to say anything she wished and had earlier "gone off" at law enforcement officers (2022).

11. The kūpuna arrested were later identified as James Albertini, Sharol Awai, Tomas Belsky, Marie Alohalani Brown, Gene Burke, Daycia-Dee Chun, Richard L. Deleon, Alika Desha, William K. Freitas, Patricia Green, Desmond Haumea, Flora Hookano, Kelii Ioane, Maxine Kahaʻulelio, Ana Kahoʻopiʻi, Mahea Kalima, Kaliko Lehua Kanaele, Pualani Kanahele, Deborah Lee, Donna Leong, Daniel Li, Carmen Lindsey, Linda Leilani Lindsey-Kaʻapuni, Abel Lui, Liko-O-Kalani Martin, James Naniʻole, Luana Neff, Deena Oana-Hurwitz, Edleen Peleiholani, Renee Price, Haloley Reese, Walter Ritte, Loretta Ritte, Raynette Robinson, Damian Trask, Mililani Trask, John Turalde, and Noe Noe Wong-Wilson (Star-Advertiser Staff 2022).

12. While this mele is most commonly called "All Hawaiʻi Stand Together"—the title used in the YouTube video of the event discussed here—it appears with the title "Hawaiʻi Loa, Kūlike Kākou" on Martin's personal website: https://www.likomartin.org/_files/ugd/5ff77e_bc8554ec8a2946c79eb80271ae17eb97.pdf.

ONE

—m—

I PA'A MAILA KE KAHUA

So That the Foundation Will Be Firm

FOUR SIGNIFICANT THEMES APPEAR THROUGHOUT this text: (1) sound-scapes, hearing, and listening, (2) musicking, (3) the connection of Kānaka 'Ōiwi to other Pacific and Indigenous peoples, and (4) haku mele (Hawaiian poetic composition). The density of these ideas and their appearance throughout this book require that they be discussed in depth to prepare the reader. The title of this chapter is borrowed from a line in Larry Kimura's (Kanaka 'Ōiwi) mele "Ke Au Hawai'i." In this mele, he calls to the ali'i (chiefs) of old to inspire the current generations of Kānaka 'Ōiwi to build a firm foundation on which they may "I mua a loa'a ka lei o ka lanakila" (move forward and gain the lei of victory).

I did not plan to write around these themes when conversing with kia'i, musicians, composers, and others about music's role on the mauna—the themes emerged organically while examining the transcripts of those conversations, as did the other ideas found in these chapters. I have been a student of haku mele since the 1990s; indeed, it was the subject of my master's and doctoral research. My interest in sound studies and soundscapes began during my collaboration with Indigenous scholars and others working in Indigenous music at the School for Advanced Research (SAR) in Santa Fe, New Mexico, in 2018. Our discussions broadened my gaze beyond musical processes, and I embraced other sonic and aural approaches to scholarship.[1] Finally, my participation in several Pacific Island studies courses at UH Mānoa in 2021 and 2022 caused me to consider the connections of this work to other places in Oceania that remain under the influence—if not overt control—of colonial powers. I hope this chapter provides a solid foundation for the reader to connect to later chapters and subjects and that the inclusion of these ideas moves this work beyond the realm of ethnomusicological query.

SOUNDSCAPES, HEARING, AND LISTENING

Ari Kelman credits Canadian composer Murray Schafer with publishing the first fully developed text to address the idea of soundscapes and includes Schafer's broad definition of a soundscape as "any aural area of study" (2010). Kelman notes that Schafer is frequently cited in works that utilize the term "soundscape" and criticizes scholars who embrace this broad definition but fail to engage with Schafer's writing more deeply: "Those who do engage with his ideas often end up totally reworking Schafer's term from the inside out to suit their own needs" (2010). Schafer laments the intrusion of human-made sounds on those of the natural world and the resulting disharmony. Such sounds have been labeled "the sounds of the Anthropocene" (Edgeworth et al. 2014).

During the months that kiaʻi occupied the Ala Kūpuna, the mauna provided a rich and varied soundscape accessible to everyone who visited it, giving each individual a significant and unique aural experience. Each experience would depend on the duration and timing of the individual's visit, their level of engagement with the soundscape, and the variety of activities they participated in or witnessed on the mauna. Indeed, the mauna did not feature a single, unified soundscape, but rather many different soundscapes, as the sounds of each location would change many times a day. Besides performances on the Ala Kūpuna, there were more private, intimate sites of musicking both on and off the mauna. These ranged from kiaʻi holding informal jam sessions in their tents to Puna resident Ikaika Marzo live streaming songs to a worldwide audience from wherever he was and bringing attention to the mauna. While the theme of the mauna as a soundscape is present throughout this book, it is most heavily discussed in chapter 2.

Humans are capable of a broad spectrum of aural engagement ranging from hearing, a passive experience in which the individual experiences sound with little or no conscious effort, to listening, which requires some effort or focus. Listening involves a range of intentionalities. In some cases, we may listen for specific sounds within a broader soundscape, such as a musical performance or even a particular instrument or voice within a performance. In other circumstances, we may focus on the entirety of the soundscape, or at least as much of it as our mental facilities allow us to absorb and process. As Barry Truax notes: "We should recall that whereas hearing can be regarded as a somewhat passive ability that seems to work with or without conscious effort, listening implies an active role involving different levels of attention—'listening for,' not just 'listening to.' The level of attention may be casual and distracted, or in a state of readiness, and its scope may be global [a general 'scan' of the entire environment] or focused on a particular source to the exclusion of other sounds. However, in each case, listening can be consciously controlled" (2001).

Hearing and listening are far more than physiological phenomena. They are moral acts with cultural underpinnings that help define the responsibility to act on what one hears: "Listening, it seems to me, is an act of attention, a willingness to focus on the *other*, to heed both their presence and their communication. It is only a necessary precursor to understanding. All women and adolescents know what it is to be *listened to* without there being any consequent understanding. Understanding, on the other hand, is an act of *empathetic comprehension*, a willing searching after the other's intention and message" (Husband 2009).

Perhaps the most attentive form of listening is what composer and music scholar Pauline Oliveros identifies as "deep listening." She defines deep listening as "a practice intended to heighten and expand the consciousness of sound in as many dimensions of awareness and attentional dynamics as humanly possible" (2005). Anthropologist and ethnomusicologist Steven Feld has done more than research and write about the soundscape of the Kaluli people of Basavi, Papua New Guinea—he recorded twenty-four hours of their soundscape. He edited the audio into a continuous, one-hour recording titled "Voices of the Forest," which takes the listener through this aural experience: "Kaluli people think of themselves as the voices in the forest. They sing with birds, insects, water. And when Kaluli sing with them, they sing like them. Nature is music to Kaluli ears. And Kaluli music is naturally part of the surrounding soundscape. . . . People's voices layer like the trees of the forest canopy. Sounds of drums or axes arch up and out like tumbling waterfalls into swirling waterpools. That's what you'll hear in these recordings" (Feld 1991).

I have listened to this recording many times, and each listening reveals sounds I had not previously heard. While one could certainly listen to the recording while working or not intently for any reason, the focus needed to truly embrace the aural experience and feel the soundscape requires deep listening and conscious exclusion of other activities or distractions. Even as I sit in my office listening to it once again, I find myself distracted by external sounds— our building's air conditioning, the sound of colleagues walking and conversing at the far end of the hallway that connects our offices and classrooms, and the squeaking of my chair as I shift my weight. My desire to listen profoundly compels me to remove as many of these other sounds as possible and hear every detail, though I realize I never will.

Feld's work and my own experience of listening to his recordings are not without issues or reasons for concern. While Feld (or any other non-Indigenous researcher) may occupy and listen to the same soundscape as the Kaluli, our listening and perception of what we hear are influenced by our prior experiences. Likewise, my perceptions of his recording differ from Feld's as I listen to it through headphones or speakers while he experienced it in the environment, albeit with an ear that was not raised or trained in that soundscape.

Dylan Robinson (Stó:lō) has coined the term "hungry listening" by combining two Halqʼeméylem words that fluent Halqʼeméylem speakers would not likely bring together. Placed together, the words identify "settler colonial forms of perception": "'Hungry listening' is derived from Halqʼeméylem words: shxwelítemelh [the adjective for settler or white person's methods/things] and xwélalà:m [the word for listening]. shxwelítemelh comes from the word xwelítem [white settler] and more precisely means 'starving person.' . . . I use shxwelítemelh to refer to a form of perception: 'a settler's starving orientation'" (2020).

While Robinson's work focuses on colonizer and settler listening habits, it applies to researchers such as Feld and me, who arrive at our soundscapes to conduct research with hungry ears. While Feld has benefited from extensive time among the Kaluli and I from decades of work in the Hawaiian community, neither of us possesses the ears of one raised in these soundscapes, nor have we acquired the cultural positionality gained through a lifetime of being nurtured in them. Feld describes the ability of Kaluli children to perceive and interpret what, to Feld, were imperceptive aural cues in the Bosavi forest: "It is only a matter of seconds before a twelve-year-old Bosavi kid can identify a bird by sound, describe its location in the forest density, and tell a good bit more about the location of its food, nests, and partners" (1991).

In Hawaiʻi, the ability to observe and—perhaps most importantly—listen and retain knowledge was a daily life skill crucial to the transmission and perpetuation of knowledge: "Children and students were trained to listen carefully, hoʻolohe, an obvious necessity in an oral culture. The wide range of verbal and literary activities mentioned above provided an ideal learning environment. Moreover, just like observation, attentive listening was a lifelong virtue" (Charlot 2005).

Hawaiian scholar and cultural practitioner Mary Kawena Pukui (Kanaka ʻŌiwi) describes how she learned many chants simply by listening to her grandmother chant at night. Prayers, legends, and genealogy were handed down in the oli (chanted) performance: "I used to wake up at night, and hear Grandmother chanting. And so I memorized the chants" (Pukui 1972).

Retired judge and current Maui mayor Richard Bissen (Kanaka ʻŌiwi) was not personally involved in adjudicating cases involving the arrest of kiaʻi on Maunakea because Hawaiʻi Island was not part of his jurisdiction. However, he was aware of activities on the mauna, including the arrest of kūpuna.[2] Bissen learned to play music as early as the fourth grade but notes that his family was largely unaware of his musical abilities until he returned from college. While he did receive some mentoring from an uncle, he attributes most of his early musical development to attentive listening: "Growing up, I just heard the same songs on the same albums on our family's record player over and over and over again. No radio commercial breaks and no random selections—just the same songs. And I think when you are away from Hawaiʻi, you tend to miss home so you pay more attention to the words and the music. So I learned a lot of songs through that method of repetition and listening" (Bissen 2022).

Gabby Pahinui (Kanaka ʻŌiwi) was one of the most revered performers of kīkā kī hōʻalu (Hawaiian slack key guitar) and singers of the twentieth century. His sons, Cyril, Martin, and James "Bla" Pahinui, also became influential performers whose careers started in the early years of the Second Hawaiian Renaissance.[3] Pahinui relates how attentive listening helped with his development as a musician: "See, at a certain time of the day, mainly the evening, the musicians would go around serenading at Kahaluu or Waikiki. Then they would always end up at the Halekulani Hotel where there would be a bun and some coffee. This guy, he sees me, a kid hanging around the streets. He says, 'Hey boy! Sit down here.' He was playing at the Hoffman Cafe. So, all I do was listen . . . as I got to know him. He says, 'Can you play guitars?' So I say, 'Sure,' and we fool around, whatever. But I'm still listening" (Pahinui in Burlingame and Kasher 1978).

MUSICKING ON THE MAUNA

The impact of musical activity on Maunakea, the kiaʻi, the movement to protect the mauna, and its worldwide audience is immeasurable. These activities exemplify what Christopher Small calls musicking: "to take part, in any capacity, in a musical performance" (2011). He proposes that music is a verb, not a noun, and that those actively involved in music production, the audience and consumers of musical works, and anyone included in these processes is engaged in musicking. Examples include but are not limited to ticket agents, stagehands, valets, janitorial staff, agents, and others involved in the logistics

Kalani Makekau-Whittaker, aka "MC Mauna," on the Ala Kūpuna. Photo credit:
Damon Tucker

of a musical performance. On the mauna, musickers included hula performers
and individuals who supplied, set up, and operated amplification systems for
musical performances and announcements, erected tents that provided shade
from the sun, prepared meals and washed dishes, made lei and other gifts, and
performed a myriad of mundane but essential tasks.

One of the better-known musickers, who was not a singer or musician, was
Kalani Makekau-Whittaker (Kanaka ʻŌiwi)—a highly competent Hawaiian
language speaker and educator drafted to make public service announcements
during breaks in the music on the Ala Kūpuna. He also operated the sound system when the regular engineer was not present. He quickly earned the moniker
"MC Mauna" and eventually became the unofficial emcee for many musical
events and programs held at the kiaʻi encampment. He describes his evolution from roadie to MC Mauna: "Pua Case was on the mic, and I think Kahele
[Dukelow] was carrying around the speaker for her, and I just told her, 'I'll do
that,' because she [Dukelow] had so many things she was trying to coordinate.
I said, 'I'll do that; I can be speaker boy.' I got the nickname [MC Mauna] and
started talking more on the mic. I just started since she [Case] couldn't talk all
the time" (Makekau-Whittaker 2020).

Makekau-Whittaker's role served many functions, as Daniel Gelo describes in his writing about the role of emcees at southern Plains Indian powwows. He describes those who perform this function as "distinctive verbal artists and agents in the continuing negotiation of Indian identity" whose "formal announcements and jovial patter construct an overtly 'Indian' space and time while fostering discourse on ethnicity" (Gelo 1999). Makekau-Whittaker has acknowledged this role, believing that the times that he spoke 'ōlelo Hawai'i to those in attendance created "a more Hawaiian environment": "I believe there was an unspoken unified goal of expressing our most authentic selves in that sacred space and to me [Hawaiian] language is a huge part of that. That was one of my contributions to that expression" (2023).[4]

Musicking occurred during the days leading up to the arrest of kūpuna on July 17, 2019. In the early morning hours of July 15, 2019, before construction vehicles were to ascend the road to Maunakea's summit, several kia'i chained themselves to the metal road grate of a cattle guard that crossed the access road to prevent vehicles and equipment from passing. During the following contentious hours, those chained to the grate and others offered music for spiritual support and nourishment (these events are described in greater detail in chap. 5). Music was also performed, in some circumstances, during the arrests of kūpuna.

The list of local, national, and international celebrities who traveled to and performed at the kia'i encampment is notable. Among the well-known Hawai'i music industry music professionals on the mauna were Natalie and 'Iolani Kamau'u, Josh Tatofi, Brother Noland (Conjugacion), Robi Kahakalau, Ekolu, Keauhou, Waipuna, Nāpua Greig, and many others. Kainani Kahaunaele is a multiple Nā Hōkū Hanohano Award-winning Hawaiian recording artist and Hawaiian language and music lecturer at Ka Haka 'Ula O Ke'elikōlani College of Hawaiian Language at UH Hilo. She and her children were fixtures on the mauna before, during, and after the arrest of kūpuna. She performed music herself and with Hawai'i Island musicians Brandon Nakano and Emma Coloma-Nakano, forming a de facto house band for visiting performers who needed musical accompaniment. In addition, Kahaunaele and her children supported the kia'i encampment by working in its kitchen, picking up rubbish, and fulfilling any task necessary. She also brought her UH Hilo Hawaiian language students to the encampment to experience life "on the mauna" firsthand.

Famous Hawaiian music performers and performers of other genres of music were not the only ones to travel to and perform on the mauna. Some individuals were less widely known working musicians, and others were not professional musicians but could offer a song and voice to entertain the kia'i. Anyone who sought to express themself musically and share their thoughts

Nā Leo Nahenahe O
Puʻuhuluhulu: Kaniaulono
Hāpai, Wehilei Lim-Ryder,
Wēkiu Lim-Ryder, Jtaime
Nakano, Kūaea Hāpai,
Koʻiahi Pūnua, Ānuenue
Pūnua. Photo credit:
Kainani Kahaunaele
(permission to use photo of
keiki granted by parents)

and talents through mele was encouraged to do so. Kahaunaele describes how keiki (children) of kiaʻi—including her son and two daughters—entertained kūpuna, kiaʻi, and visitors to the encampment to lift spirits.

> One of my favorite developments of that time was the serving of music by our children. As children of musicians, they really had no choice but to participate. They came together with some strengths in vocals, harmonies, instrumentation, hula, oli [chant], and a pretty good collective mele catalog. With lots of loving encouragement and direction from their parents, they started to sing together on the mics. They found a nice blend and eventually started rehearsing, leading our mele sessions and giving their parents a chance to sing back-up or hula. The kūpuna loved it. We parents loved it. Our children started to love it too, and they ended up forming a band called *Nā Leo o Puʻuhuluhulu*. (2020a)

National and international recording artists such as Steel Pulse, Damian Marley, and Hawaiʻi-born Jack Johnson traveled to Maunakea to perform and lend their support and voices to the movement. Actors Dwayne "The Rock"

Johnson and Jason Momoa, both with strong Hawai'i roots, traveled to the mauna to voice their support for the kia'i. Momoa is also Kanaka 'Ōiwi. Both shared their activities on the mauna with sizable audiences via their social media accounts and in the press. Janet Jackson supported the kia'i at her concert at the Blaisdell Center in Honolulu on November 19, 2019. During the concert, she made a public statement supporting the kia'i and displayed the hand gesture that supporters of the movement have widely used. This gesture is often followed by the exhortation "Kū kia'i mauna!" (stand in defense of the mountain!) (KITV 4 Web Staff 2019). The following chapters describe many other acts of musicking by people performing different roles on the mauna and elsewhere.

Andre Perez was one of the organizers of the activities that preceded the occupation of the Maunakea Access Road and one of acknowledged kia'i leaders throughout the standoffs with law enforcement. He plays guitar and 'ukulele and is learning to play bass. While not a professional musician, Perez notes the significant role that musicking has played in his life. He shares his feelings on the crucial role that music served on the mauna.

> It is evident that music was a critical part [of the movement to protect Maunakea] because so many Hawaiian musicians came, and what was interesting to me was people who we might not have known their political position on the issue kept coming back. For example, I kept seeing Brother Noland [Conjugacion] up on the mountain four or five times. He would come up and jam, and it was really awesome. Here is the main point: it was evident when you have international stars like Steel Pulse and Damian Marley, you know when these groups came up to play, there's something to be said about the power of music and how it awakens people, how it moves people. (2020)

CONNECTIONS TO PACIFIC AND BROADER
INDIGENOUS MOVEMENTS

"There is a world of difference between viewing the Pacific as 'islands in a far sea' and as 'a sea of islands.' The first emphasizes dry surfaces in a vast ocean far from the centers of power. Focusing in this way stresses the smallness and remoteness of the islands. The second is a more holistic perspective in which things are seen in the totality of their relationships" (Hau'ofa 1994).

In the following chapters, I discuss the protective actions of Tāngata Whenua (the Māori people) at Ihumātao in Aotearoa (New Zealand) and other Pacific connections to the ideas presented in this book. At Ihumātao, lands once occupied by Tāngata Whenua were taken from them by British settlers in 1864. In 2016, a private land developer purchased the land and planned to build expensive homes at Ihumātao, resulting in strong resistance from and occupation by Tāngata Whenua. Their actions ultimately resulted in the government purchasing the land and agreeing to consult with Tāngata Whenua on its future use. Music played a decisive role in these confrontations.

Epili Hauʻofa (Tongan/Fijian) formulated his ideas about the true nature of Oceania during a drive from Kona to Hilo to attend an academic conference. During the drive, Hauʻofa may have driven past Puʻuhuluhulu.[5] He describes what he saw on that drive: "I saw such scenes of grandeur as I had not seen before: the eerie blackness of regions covered by recent volcanic eruptions; the remote majesty of Maunaloa, long and smooth, the world's largest volcano; the awesome craters of Kilauea threatening to erupt at any moment; and the lava flow on the coast not far away. Under the aegis of Pele, and before my very eyes, the Big Island was growing, rising from the depths of a mighty sea. The world of Oceania is not small; it is huge and growing bigger every day" (Hauʻofa 1995).

Hauʻofa encourages the development of a stronger regional identity for Pacific nations to supplement—not supplant—individual Pacific Island identities (such as Kānaka Maoli, Tāngata Whenua, and Ni-Vanuatu) in addressing urgent shared challenges. These issues include nuclear vessels traversing the region, the use of Pacific Islands as dump sites for nuclear waste, the extraction of resources, overfishing by vessels from abroad, and the continued threat of colonial and new regional powers. He expands on this important concept: "The term Pacific Islands Region refers to an official world of states and nationalities. John and Mary cannot just be Pacific Islanders; they must first be Ni Vanuatu, or Tuvaluan, or Samoan. For my part, anyone who has lived in our region and is committed to Oceania, is an Oceanian" (Hauʻofa 1998).

While I am not inclined to claim the Oceanian identity that Hauʻofa generously offers to settlers and settler descendants such as myself, this book marks my first attempt to be a better resident of and contributor to Oceania. My thoughts are influenced by the writings of poet and author Albert Wendt (Sāmoan): "I belong to Oceania, or, at least, I am rooted in a fertile portion of it and it nourishes my spirit, helps to define me, and feeds my imagination" (1982). For these reasons, I look to our sea of islands to identify ideas and actions relevant to this examination of music's role on Maunakea.

I also fix my gaze to the east, to the Indigenous peoples of North America, while acknowledging that some of my ancestors were among the first to colonize the area now known as New England. Efforts to protect Maunakea mirror those in North Dakota, where the Standing Rock Sioux people and allies attempted to prevent the construction of the Dakota Access Pipeline. They argued that potential breaks in and oil leaks from the pipeline would endanger

Māori visitors to Puʻuhuluhulu showing support, bearing the tino rangatiratanga (absolute sovereignty) flag. Photo credit: Damon Tucker

drinking water supplies. Unfortunately, legal challenges and acts of resistance failed to halt construction; the oil pipeline was completed in 2017.

Pua Case (Kanaka ʻŌiwi) notes that her travels and the travels of other kiaʻi from Maunakea were essential to developing relationships with Indigenous movements and protectors in North America: "A number of us over the years had traveled to different movements and stood with them on their front lines, and many others who could not physically go had supported from here.... [6] We had truly become the Maunakea Movement, a visible and worldwide symbol of collective unity" (P. Case 2020).

The protective actions and mutual support offered to kiaʻi on Maunakea, Tāngata Whenua in Aotearoa, and water protectors in North Dakota do not diminish the individual identities of these people or homogenize their actions. Pua Case's cousin Emalani Case (Kanaka ʻŌiwi) describes the evolution of her thinking on solidarity between Indigenous movements. One of her students expressed concern about conflating social movements with significant differences that may share some similarities: "In reflecting on the recent Indigenous movements at Mauna Kea and Ihumātao, he asked about whether or not expressions of solidarity can detract from individual movements and blur their specific contexts and circumstances. In other words, with social media and hashtags, has it become too easy—and perhaps even normalized—to conflate issues?" (E. Case 2021).

Another concern is the amount of media and scholarly attention given to movements and conflicts in major population centers (by Pacific standards) like Aotearoa and Hawaiʻi. These movements can easily overshadow those of other locales. Some scholars in Pacific studies have lamented "Polycentrism" in the field and in different scholarly disciplines. They argue that a disproportional amount of attention is given to Polynesian Islands and cultures over those of others in Oceania. David Hanlon notes that in the case of Micronesia, "it is ironic, then, that a region of Oceania or the Pacific so profoundly affected by American colonialism is largely absent from the American literary imagination" (2009). Hawaiʻi, by contrast, is never far from the American and international imagination as a popular and "exotic" yet still American visitor destination and an important strategic location for US military forces.

The roles that musical composition and performances served on Maunakea mirrored those at Ihumātao, with a litany of new compositions, recordings, and performances supporting the efforts of protectors of iwi (tribal) lands and their claimants. Renowned Māori tito waiata (composer) and performer Rob Ruha (Te Whanau a Apanui, Ngāti Porou) composed "Ka Mānu" ("Remain afloat") on hearing the news of the confrontation at Ihumātao while traveling in Japan: "I'm showing my support because our people aren't in the wrong. The Crown has failed them; they must fix the problem. Who gives them the right to tell these people what to do? When in reality, they [the Crown] put our people in that situation in the first place. So that's why we're here" (Ruha cited in Black 2019).[7] The subsequent audio recording and music video Ruha released includes prominent Māori recording artists such as Maisey Rika, Bella Kalolo, Ria Hall, Seth Haapu, and Troy Kingi. There are similar issues and concerns at play at Maunakea and Ihumātao. Perhaps the most significant is the contested development of lands. In both situations, there are unresolved claims by Indigenous people who rightly believe their voices were ignored or disregarded during decision-making processes.

Perez describes his experience at Standing Rock, sharing the knowledge he learned from protectors standing against efforts to build the Dakota Access Pipeline. Like Maunakea, there was no shortage of musical experiences.

> I spent five weeks at Standing Rock. There were lots of musicians that came
> up to jam: Neil Young, a lot of hip-hop artists, particularly a lot of native
> hip-hop artists. But the one thing that stood out to me because it was

unusual—the native tribes, the drumming, and singing that went on all night. I remember the camp was about fifty acres, sometimes five thousand people there, and you hear these drums and people singing and flutes coming from all different areas, sitting around the campfires. It is traditional music or music that is rooted in your language. I think that is a feeling of connection to the ancestors. And that brings a feeling of reassurance, a feeling of not being alone and having hope. (Perez 2020)

In his examination of kīkā kī hōʻalu, Kevin Fellezs (Kanaka ʻŌiwi) uses the trans-Pacific seafaring of Pacific peoples as a metaphor to reorient the view of Hawaiʻi. Hawaiʻi is seen as the edge of "America's Far West" in an American-centric view of the world or as the easternmost islands in Oceania. Instead, Fellezs centers Hawaiʻi and the movement of kīkā kī hōʻalu west to Japan and east to the continental United States. He posits that by doing so, Hawaiʻi is no longer the "most isolated inhabited archipelago in the vast Pacific Ocean, but is the locus of movement from, rather than simply a crossroads through, a space of originary power and cultural meanings, a land of beginnings rather than endings, of possibilities both fulfilled and yet to be realized" (Fellezs 2019). Fellezs's reorientation of Hawaiʻi is similar to what Hauʻofa describes as redefining Oceania's boundaries as its people respond to a changing world: "They have since moved, by the tens of thousands, doing what their ancestors did in earlier times: enlarging their world as they go, on a scale not possible before. Everywhere they go, to Australia, New Zealand, Hawaiʻi, the mainland United States, Canada, Europe, and elsewhere, they strike roots in new resource areas, securing employment and overseas family property, expanding kinship networks through which they circulate themselves, their relatives, their material goods, and their stories all across their ocean, and the ocean is theirs because it has always been their home" (Hauʻofa 2017).

The relationships developed between protectors at Maunakea, Ihumātao, and Standing Rock have fostered mutual support and the sharing of strategies to achieve goals. All three groups have benefited from these relationships and musicking in these locations. These groups have created a community bound not by regionalities but by a shared purpose: to protect sacred lands against the incursion of continuing settler-colonial activity and aspirations for those lands and resources. Edvard Hviding has noted the "challenge of developing mutually inspiring communication among knowledges" while acknowledging "a wonderful diversity of human lifeworlds that can hardly be interpreted within a single-discipline framework" (2003). While his writings focus on these challenges within the context of Pacific Island studies, I experienced the same challenges in this multidisciplinary approach and discussion of diverse peoples, practices, and epistemologies in examining music's role in protecting Maunakea.

MELE AND HAKU MELE

"I think the mele were such an essential part of galvanizing and expressing the naʻau [entrails, the seat of emotion in Hawaiian thought], the heart, the love, you know, the conflict that each of us were living, but knowing that they will get through it with aloha and with the beauty and majesty of Maunakea" (Beamer 2020).

It is impossible to overstate the importance of ʻōlelo Hawaiʻi in composition and performance on the mauna and in many other contexts. Hawaiian scholar and poet Larry Kimura has argued that ʻōlelo Hawaiʻi is used on many different levels, but Hawaiian poetry is the most important and highest level (Kimura 2002).[8] In performance, the most important elements are the mele (poetic text) and leo (voice) (Stillman 2005). Elizabeth Tatar agrees, noting that the voice is "the most important instrument of musical performance" (Tatar 1982). Mele also document the genealogical connection between Maunakea and Kānaka ʻŌiwi explored in this book. In the most fundamental sense, haku mele is the Hawaiian term for both the act of writing Hawaiian poetry and the composer of Hawaiian poetry.[9] The mele is the poetry itself—the words, meanings (both literal and metaphorical), and poetic devices used by the composer.

Mele also describes any vocalization of the lyrics, though more specific terms exist for the performance of older chanted and newer singing styles influenced by introduced musical forms. The distinction between lyrics and performance style also exists in English: "A song is sung, a chant is chanted, a poem is recited" (hoʻomanawanui 2005). Mele does not mean "music." There is no evidence of a pre-Western-contact Hawaiian term directly corresponding to the English concept of music.[10] Hawaiʻi is not alone in that respect—other cultures also lack a term synonymous with music. However, the Hawaiian language does contain many terms related to mele and its performance, including terms for the subject of mele, names for various performance styles, and terms for performance characteristics and adornments (Kamakau 1867).

Over the years, some organizations have encouraged the composition of new mele. For example, the City and County of Honolulu Department of Parks and Recreation started an annual songwriting competition in 1950 that continued into the mid-1970s (Department of Parks and Recreation, City and County of

Honolulu 1977). This competition included entries by many native speakers and some of the best-known haku mele of that era—Mary Kawena Pukui, John Kameaaloha Almeida, Alice Nāmakelua, Randy Oness, and Dorothy Kahananui. Honolulu radio station KCCN established the Nani Awards in 1978; a popular vote determined the winners. In 1982, the academy became an industry association known as the Hawaiʻi Academy of Recording Arts (HARA), and the Nani Awards became the Nā Hōkū Hanohano Awards and a vehicle for peer recognition within the Hawaiʻi recording industry. HARA presents an award for haku mele (best new Hawaiian language composition), Hawaiian language performance, and several other awards for Hawaiian language recordings at the annual Nā Hōkū Hanohano Awards held in Honolulu (Hawaiʻi Academy of Recording Arts 2022).

The prospect of awards or financial gain did not inspire haku mele and those composing songs in English to express their support for the kiaʻi and the mauna. Instead, the beauty of the mauna, the desire to see it protected from further desecration, its historical and genealogical significance to Kānaka ʻŌiwi, and admiration for the kiaʻi provided inspiration to compose. The composition and performance of mele on Maunakea Hawaiian reflect a Hawaiian epistemology, a Kānaka ʻŌiwi philosophy of knowledge, which was pervasive in the words and actions of kiaʻi on Maunakea. Manulani Aluli Meyer (Kanaka ʻŌiwi) notes that

> It is not the short term we look for as Hawaiians, it is the long. Anything else is a mistake pushed by minds that do not understand the essence of water or the finite nature of our human resources. It will always, always be a mistake to base a movement on money. Always. This is an epistemological point—that relationship is more valuable than the more modern sense of efficacy, money. Hawaiians know this, and as we struggle to see how best to be of use, we have only to relate hermeneutics to the equation to understand why and how things went wrong. But that's another story.[11] (2001b)

Meyer wrote this passage many years before events unfolded on Maunakea, and her thoughts resonate deeply in the context of kiaʻi actions there. I have written several mele for the mauna—and will undoubtedly write more. Whenever my thoughts return to the mauna and the many friends I have who stood as kiaʻi, when I watch videos of their actions or see pictures documenting the events of July 17, 2019, the inspiration to compose is never far behind.

NOTES

1. These scholars are named and thanked for contributing to this work in the acknowledgments section.

2. Bissen notes that he adjudicated some cases on Maui of individuals arrested for their actions in defense of Haleakalā and in opposing construction of the Daniel K. Inouye Solar Telescope near its summit.

3. In the late 1970s, Dr. George Kanahele noted renewed interest in many Hawaiian cultural practices beginning in the 1960s, which he referred to as the "Hawaiian Renaissance." In recent years, many have started referring to this era as the "Second Hawaiian Renaissance." This choice recognizes the significant renaissance of Hawaiian practices that occurred during the nineteenth century reign of King David Kalākaua. The Second Hawaiian Renaissance is discussed in more detail in chapter 6.

4. Gelo does not discuss the use of Indigenous languages in his writing about the emcee's role in powwow other than to note that many of the exhortations expressed by emcees in the course of their duties "have a direct basis in the native language" (1999).

5. It is not clear from Hauʻofa's account of this journey whether he took the former Saddle Road (now the Daniel K. Inouye Highway) that sits between Maunakea and Maunaloa, the northern route around Maunakea, or the southern route around Maunaloa. His mention of observing volcanic activity at Kīlauea crater suggests that he took the southern route, which would have brought him close to Kīlauea. I thank Halena Kapuni-Reynolds for drawing my attention to that possibility.

6. Some of the travels Case refers to in this conversation were to support the Winnemen Wintu in their efforts to bring the salmon back to their rivers, the Lisjan ʻOhlone for protection of their ancestral shell mounds, and the water protectors at Standing Rock in North Dakota. She also notes visits to Maunakea by Chief Arvol Looking Horse, a Cheyenne-Lakota spiritual elder, and Ladonna Bravebull Allard of the Sacred Stone Camp and the Standing Rock Reservation.

7. Te Whanau a Apanui and Ngāti Porou are Ruha's primary iwi affiliations, though he does have ancestry from other iwi. Iwi are sometimes referred to as tribes, though there are significant differences. I give the iwi associations of those of Māori ancestry, when known, following their mention. Ruha performed at the Maui Arts and Cultural Center on January 25, 2018, with fellow Māori artists Maisey Rika, Seth Haapu and Horomona Horo in a concert billed as "Aotearoa's Finest." During his set, Ruha dedicated a waiata (song) to UHMC Professor of Hawaiian Studies and kiaʻi Kaleikoa Kaʻeo, who previously had been arrested for his actions in defense against development on the summit of Haleakalā. When Kaʻeo invoked his right to use Hawaiian in court and refused to identify himself in English, presiding Judge Blaine Kobayashi refused to acknowledge Kaʻeo's presence and issued a bench warrant for his arrest. Kobayashi retracted the warrant on July 26, 2018, the day after the Aotearoa's Finest concert. The original charges against Kaʻeo were dismissed in July, 2018, because of the court's failure to try him in a timely manner.

8. Kimura's statement regarding the status of mele appears in his master's thesis, which was written in ʻōlelo Hawaiʻi. The text in the passage above is my translation and summation of his statement.

9. Hawaiian words do not take the letters *s* or *es* to indicate plurality. In the opening of this sentence, the word mele is plural. I attempt to present these plural forms in such a way that their plurality can be determined contextually.

10. The term puolo was coined by the *Kōmike Huaʻōlelo Hou* (Hawaiian Language Lexicon) in the 1990s to address this need. It was adapted from the Māori word puoro, which has the same meaning (Kōmike Huaʻōlelo 2003).

11. Examining and explaining what defines a Hawaiian epistemology is beyond the scope of this work. I refer the reader to Meyer's exhaustive writings on the subject (1998; 2001a; 2001b; 2003; 2008).

TWO

—⁓—

LOHE ʻIA MAI ʻŌ A ʻŌ

The Soundscapes of the Mauna

The idea of sensuality helps me step outside the box of my colonial context and brings me to the sights, sounds, smells, touches, and tastes of a deeper experience of this world. Sensuality is the first category for this paper on human potential because it is the grounding and the foundation for what I call "cultural empiricism," the idea that knowledge that comes from our five senses is shaped by a distinct relationship we have had with the world as cultural people. This experiencing we still have, and it is the finding of what this is that has most shaped my human potential. (Meyer 2003)

In this chapter, I describe the soundscapes of Maunakea, including but not limited to soundscapes of confrontations between kiaʻi and law enforcement officials. I discuss listening and hearing as physiological, cultural, and moral phenomena. This understanding is essential, as any time spent on Maunakea, particularly at the kiaʻi encampment, was an intensely sensual experience. Experiences included feeling the movement of the wind, the rain, and the touch of skin as people shared embraces; smelling food being cooked, the fragrance of lei, and the petrichor that precedes and accompanies rain; and seeing Maunakea and the surrounding areas, the sky, clouds, sun, and moon, forests, and roadways. There was also the sight of kiaʻi wearing brightly colored clothing and carrying flags from many lands, contrasting the black, gray, and blue uniforms worn by law enforcement officers. Some of the most impactful sensual experiences on the mauna were aural: the sound of the wind and rain and hushed conversations at night, occasionally interrupted by music or motor vehicles passing by on the highway. These nocturnal experiences contrasted the sound of pahu (drums), ipu (gourds), and other Hawaiian instruments at the ʻaha (protocol gatherings) held four times daily, the shuffling of feet on the paved portions of the Maunakea Access Road and on the fields of rocks that surrounded the encampment, the amplified sound of announcements and musical performances utilizing modern instruments and electronic instruments, the blaring of megaphones used by law enforcement communicating with the crowds of kiaʻi, and the sound of unamplified voices and instruments from informal jam sessions. Traffic on the Daniel K. Inouye Highway increased during the day, with many passing drivers beeping their horns in support of the kiaʻi. There were also periods of relative silence, some occurring naturally and others requested at specific times by kūpuna and kiaʻi leaders. While I address musical performance to some degree, the focus is more on the experience of listening to and hearing musical performance, silence, and other elements of the mauna's soundscape.

Several individuals who shared their experiences on Maunakea with me related the experience of "listening to the mauna." Regardless of the time of day or night or the level of human activity on the mauna, there were audible events to be experienced. The accounts of experiences were not simply aural but multisensory, as described by scholar and kiaʻi kuʻualoha hoʻomanawanui (Kanaka ʻŌiwi).

> To me, listening to the mauna is a way of paying attention, right? Starting with your ears. But also, it's feeling with your body. So, in poetry—I teach poetry—I talk about the seven senses. So there's sight, sound, smell, taste, touch—the visible ones. Then there's kinesthetic, which is movement, like hula. Then there's organic—internal feeling or sensation. And so, for me, it's usually multisensory that, on one hand, you're listening, but you're also feeling the touch of like things like temperature or very subtle movement on your skin, but it's also connected to that organic, which is also how we talk about now—feeling that they're very much working in harmony. (hoʻomanawanui 2022)

Kenneth Makuakāne (Kanaka ʻŌiwi) grew up in the community of Keaukaha on Hawaiʻi Island, and Maunakea has been a constant physical and spiritual presence in his life. The mauna has also been a source of inspiration for his spirituality and musical compositions. He likens his experience of "listening to the mauna" to the wisdom passed on to him by his father in times when Makuakāne was not necessarily attentive to what his father was telling him.

> I have found that since he passed, all of those recollections, those things that he had imparted to me are so vivid, and the things that I use today, every single one of those things has come from sitting down and listening to him not knowing that I was absorbing what he was saying. We only take

what we need at the time, and the rest goes back into the repository. So if my father and what he talked about didn't mean anything to me at the time, when he passed, all of a sudden, those things came to the forefront. I look at all of creation as doing the same thing. When I needed it, that is when the mountain called to me, and that was the most incredible thing. It happened. When I needed it, it was there. Because even when I didn't need it, it was still there. But only when I needed it did that voice align, and I heard it. I don't know how I heard it, but I certainly felt it. All I know is that there's a spiritual space in me that is open to receiving that information, that interconnectedness, that oneness with creation that I definitely am a part of. And that is how I feel about what places like Maunakea and a lot of other places mean to me. (2020)

Isaac Maluhia Castillo (Kanaka ʻŌiwi) relates memories and emotions that became embodied because of aural experiences on the mauna, and how hearing mele like "Kū Haʻaheo e Kuʻu Hawaiʻi" allowed him to relive those experiences and feelings even after he departed: "I think the most powerful thing about the music is not just that it was a pretty song about a moment in time that we're going to look back on. It's like when I heard that song, I cry every time I hear it. When I hear people singing ʻKū Haʻaheo,ʻ it takes me to a place where I'm standing on the mauna, and everybody's learning all the words, and we're all singing it because we understand this is how we're going to be steadfast in our place" (2020).

Castillo also found that listening to Josh Tatofi's Tongan "For the Lāhui" enabled him to embrace the Hawaiian name (Maluhia) given to him by his birth parents shortly after he met them and before he visited the kiaʻi encampment. He acknowledges hesitance to use this name because he did not understand its meaning. But a conversation with a fellow kiaʻi and hearing Tatofi singing "For the Lāhui" empowered him to embrace the name: "I'd never heard maluhia [peace, tranquility] used in the context of a song, and it's in that song, you know, maluhia, and it just kind of codifies this entire movement for me. It's not about fighting. It's about coming to some sort of way of strength in a peaceful manner, and the music keeps me grounded in that. I'm not a fighter, I'm not very big, but I've played songs that have made some big dudes really cry, and that feels like we're connecting in this other way to this other strength" (2020).

Meyer has written about the Hawaiian cultural implications of the senses.[1] Like Pauline Oliveros, she identifies a third term that describes a more profound sensual experience than simply listening. Lohe is the Hawaiian term meaning "to hear," and hoʻolohe means "to listen."[2] There is also a term not used as frequently, in my experience, in everyday conversations in ʻōlelo Hawaiʻi: hoʻolono. According to Meyer, hoʻolono infers an even deeper engagement with sound and evokes the Hawaiian deity Lono:[3] "Listening, too, becomes something that is lifted beyond the mundane. To pay attention, to really listen (hoʻolono) is to invoke a spirit, a deity.[4] Listening, then, becomes a spiritual act. Doing it well is tied to what Pua Kanahele said to us earlier: 'You, yourself, cannot make any of this happen.' It is intimately tied to others and how we invoke our own genealogy to learn what is most critical. Listening well is found in the act of focus, and focusing is part of what culture helps to define" (2003).

Heoli Osorio recalls details of a visit to Kīlauea crater with her "Granny Groovy" (Clara Kuʻulei Kay), with whom she hiked through a forest trail and experienced the sensual stimulation of the journey.

> When I was eight years old, I went to visit Granny Groovy alone. Forty years after my father walked back along that long, quiet, and devastating trail from Kīlauea Iki, I took my first solo airplane trip to Volcano for the summer. Granny Groovy and I gardened, ate papaya, said grace, strung lei—and hiked to Kīlauea Iki. We saw what was left after Pele's path had cut through the forest, marveled at Puʻu Puaʻi, and felt the heat of Pele's kiss on our cheeks. I did not ask about Pele. I did not think I was allowed to. I only watched, listened, and felt her presence. This is how I know that sometimes silence can be passed down through generations until it becomes tradition. (J. H. Osorio 2021)

Osorio could not have embraced the specific, intense, and intimate experiences she describes in this passage anywhere else on Earth. She allowed herself to engage with the silence of her journey to Kīlauea and to be transformed by her sensory experience. It was far more than a journey of nostalgia, retracing the steps taken by her father forty years prior. Her experience was unique and grounded her in her genealogy, her pilina (relationship) to the ʻāina; it prepared her to move forward in life and in her role as a kiaʻi of Maunakea.

The depictions of Makuakāne, Castillo, Osorio, and others speak to the deeply sensual, spiritual, and culturally based experiences of those on the mauna. While it would be worthwhile to examine the aural experience of those who mainly, if not exclusively, watched and heard events via streamed audio, doing so is beyond the scope of this work.

KE ALA KŪPUNA AS A LANGUAGE CONTACT ZONE

As described above, engaging in a deep, multisensory experience allowed listeners to transcend a common challenge on the mauna: the proceedings during the ʻaha and many musical performances were largely conducted in ʻōlelo Hawaiʻi. Many kiaʻi and supporters are multilingual—competent in English,

Hawaiian, Hawaiian Creole English ("Pidgin English"), and proficient in other Indigenous and colonial languages. I do not make this statement to disparage law enforcement, government, and university officials, who may also be multilingual. However, the language of Hawaiʻi's colonizers (English) remained the primary means of communication among pro-TMT forces and in their communications with kiaʻi. Many kiaʻi chose to use ʻōlelo Hawaiʻi as much as circumstances allowed—in communication among themselves, in classes at Puʻuhuluhulu University, to Hawaiian-speaking supporters around the world, and, most pertinent to this work, in their compositional and performance practices on the mauna. In some cases, kiaʻi refused to speak English during court proceedings for offenses related to their protective actions. As the State of Hawaiʻi Constitution affirms ʻōlelo Hawaiʻi as an official language, they were certainly within their rights. State judiciary policies compel the courts to hire interpreters for translation services for Hawaiian speakers.

The Ala Kūpuna was also a multicultural contact zone where Kānaka ʻŌiwi welcomed Indigenous "cousins" from other areas of the Pacific and North America and non-Indigenous peoples, both their supporters and supporters of TMT.[5] Music played a role in these multicultural interactions, as there were opportunities for everyone to share music regardless of race, ethnicity, or place of origin. In the context of Native North America, John-Carlos Perea (Mescalero Apache, Irish, German, Chicano) has observed the intertribal nature of powwow, where performances often include songs and dances that are tribe specific and depend on the performance's function and context. These performances can include non-Indigenous participants if the powwow committee and master of ceremonies agree. Intertribal dancing, he argues, "becomes a moment during the pow-wow where difference is negotiated and community is created through social activity of music and dance" (Perea 2014). While those on the Ala Kūpuna did not share the same kind of tribal affiliations that Perea describes, aspects of negotiating difference and creating community were certainly in play.

A half-century ago, the Hawaiian language seemed destined for extinction. Intergenerational transmission of the language had all but vanished. In 1896, a law was passed to prohibit schools from conducting classes through the medium of ʻōlelo Hawaiʻi or any language other than English. By the 1970s, a cultural rebirth led to renewed interest in Hawaiian language, cultural practices, knowledge, beliefs, and cultural pride restoration. As Suzanne Romaine notes that language plays a crucial role in the transmission of culture, as "the world is not simply the way it is, but what we make of it through language" (2000). Music also plays a significant role in documenting, preserving, and transmitting knowledge. Music helped to increase awareness and support social change in the islands. Many young composers and musicians began to seek out older texts and recordings and consult with the aging and rapidly diminishing population of native speakers. In the past fifty years, the Hawaiian language has made "a small but determined comeback" (hoʻomanawanui 2005).

In 1978, a state constitutional convention made Hawaiian an official language in Hawaiʻi, giving it the same legal standing as English. In 1986, the Hawaiʻi State Legislature repealed the territorial-era legislation that outlawed the use of Hawaiian as a medium of instruction. Since then, a thriving immersion program extending from nursery school to the doctoral level has helped reverse the decline in Hawaiian language use among the young. After nearly three decades of Hawaiian medium education, many people are once again transmitting the Hawaiian language to their children and grandchildren. With the exception of the Niʻihau community, this intergenerational transmission of ʻōlelo Hawaiʻi had rarely been seen in Hawaiʻi since the first half of the twentieth century. Over two decades have passed since the first students graduated from Hawaiian immersion high schools. Some have become respected haku mele, performers, and recording artists, including Kaumakaiwa Kanakaʻole, Kamakakēhau Fernandez, Kalani Peʻa, and Kaniela Masoe. Many were among the kiaʻi.

While the ability to understand ʻōlelo Hawaiʻi undoubtedly enhances and deepens the experience of performances conducted in ʻōlelo Hawaiʻi, those who do not understand ʻōlelo Hawaiʻi can still appreciate its beauty and communicative intent. As noted by kumu hula and educator Hōkūlani Holt (Kanaka ʻŌiwi), "Often when music affects a person, they're drawn to the vocalization if they are drawn to the sound first. That produces some kind of emotional response, and then they listen, or they are drawn into what are the words are saying, whether it be English or another language. Sometimes you don't even have to know the other language and it just produces this emotional response. So, I think that it's kind of an interesting thing to think about because Hawaiian music, creative arts, and such draw people to it and they don't even know why" (2020).

Kānaka ʻōlelo Hawaiʻi (Hawaiian speakers) on the mauna included members of kiaʻi leadership, others who resided on the mauna for extended periods, those who regularly commuted to the mauna, and those who visited to support the kiaʻi and learn more about issues surrounding the mauna. Some law enforcement officers on the mauna were likely conversant in Hawaiian, and at least one addressed kiaʻi using ʻōlelo Hawaiʻi. My observation and the supporting statement by Holt highlight the importance of the aesthetics of aural experiences to being drawn into language experiences. In cases where composers and performers chose to compose and sing in ʻōlelo Hawaiʻi, multiple considerations were at play, as posited by ethnomusicologist Harris Berger: "Questions of language choice are a crucial part of musical experience. Musicians, listeners, and cultural workers must constantly ask themselves such questions as Which languages or dialects will best express my ideas? Which will get me a record contract or a bigger audience? What does it mean to sing or listen to music in a colonial language? A foreign language? A ʻnativeʼ language?" (2003).

Elizabeth "Bam" Post is a former lecturer in psychology at the University of California Davis and has hosted a weekly Hawaiian music radio program in Davis entitled "Na Mele o Hawaiʻi" since August 2011. She considers herself an ally to the kiaʻi and Kānaka ʻŌiwi and offers her thoughts, as someone who does not speak ʻōlelo Hawaiʻi, on the issue of language comprehension in mele performed and recorded for the mauna.

> Music carries a message rapidly; it carries a message like a semaphore. It carries the message quickly and pleasingly, aesthetically. Youʼve got a message in a bottle with a song, and you can just put it out there because the music is understandable, the tonality is understandable, and every [hearing] human brain can hear when you attach a message—youʼre already in the brain. Clearly, the music is out there for people who are already willing to listen, and, if in fact theyʼre already willing to listen, they are probably willing to try to find out what the translations are, what it means. (Post 2022)

The choice to compose and sing in ʻōlelo Hawaiʻi may express oneʼs cultural identity and proficiency and rejection of the colonizerʼs language and its associated trappings. The language communicates even if the listener does not understand it. It sends a clear message to everyone whether or not the specific meaning carried by its words and grammar are comprehended—"We are the people born of this ʻāina; we speak the language that was born of this ʻāina, and only we have authority to speak for this ʻāina." Simply put, ʻōlelo Hawaiʻi speaks for the ʻāina in a way that English cannot because, as Osorio argues, the cultural coding inherent to verbal expression in ʻōlelo Hawaiʻi is stripped away by English. Mele can reach and impact an audience that is currently unable to understand the meanings and thoughts expressed but desires to do so (J. H. Osorio 2021).

THE CULTURAL UNDERPINNINGS OF SILENCE

"Silence is an actual, meaningful means of communication, and it has various functions in a different context and different cultures.... To have a clear vision about silence, one should not consider language as spoken or written words.

Interaction is any means by which people of any culture communicates or understands each other." (Amer, Naser, and Abdulmajeed 2019).

Silence is more than the lack of artificial sounds, and its implications and value vary from culture to culture. Indeed, while there may be similarities between perspectives on silence among Indigenous and Pacific peoples, there are also differences in its role within the culture. While the ability to communicate using language may distinguish us from other animals, animals also communicate, and humans share many nonverbal means of communication. Chris Griffin differentiates between communicative and noncommunicative silences, noting that even silences that lack communicative intent can also carry meaning: "Broadly speaking, silences are of two sorts: those in culture, which are by definition communicative, and those in nature, which because of the absence of human agency or an intention-making party are 'non-communicative'—even when they are capable of rendering 'meaning' to human beings [as in the case of a 'silent night' or the 'silence of the hills']" (2003).

Silence has been used strategically during protests in Aotearoa. In 1994, the Crown (the settler-established government of Aotearoa New Zealand) proposed a settlement intended to address the historical claims of the Māori people known as the Fiscal Envelope. The Crown framed the proposal as an attempt to settle Māori grievances fairly forever. In fact, it was "an attempt by the Crown to weasel out of its responsibilities under the Treaty" (Treaty Times 1995). Crown representatives engaged with iwi (tribe-like entities) throughout the country and faced stiff resistance to the proposal:[6] "The most unsettling protest action for the then Chief Executive of Te Puni Kōkiri [Ministry of Māori Development], Wira Gardiner, occurred at Owae marae in Waiariki. A group of about 300 mainly young protesters sat motionless and impassive on the ground, wrapped in grey blankets. There was no heckling, no yelling, no chanting as the Crown contingent passed onto the marae—just silent disapproval. At the same hui, a New Zealand flag was burned, underlying the strength of opposition" (Harris 2004).

Te Ururoa Flavell (Ngati Rangiwewehi, Ngati Kahu, Ngati Huri, Ngati Raukawa, Ngati Te Ata) was one of those young protesters and later became a member of the New Zealand Parliament for Waiariki, serving from October 2005 to October 2017. He also served as coleader of Te Paati Māori o Aotearoa (the Māori Party) from July 2013 to July 2019. He describes the intent and strategy behind the protesters' silence.

> We had a wananga [discussion] at Kairau marae the night before so everyone knew what we were protesting about and set off at 6:30am for our hour walk

to Owae. Wira [Gardiner] came on to marae with the Minister. Imagine all these people wrapped in blankets sitting on the marae in complete silence. I pictured it like when our people would have to wait outside the Land Court waiting for their cases to be heard, sometimes for days. At lunch time, Wira came out and told us to come for kai [food]. No one moved! We kept our places until they left. Wira was to say in one of his books that it was the most effective protest he had encountered; he said it tapped his heart. I felt proud of that because that was the intention. And he got it. (Flavell 2022)

The book ʻŌlelo Noʻeau: Hawaiian Proverbs & Poetical Sayings is an invaluable and frequently cited source of proverbial sayings that reflect Hawaiian worldview and cultural values (Pukui 1983). There are numerous references to silence within the book, describing when it is valued and not. I share two here. For each of these sayings, I provide the expression in ʻōlelo Hawaiʻi as it appears in ʻŌlelo Noʻeau followed by a literal translation and, in parenthesis, a deeper interrogation of its meaning as provided by Mary Kawena Pukui, the author.

E hāmau o makani mai auaneʻi. Hush lest the wind arise. [Hold your silence or trouble will come to us.] (Pukui 1983)

Pukui notes that this phase references the practice of gathering pearl oysters at Puʻuloa, Oʻahu, an area now known as Pearl Harbor. The phrase "nā iʻa hāmau leo o ʻEwa" (the silent fish of ʻEwa) is also a well-known reference to these oysters.[7] Pukui notes that when people went to gather oysters, they would do so in silence so as to not generate a wind that would alert the oysters of their presence. This practice is not specific to Puʻuloa—not speaking about one's intention to go fishing continues today. Meyer notes the scorn one would receive for asking if someone was going fishing: "This is why we never asked if uncle was going fishing. The sound of the words scared the fish away and uncle would then put down his gear and do something different, usually with a scolding to the ignorant questioner first" (2001a). Alberta Pualani Anthony notes that Hawaiian children are taught from a young age to glance downward and remain silent when spoken to by someone older (1979).[8]

On the other extreme, it is considered rude to remain silent and not call out to someone approaching your home.

Mū ka waha heahea ʻole. Silent is the mouth of the inhospitable.[9] (Pukui 1983)

Kaimana Barcarse (Kanaka ʻŌiwi) is an employee of the Kamehameha Schools who has also worked for years as a disc jockey for the Alana I Kai Hikina Hawaiian language radio program broadcast at KWXX radio in Hilo.

He previously worked at the ʻAha Pūnana Leo and currently serves on the State of Hawaiʻi Board of Education. Barcarse grew up on the slopes of Maunakea and, in his youth, gathered food there, including hunting birds, sheep, goats, and pigs. Barcarse has traveled on waʻa kaulua (double-hulled canoes) between the Hawaiian Islands, the Pacific, and Africa. He discusses the cultural implications of silence in personal interactions, particularly by kūpuna when he is in their presence.

> Silence is a space, and it is about bringing people up there [to Maunakea] so that they can have a connection with the person that they're supposed to connect within a silent space, but away from others that might see this leader and want to share their thoughts. But that's not necessarily the reason for being there, even though you have a right to speak. Being in the audience of certain people, knowing that your silence speaks even more. In my opinion, my silence is actually supporting this kupuna in their opinion. Just with the head, just with your lawena [body language and mannerisms], that silence, to me, speaks volumes. The silence before kupuna speaks, when they're asked a question—that silence speaks volumes, you know. I look at it as more like a kōnane move.[10] It's not that older kūpuna are slow to think and they have to get their thoughts together. What I see in that kupuna is they are waiting until you are ready [to listen]. (Barcarse 2022)

Kalani Makekau-Whittaker notes that silence was sometimes invoked during the ʻaha held four times daily on the mountain. This silence would allow participants to focus their attention on the reason why they had gathered at the ʻaha—Maunakea: "During the ʻaha, Kekuhi [Kanahele], who usually ran the ʻaha, would once in a while take these moments as we connected through mele, and she would pause at the end of certain chants. And because she was controlling the ʻaha on the mic everyone would follow along, and then there was this silent connection with the mauna. We usually would be facing the mauna chanting and then would stop and pause and just sort of take it all in" (Makekau-Whittaker 2020).

WHEN SILENCE IS NOT SILENT

The eighteenth-century Austrian composer Wolfgang Amadeus Mozart is frequently quoted as having said, "The music is not in the notes, but in the silence between." This quote routinely surfaces as a meme across social media sites, although some attribute it to Claude Debussy, John Cage, or other notable composers or musicians. Who originated this statement is not significant, mainly because it is inaccurate. The vibrations and sounds of many instruments, such as violins, guitars, pianos, and drums, continue after the performer stops playing. The acoustics of many venues echo the sounds of instruments and the human voice for a significant amount of time after performers have ceased playing or singing. These echoes either join the sounds of subsequent performative acts or fade into nothingness or rounds of applause at the end of the performance. Neuroscientist Seth Horowitz notes that even if we were to isolate ourselves in a soundproof chamber with walls made of materials incapable of the reflecting sounds we make, humans cannot experience silence.

> There is no such thing as silence. We are constantly immersed in and affected by sound and vibration. This is true no matter where you go, from the deepest underwater trenches to the highest, almost airless peaks of the Himalayas. In truly quiet areas you can even hear the sound of air molecules vibrating inside your ear canals or the noise of the fluid in your ears themselves. The world we live in is full of energy acting on matter—it's as basic as life itself. And the reasons the constant thrumming doesn't drive us all insane are the same reasons we get distracted by radio jingles and can't read when the TV is on: we are good at choosing what we hear. But even if we don't hear a sound, someone else does. (2012)

Many individuals who spent time on the mauna spoke of periods of silence, both naturally occurring and requested during the protocol and specific activities and events. It is clear from my conversation with many of these individuals that they were not seeking absolute silence but, more generally, the absence of artificial and intrusive sounds generated by human activities: "I feel like those times of silence are the perfect time to reflect. I mean, we're going through these ceremonies three times a day. People are excited to participate. There are lapses in between within the ceremony and outside of the ceremony. But I think because having the training of practicing kapu aloha, having silent time becomes normal, and it's different from like gaps of nothingness. That silence is also time to strategize, time to feel, time to contemplate" (Kahaunaele 2020a).

There was a time when the sounds of kānaka activity were not so out of place in nature, which is still the case to some degree. For example, in recordings made by anthropologist and musician Helen Roberts in 1923, James Kapihenui Palea Kuluwaimaka chanted many older mele. Kuluwaimaka was born in 1845 in Kaʻū on Hawaiʻi mokupuni and served in the courts of both Kamehameha IV and Kalākaua. In Kuluwaimaka's recorded performances, the listener can clearly hear the manu (birds) chirping while he is chanting. Their continued sounding during what might otherwise be construed as a disturbance of the forest's relative silence suggests the birds' familiarity with and lack of concern over his presence and the sound of his voice.[11] Hawaiian cultural practitioner and author Leilehua Yuen recalls hearing birds singing as she and "Aunty" Nona Beamer practiced chanting each morning after breakfast in East Hawai'i Island.

> Just before sunrise, the birds would begin their morning song. Once it warmed up a bit, we would move from the toasty kitchen to the parlor, where the piano still sat [as it does today], along with my pahu drum, assorted ipu hula [gourds], guitars, 'ukulele, kalā'au [sticks], 'ili'ili [rock castanets], pū'ili [bamboo rattlers], and etc. When we started our hakalama the birds would fall silent.[12] Then, as we began our oli, they would begin again to sing. 'Dahling!' Aunty Nona would cry out, a delighted look on her face. 'Listen to the birds! You know, I do believe they enjoy the oli. Let's do it again, as sweetly as they.' (Yuen 2022)

Sam 'Ohu Gon, a senior scientist and cultural advisor at the Nature Conservancy of Hawai'i, also notes that he is often joined by the sounds of manu when performing oli in the natural world: "I do notice that when chanting forest entrance and the forest is silent at the start, there are often answering calls by birds by the time the oli is finished. It is interesting to me that my favorite forest entrance, 'Kau ka Hali'a,' includes the line: 'Ho'āla ana 'oe, 'o 'oe 'o Halaulani, 'o Hoakalei, me he manu e kani nei i ke kuahiwi, i ke kualono' [That upon your rising, you were indeed in the sacred, expansive forest rising as a wispy cloud, with birds chirping in the mountain top, ridges]"[13] (2022).

When discussing Thomas Lindsey's composition "Honesakala" with me in 2009, Larry Kimura spoke to the normativity of sound in the native forest, specifically the voices of birds. The following lyric appears as the third line of the chorus:

'A'ohe kani leo na manu o 'Ōla'a But the birds of 'Ōla'a no longer sing

"Honesakala" is set in Kohala on north Hawai'i Island, while 'Ōla'a is many miles away on the eastern side of the same island, south of Hilo. Kimura states that 'Ōla'a was famous for its forest filled with native birds that sounded constantly. Therefore, this line discussing the silence of the forest indicates something is out of the ordinary: "Ke loa'a ka 'eko'a, 'a'ole kani leo, 'oi ka ikaika, 'eā? Ka 'eko'a ka mea e 'oi a'e ka ikaika o kēlā mana'o. No laila, 'a'ole lohe, he mea 'ē loa [When you have the opposite and no sound is heard, the emphasis of that thought is amplified, right? So, they are not heard, and that is very strange] (Kimura in Donaghy 2010).

These accounts document how certain nonintrusive sounds do not infringe on perceptions of silence in the natural world. Nor do all human-generated sounds disrupt these perceptions. Unfortunately, the same cannot be said for human-generated sounds such as motor vehicle traffic and megaphones—particularly the military-grade LRAD (long-range acoustic device) brought to Maunakea by law enforcement agencies during the standoff with kiaʻi.[14] For these reasons, my use of "silence" in the remainder of this chapter does not refer to an unattainable, pure silence. Instead, I use the word to describe a soundscape in which disruptive sounds that humans generate, often mechanical or electronically amplified, are absent or minimized. Nevertheless, the sounds of the natural environment are still present and audible—even above some sounds made by humans.

On Maunakea, kiaʻi leaders invoked silence purposefully and strategically in two situations discussed in this chapter. The first was during confrontations with law enforcement. Pua Case shares the challenges of preparing kiaʻi and visitors to maintain silence when needed.

> It's a discipline, and we're not disciplined, and so having silence was a manner by which we were listening instead of talking. We're so good at chanting, praying, but we're not good at receiving the response to that, and it's uncomfortable. One of the reasons that we would go into so much silence is it was actual nonviolent direct action training, where I would say, "We're going to sit in silence for a half hour because you might be here with the police for the whole day." And if you're not used to being silent, you're not going to be able to. So we're going to practice silence, and hopefully, we're going to be receiving when we're practicing. So there's a lot of reasons for silence, but that's why we have he mū ʻo ia—everybody just be quiet and just and just observe.[15] You cannot do all those other senses when you're talking. It's really just a Kānaka Maoli kind of teaching—just be quiet the whole time, and it's not even meditating. It's just listening, observing, feeling, you know, the heart is receiving. So that's a discipline that a lot of people don't have, but that also is part of what is practiced on the mauna. (2020)

Zachary Alakaʻi Lum (Kanaka ʻŌiwi) is a haku mele, singer, arranger, music producer, educator, and a member of the multi-Nā Hōkū Hanohano Award-winning group Keauhou. Several of his compositions have earned him the coveted Haku Mele Award at the annual Nā Hōkū Hanohano Awards, and he has produced multiple recordings with aloha ʻāina themes. He notes how he uses silence while teaching large numbers of students during choral practice to get their attention: "We use it in school, too. Because when we're running a rehearsal with 1,800 kids, the way to get them to stop talking is to get their attention and then be completely silent. I think silence is implicit with attention. If aloha ʻāina is the idea that you are supposed to be reverent or respectful to the bigger picture, silence will do that because at that point you're seeing: I'm silent because I know something else is happening because it's not about me right now" (Lum 2020).

While noncommunicative, the second reason for the invocation of silence was also significant—to provide an atmosphere allowing kiaʻi and visitors to contemplate their reasons for being on the mauna without being distracted by sounds created by man. Noe Noe Wong-Wilson (Kanaka ʻŌiwi) is the executive director of the Lālākea Foundation in Hilo, a member of the new Mauna Kea Stewardship and Oversight Authority, and one of the leaders at the kūpuna encampment.[16] She relates that kiaʻi leadership instituted a ten o'clock p.m. curfew on the mauna, not simply to allow others to sleep but also to allow individuals to experience the mauna in a meaningful way.

> We wanted people to be quiet, and we didn't want to hear people. If you weren't ready to go to sleep, you could be in your tent or you could be gathered in small groups, but we didn't want to hear you. Keep the noise down and sit in a chair out there. That because it's freezing cold, it doesn't matter what time it was, but just sit there and watch the stars. Just watch the clouds move, just to hear the silence and see the mauna. Maybe the moon would come up, and you can see the outline of the mountain, and it's only you and what you're looking at. It's just you and the universe, and nobody else matters, and to just sit there for long periods of time in that silence is really spectacular. (Wong-Wilson 2022)

Silence played multiple roles on the Ala Kūpuna, especially during the arrest of kūpuna on July 17, 2019, and there were various reasons for kiaʻi leaders to invoke silence. Case clarified differing accounts I had previously heard regarding the invocation of silence while law enforcement officers arrested kūpuna and the kūpuna's insistence that they be arrested first. Their reason? To protect the younger kiaʻi and their leaders who were prepared to be arrested. This decision was intended to minimize the potential impact of arrest on younger kiaʻi's future lives and endeavors. Another possible reason, though not brought up by anyone I spoke to, was that the arrest of the younger kiaʻi could have negatively impacted decision-making, morale, and strategy among kiaʻi.

> The kūpuna themselves asked us to be silent. I took the directive from them because I was requested to be the one on the microphone to guide and remind people of the instructions set by the kūpuna that day. Silence was

Kaumakaiwa Kanakaʻole (far left, in black shirt and pants) and others performing hula on the Ala Kūpuna. Photo credit: Damon Tucker

the method by which we could honor them, keep all attention on each one of them as they were carried or led to the vans. The kūpuna had decided together to be the front line that day. We listened to them, and they said this is their sentiment, that this was their turn to do what many of them had not ever been able to do—to stand in the front. Plus, they didn't want any young people to be arrested if possible that day or any other day. There's a film where Aunty Max [Maxine Kahaʻulelio] talks about what she tells Kahoʻokahi [Kanuha] before the arrests begin that day. She says, "You will not be arrested. I will be arrested in your place. Enough young people, we need you. We need you at home. We need you working. We need you leading. We are old; most of our life is over already. This is our time and our turn." As the arrests continued that day, some of the kūpuna did speak, chant, and call out to the masses assembled, "Don't give up. Don't leave the mountain!" And until the mountain was safe, nine months later, we listened and never left. (P. Case 2020)

The decision made by the kūpuna and honored by the younger kiaʻi is similar in many ways to how Chris Griffin characterizes the role of silence in Fijian culture—one that articulates one's place and position in society and embraces cultural values: "It is hard to exaggerate the part silence plays in Fijian culture. Silence speaks of rank and hierarchy and marks the normative boundaries between groups, and individuals, even more effectively than does the spoken word. It forms, so to speak, part of the text, and in some instances is a component of those wider taboos or avoidances that mark people's relations with others. . . . Above all, though, silence or quietness is a mark of cultivation, part of that humility [yalomalua] that defines all cultured Fijians irrespective of rank" (2003).

The contexts that Griffin describes reflect the communicative purposes of silence mentioned earlier, as did the decision made by the kūpuna and honored by the younger kiaʻi: their behavior clearly communicated to law enforcement officers that the younger kiaʻi would not engage with them verbally in any manner, nor would they be lured into verbal or physical confrontation that could lead to their arrest.

Hāwane Rios was on the Ala Kūpuna when decisions were made to allow the kūpuna to be arrested. She reflects on the events of that day and notes the communicative and strategic effectiveness of this tactic and its spiritual and cultural significance.

> There is time for healing in sound and unity and sounds. There's also time
> for unity and healing in silence and the strength that comes from that.
> That day that the kupuna got arrested, my mom [Pua Case] turned to me;
> she said we're not chanting or singing unless we're asked to by the kūpuna.
> We're going to honor them today and keep the people safe because there are
> so many people there. We need to keep the people calm, and for me, that is
> not just from a nonviolent direct action standpoint but also from a cultural
> standpoint, a spiritual standpoint. That all came together in a very powerful
> and needed way because it could have been a really dangerous situation that
> day. (Rios 2020)

Wong-Wilson shared how her training as a Hawaiian cultural practitioner helped prepare the kiaʻi to be aware of their soundscape while enabling them to hear everything happening during confrontations with law enforcement. This training and the resultant silence reflect the noncommunicative nature of silence described by Griffin. Though noncommunicative, such silence is no less significant.

> That's just the way we're trained: so that our voices are not louder than
> the sound of the wind. That's what our training is: whatever the natural
> environment sound is because sometimes the wind is noisy. The sound
> of the environment and the sound of nature around us is what we want to

hear, not somebody's chatter and not talking about something that is just inappropriate for the moment that you want to be in. Silence is forcing yourself to be in that place. If you keep your mouth shut, it allows for your ears to open and for you to hear the sounds that are around you. And those sounds are part of the hōʻailona [signs] we look for, whether it's the sound of the birds or the wind or just the sounds of nature, the sound of the environment. (Wong-Wilson 2022)

In practice, this tactic allowed the kiaʻi to hear communications from law enforcement officers clearly. It also allowed the wishes of the kūpuna to be communicated to all kiaʻi. Most kiaʻi honored the request for silence and maintained it during the arrests. There were moments when kiaʻi were challenged to maintain their silence, and occasionally some could be heard crying and shouting in exasperation. In response, fellow kiaʻi would approach them and remind them that it was the request of the kūpuna. If they could not maintain silence, they were gently asked to leave the Ala Kūpuna. Ultimately, thirty-eight kūpuna were arrested, and no other kiaʻi were arrested for their actions that day—a testament to the effectiveness of their strategy and discipline.

HŌʻULUʻULU MANAʻO (SUMMARY)

As discussed in this chapter, the definitions of listening and hearing extend beyond the mere sensory experience of sound reaching one's ear. They also include the hearer's reception of information, the subsequent analytical processes, and the hearer's response (or lack thereof). Listening and hearing are far more than physiological phenomena; they are moral acts that help define one's kuleana. Josh Tatofi speaks of the desire of kiaʻi and their supporters to be heard. This hearing extends beyond the simple grasping of their words and meanings to their communicative intent and expected results—that their concerns be addressed in a meaningful way: "I think that the biggest thing about what this whole thing is the fact that we just want to be heard, as a people, heard as Polynesians, as Hawaiians, and let it be known that we are very much aware of our culture" (Tatofi 2020).

The state and university have yet to listen to these voices to understand and become good partners with the Hawaiian community by addressing its concerns. Instead, they wait for their opportunity to respond and make counterarguments over the stewardship of Maunakea and the construction of TMT. Failing to hear the people, be attentive to them and their well-being, and act in their best interests have had unpleasant consequences for political leaders in Hawaiʻi's history. For example, before the time of Kamehameha, in the moku (a large land division) of Kaʻū on Hawaiʻi Island, the lives of three despotic aliʻi—Koʻihala, Kohaikalani, and Halaʻea—were ended by the people of Kaʻū in creative and horrific ways as punishment for their mistreatment (Judd 1890).[17] While I would never advocate such action against anyone under any circumstances, I note these incidents hoping that those in power genuinely heed the voices of those who have risked their livelihoods, health, and even lives protecting Maunakea and not privilege outside interests. To continue to hear yet disregard these voices has damaged our community and the mauna's pristine environment. Should TMT be built, the damage to both will be irreparable.

NOTES

1. Interestingly, the Hawaiian dictionary does not identify a single word that represents the collective senses. Instead, it attributes ʻike (knowledge) to the use of each of the listed senses: ʻike i ka maka (seeing, or knowledge by means of the eye) (Pukui and Elbert 1986). The Hawaiian Lexicon Committee, whose work is described in chapter 4, has coined the term lonoa for "sense" (Kōmike Huaʻōlelo 2003).

2. The prefix hoʻo- is common in Hawaiian and is causative in nature. For example, lohe is the experience of hearing, where hoʻolohe implies an agency on the part of the person and intent to experience sound.

3. Other Polynesian languages contain cognates of lono and hoʻolono, and they also have gods with similar names and domains to Lono. For example, rongo is the Māori cognate of lono, and whakarongo is the Māori cognate of hoʻolono. In the Māori language, rongo (the cognate of lono) is used not just for hearing but for all senses except for sight (Moorfield 2003). Rongo is also a Māori deity associated with similar domains as Lono in Hawaiʻi.

4. Lono is one of the primary Hawaiian gods, best known as the god of fertility, rainfall, agriculture, and music. He is also referred to as the "god of sound" in *Hawaiian Mythology* (Beckwith 1976). In Beckwith's recollection of the story of Kiha, Lono blew into a shell trumpet named Kiha-pu that was in the possession of Kiha, an aliʻi of old Hawaiʻi. By blowing into it, Lono gave it "the voice of a god" (Kalakaua and Daggett 1888).

5. I have frequently heard Kānaka ʻŌiwi refer to other Pacific peoples as their cousins due to the history of the settling of the Pacific Islands and their mutual histories of voyaging and moʻokūʻauhau—kinship connections. I also noted this term used to reference kiaʻi supporters by other Indigenous communities, such as those from Native North America.

6. The Crown refers to the settler-established government of New Zealand, though in everyday use it specifically refers to its executive branch. It is a constitutional monarchy that has retained the ruling monarch of England as its sovereign ruler. The attempts to permanently settle Māori claims via this process are too nuanced to be discussed in depth here and are described in Wira Gardiner's *Return To Sender* (1996).

7. Puʻuloa was once famous for its beds of pearl oysters, which have vanished due to the activities of the US Navy in the estuary. These shells were the subject of the mele "Pūpū O ʻEwa," the basis for the song "Pearly Shells."

8. Anthony is better known in the Hawaiian community as Pua Hopkins, Anthony being her married name. She was foundational in establishing the Hawaiian Studies program at UH Mānoa and created two popular Hawaiian language textbooks. I thank kuʻualoha hoʻomanawanui for bringing this paper to my attention, as she took a class in nonverbal Hawaiian communication from Anthony in 1988.

9. Pukui discusses the importance of welcoming a guest into one's home by heahea in *Polynesian Family Systems of Old Kaʻu* (Handy and Pukui 1958).

10. Kōnane is an older Hawaiian game resembling checkers, where small pebbles are placed on a board made of either wood or stone (Pukui and Elbert 1986).

11. The idea of the birds continuing to sing (or perhaps, singing along) while chants were being performed as indicative of their familiarity with chanting is not my own. It was suggested to me several decades ago by a friend, though I've forgotten his or her identity. I confirmed the sound of birds in Kuluwaimaka's chants by listening to these recordings as found on the audio CD *Nā Leo Hawaiʻi Kahiko* (Bishop Museum 1997).

12. The hakalama is a Hawaiian syllabary that contains every combination of vowels and consonants found in the Hawaiian language. It is used in Hawaiian education programs, and I have used it regularly to train singers to properly pronounce Hawaiian words.

13. This translation comes from the document "Nā Oli no ka ʻĀina o Kanakaʻole (The chants for the Kanakaʻole Lands)" (Edith Kanakaʻole Foundation 2017).

14. The LRAD, also known as a sound cannon, is capable of generating sounds up to 160db. Most often used for communications over a long distance, it also has the potential to be a sonic weapon causing pain, discomfort, and long-term hearing problems. The American Civil Liberties Union (ACLU) of Hawaiʻi demanded that the state attorney general, Clair Connors, offer assurances that the LRADs in the possession of law enforcement officers would not be used as weapons against kiaʻi. Connors issued several communications that fell short of ACLU Hawaiʻi's demand for assurances, stating only that the LRAD would be used as means to communicate with kiaʻi (Osher 2019).

15. "He Mū 'O Ia" is a chant taught to kia'i and performed frequently on the mauna. Mū means to be silent, and it was one of the kia'i strategies of nonviolent direct action. A recording of Pua Case teaching this chant can be viewed on YouTube: https://www.youtube.com/watch?v=bJwocfIyQE4.

16. The Mauna Kea Stewardship and Oversight Authority was established in 2022. I discuss the establishment of the authority in the conclusion.

17. These events are documented in a composition and musical recording by Kekuhi Kanahele entitled "Ka'ū Kū Mākaha," released on her CD *Kekuhi* (1998).

THREE

—ₘ—

KOLO KE EWE I KE EWE

Rootlets Seek out Other Rootlets

IN THIS CHAPTER, I DISCUSS the genealogical connection between Kānaka 'Ōiwi and 'āina, the importance of this connection in regard to the protective actions of kia'i on Maunakea, and the extent to which this connection was documented in mele and mo'olelo. I consider historical and modern uses of the terms aloha 'āina and aloha 'āina 'oia'i'o and how these terms are fundamentally and irrefutably based on genealogical connections between 'āina and Kānaka 'Ōiwi. Finally, I examine three mele: "Mele O Kaho'olawe," composed during the struggle to end the bombing of Kaho'olawe by the US Navy, "Aloha 'Āina 'Oia'i'o," composed by Kainani Kahaunaele, and "For the Lāhui," composed by Josh Tatofi with Hawaiian lyrics by Hinaleimoana Wong-Kalu. The latter two mele were composed in the early days of the confrontation on Maunakea.

MO'OKŪ'AUHAU MA KE MELE: HAWAIIAN POETIC EXPRESSIONS OF GENEALOGY

Every time I reflect on why we're standing to protect Maunakea, I always return to the "Mele Ko'i Honua o Kauikeauoli," the birth chant of Kamehameha III. This chant leads us right back to the very core of our existence as a people. The genealogy of Mauna a Wākea from the mele "Hānau 'o Kauikeaouli" tells us that the mountain is our ancestor. From the union of our sky father, Wākea, and the powerful manifestation of Haumea, Earth Mother, through the form of Papawalinu'u, born was sacred mountain Mauna a Wākea. From the union of Wākea, and the mother of many of our islands, Papahānaumoku, born was Ho'ohōkūkalani, goddess of the star realm. From the union of Wākea and Ho'ohōkūkalani, was Hāloanakalaukapalili, who was stillborn and buried at the east of their home.

Pua Case (*left*) with daughters Kapulei Flores (*middle*) and Hāwane Rios (*right*).
Photo credit: E. Kalani Flores

From that burial grew the first kalo [taro], the sustenance of our people.
From the reunion of Wākea and Hoʻohōkūkalani, born was Hāloa, named
after his elder brother, meaning "the eternal breath." From Hāloa comes the
Kānaka ʻŌiwi people, the original peoples of Hawaiʻinuiākea [great and
broad Hawaiʻi]. This chant connects me and every single person who has
Kānaka ʻŌiwi blood running through their veins and genealogies to a sacred
ancestral knowledge that teaches us of our relationship to everything that
gives and sustains life. And it is this very teaching that grounds me and my
family to our sacred commitment to protect the sacred. Maunakea is my
ancestor, and because of that truth, it is my birthright to uphold my kuleana
[responsibility, right], my lineal responsibility to show up, stand up, and
speak up for the rights of this place that has given and will continue to gift
me, my kūpuna, my ʻohana, our lāhui, and our descendants' life. So when I
say, "We are Maunakea," I mean it with everything that I am. (Rios 2020)

Hāwane Rios is a native of Waimea, a small town located in the saddle area
with the Kohala Mountains to its north and Maunakea to its southeast. She
is a haku mele, singer, recording artist, and kiaʻi. She considers Maunakea

her ancestor and muse—the source of inspiration for her compositions. Her mother, Pua Case, has spent her entire life in Waimea. Case's father, William, was the water supervisor for Parker Ranch—one of the major private land-owners on Hawai'i mokupuni (Hawai'i Island).[1] Because of this family history, Case considers herself a water protector by birth. She cites her genealogical connection to Maunakea through Manaua—a rain rock located in Waimea that she, her 'ohana, and others with genealogical ties to it care for. Rios, Case, and other family members have been involved in legal actions against the state for over a decade to halt the development of TMT and rectify the substantial environmental damage caused by the astronomy industry on Maunakea. Between the 2015 confrontation at the TMT groundbreaking and the July 2019 arrest of kia'i for their role in preventing construction equipment from ascending to the TMT construction site, Rios and Case traveled the world to increase awareness of the issues on the mauna. Both returned to Hawai'i mokupuni before the state and TMT partnership's renewed attempt to begin construction in the summer of 2019. As they are kupa o ka 'āina (citizens or long familiar with or born on the land), Case and Rios can trace their genealogical connection to Maunakea back many generations and are but two of countless Kānaka 'Ōiwi who share these same connections and who have stood in defense of Maunakea and other lands.

Two types of mele are genealogical in nature. Mele of the first type, mele ko'ihonua (cosmogonic genealogies), express the connection between Kānaka 'Ōiwi, the akua, and the land. Several mele ko'ihonua document the creation of the Hawaiian world and Kānaka 'Ōiwi. Some are variations of the same telling, and others address creation differently. While they differ and sometimes contradict each other, many acknowledge the genealogical relationship between the 'āina, akua, and kānaka. The mele ko'ihonua Rios refers to is known by several names: "He Kānaenae no ka Hānau 'ana o Kauikeaouli" (An affectionate chant for the birth of Kauikeaouli), "Hānau a Hua ka Lani," and "O Hānau ka Mauna a Kea." Silva explains that "O Hānau ka Mauna a Kea" is the most common name used today as this is the first line of the verse that identifies Mauna Kea as the sacred, first-born child of Wākea and Papahānaumoku (2023).

The Kumulipo is the best-known mele ko'ihonua, and Kame'eleihiwa explains its significance: "Hawaiian identity is, in fact, derived from the Kumulipo, the great cosmogonic genealogy. Its essential lesson is that every aspect of the Hawaiian conception of the world is related by birth, and as such, all parts of the Hawaiian world are one indivisible lineage. Conceived in this way, the genealogy of the Land, the Gods, Chiefs, and people intertwine with one another, and with all the myriad aspects of the universe" (1992).

The Kumulipo contains over two thousand lines and was composed around 1700 by Keāulumoku for Kaʻīimamao to trace his genealogy to the earth's creation. Kalākaua later used the Kumulipo to affirm his claim to the throne and facilitate his sister Liliʻuokalani's subsequent ascendance to the throne when he died in 1891 (Oliveira 2014).

The second type, mele kūʻauhau, documents genealogy—connections to human ancestors (Brown 2016; Silva 2016). Oliveira argues that mele koʻihonua "are crucial to understanding a Kanaka worldview, and through these cosmogonic genealogies, we learn of the formation of the ʻāina, the first living organisms, and the birth of akua [gods] and people" (Oliveira 2014).[2] As such, moʻokūʻauhau is "a foundation of ʻŌiwi culture, identity, and worldview" (hoʻomanawanui 2014).

One ʻōlelo noʻeau (proverbial saying) associated with Maunakea is "Maunakea piko kaulana o ka ʻāina."[3] Kumu Pono Associates utilized this phrase as the title of their 2005 report to the University of Hawaiʻi Office of Mauna Kea Management. They translated the phrase as "the famous summit of the land" (Maly and Maly 2005). While this translation is not inaccurate, it does not consider the more significant meaning of piko as the umbilical connection between the mauna and the heavens and between the mauna and Kānaka ʻŌiwi. However, the report later acknowledges this meaning and the historic practice of taking a newborn child's ʻiewe (placenta) for burial at Puʻu Pōhaku to ensure the health and long life of the child (Maly and Maly 2005). This practice continued for many years into the twentieth century.

In the late 1990s, the State of Hawaiʻi's Department of Health (DOH) instituted an administrative rule change forbidding the return of any human tissue, including the placenta, due to concerns over HIV and other infectious health issues. However, the DOH and hospitals did not consistently apply this rule. The issue came to a head in 2005 when Kaiser Medical Center denied a request to return the placenta of a Kanaka ʻŌiwi couple's newborn child. The couple, supported by the Native Hawaiian Legal Corporation, sued for the return of the placenta. Eventually, the rule preventing the return of ʻiewe was changed (Altonn 2006). The practice of burying ʻiewe near the summit of Maunakea continues today. Kalani Makekau-Whittaker, better known as "MC Mauna" at Puʻuhuluhulu, considers himself "He kauā hoʻokō no ka lāhui" (A hardworking servant for the nation) and describes the significance of placing of his children's umbilical cords on the mauna.[4]

> I'm originally from Oʻahu, but my wife and her family are from Hilo. We live on the slopes of Maunakea, and we always taught our children the importance of connection to place, and so they would refer to it as "my

mauna." So it's a very intimate, personal connection for them. And not just in that way, but also all three of our keiki [child/children] have their piko [umbilical cord] up there. So there's that connection. Also, before our eldest [child] left for college, in fact, I think that was the day before she left, we went up there and just did a ceremony at Waiau to make sure that she keeps connected no matter where she goes in the world. So there's that kind of connection to Maunakea for us. (Makekau-Whittaker 2020)

A reference to ewe (a variant spelling for ʻīewe) is found in the fourth line of the mele koʻihonua for Kauikeaouli and other older mele but is less common in modern compositions. Kimura does include such a reference in his mele aloha ʻāina "Kulaiwi": "ʻaʻohe mea, nāna e kūʻai i ke ewe o kuʻu mau iwi" (poetically, "no one can purchase my birthright, my very being"). Kimura composed this mele, now considered a standard of the Hawaiian music canon, in the 1970s after attending a gathering with a group of Native Americans. They questioned him about the lands that had once belonged to the Hawaiian Kingdom but were illegally seized after the overthrow of the monarchy and later transferred to the state and federal governments. Their question implied that Kānaka ʻŌiwi no longer had collective lands to call their own. "Kulaiwi" was Kimura's response to this question. Kulaiwi means "field [or plain] of bones" but metaphorically refers to all lands inhabited by the ancestors of today's Kānaka ʻŌiwi. In Kimura's translation, all of Hawaiʻi's lands are the birthright of Kānaka ʻŌiwi.[5]

Manulani Meyer notes that a Hawaiian cultural identity recognizes a link "to place, to our role in history and our own sequence in genealogy" (2003). She adds that the importance of genealogy is not unique to Hawaiian culture; what is significant is "its priority in how it was shaped and how it also formulated what was worth knowing and thus carried on" (Meyer 2003). Scholar and kiaʻi hoʻomanawanui articulate how moʻolelo (stories) document genealogical connections to the ʻāina, reflect the term Kānaka ʻŌiwi used to identify themselves as a people, and differentiate their place in this world from later colonizers and settlers:[6] "Within a Kanaka Maoli context, traditional moʻolelo recount our origins as being descendants of our Earth Mother, Papahānaumoku, and Sky Father, Wākea; thus, Kānaka Maoli are the Indigenous population of the Hawaiian Islands. Our names for ourselves, Kānaka Maoli, ʻŌiwi, and Hawaiʻi are reflective of the primacy of moʻokūʻauhau in our worldview and its connection to our ʻāina" (2019).

Marie Alohalani Brown notes that moʻolelo, mele, and kaʻao (explanation to follow) are forms of Hawaiian literature that overlap—"mele koʻihonua such as the Kumulipo, which is a genealogy and a sanctifying prayer for an ali'i, may inform mo'olelo, which in turn may inform ka'ao" (2016). As such, ho'omanawanui expands on why characterizing any of these literary forms as fiction, legend, or myth is improper and inaccurate: "Within a Kanaka 'Ōiwi cultural context, however, concepts such as mythology and folklore are not merely fictitious inventions of imagination, but are also historically and genealogically based on real figures and ancestors, some of whom become deified because of their extraordinary feats" (2017).

Rios explains how her genealogical connections to Maunakea are amplified through mo'olelo and ka'ao, citing the mo'olelo of the romance between Hawaiian deities Kūkahau'ala and Lilinoe.

> I was in makahiki 'elua [second-year Hawaiian language studies], and I was just starting to understand our language. Auntie Ku'ulei Keakealani told the story ma ka 'ōlelo Hawai'i [in the Hawaiian language], and I understood it. And not just on a basic level of understanding Hawaiian, but I could feel it. I could feel that love of Kūkahau'ula traveling all the way across from Kahiki and settling in Kawaihae and going up to that mauna every single day and being met with like the blistering cold. Having that relationship with that story and getting up every morning and seeing the mountain that I was raised looking at change color at sunrise and sunset and now knowing why. Because I know Kūkahau'ula was making his way up to love Poli'ahu. And so connection to 'āina has been such a huge medicine for me, such as in my reclaiming of my own ea [sovereignty, independence, breath] and my own mauli [spiritual essence] and falling in love with 'āina through love stories that our kūpuna passed. (Rios 2020)

Rios makes a significant point in this story: the importance of one's ability to hear these stories and genealogies in 'ōlelo Hawai'i and to understand their meaning without reading someone else's interpretation, regardless of how skilled or poetic the translation may be. Heoli Osorio speaks to the impossibility of accurately translating texts into English: "As Kanaka Maoli scholars, we constantly recognize that it is impossible to convey all of the cultural coding that English strips away, and equally impossible to avoid the western cultural coding that English adds" (2021). In the process of hearing and making her own meaning, empowered by her ability to understand 'ōlelo Hawai'i and her cultural knowledge, Rios connected deeply and personally with the people and places expressed by Keakealani in a way that may not have been possible with the cultural coding inherent in an English translation of the story.

KE ALOHA ʻĀINA AND KE ALOHA ʻĀINA ʻOIAʻIʻO

The historical authenticity of the term aloha ʻāina was challenged by Western academics in the 1980s—a challenge that was vigorously contested and soundly undermined by Kānaka ʻŌiwi scholars, particularly Haunani Kay Trask.[7] Pukui and Elbert note in their definition of the term that "aloha ʻāina is a very old concept, to judge from the many sayings [perhaps thousands] illustrating deep love of the land" (Pukui and Elbert 1986). While there are many examples in Hawaiian literature from which to choose, I cite one from the late nineteenth century. Iosepa Kahoʻoluhi Nāwahīokalaniʻōpuʻu was a lawyer, legislator, educator, and newspaper publisher born in Kaimū, Puna, on Hawaiʻi Island in August 1842. Nāwahī and other former legislators under the monarchy founded Ka Hui Hawaii Aloha Aina (the Hawaiian Patriotic League) on March 14, 1893—less than two months after the overthrow of the monarchy. In 1895, Nāwahī and his wife, Emma, founded and published a newspaper named *Ke Aloha Aina*. They published many articles on the concept and meaning of aloha ʻāina in its pages (Silva 2004). While Nāwahī died in 1896, *Ke Aloha Aina* enjoyed "immense popularity" under Emma's leadership until she died in 1910. *Ke Aloha Aina* ceased publication in 1920 (Chapin 1996).[8]

Silva describes aloha ʻāina as a "complex concept that includes recognizing that we are an integral part of the ʻāina and the ʻāina is an integral part of us" (2017). For Emalani Case, aloha ʻāina is "a fierce love of place" instilled in her by her father (2021). She adds that to embrace aloha ʻāina is to embrace the cosmologies represented in moʻolelo, moʻokūʻauhau, and mele koʻihonua, which leads to understanding that ʻāina is an ancestor of Kānaka ʻŌiwi and committing to care for and protect it as an ancestor. University of Hawaiʻi Maui College Professor Kaleikoa Kaʻeo expands on this concept.

> You have to understand the meaning of where ʻāina comes from, yet the basic meaning—that which feeds or you, providing life and sustenance. Then you look at the Polynesian meaning of the word ʻāina, the ancient meaning itself coming forward—kāinga—and for what this kāinga means in Polynesian languages.[9] It's a familial relationship; it's family. So you can see, even in Polynesian what we call land or ʻāina has a deeper meaning, which is, of course, family, but the idea of the land itself. We have this familial relationship in the same way. You are of a family in that same way you are all that land. So that teaches us something about how we saw who we are as Kānaka. We are of the land itself, very different than the kind of meanings that have been imposed upon us as a people. (Kaʻeo 2019)

Hawaiian composer, singer, and scholar Jon Osorio (Kanaka ʻŌiwi) expands on the idea of aloha ʻāina being land-specific more broadly to nature and all the ʻāina provides for humanity: "Aloha ʻāina is a relationship not just with the land but really with nature itself and in particular, that part of the land and sea and streams and water that actually sustains life. ʻAi [to eat/food] is the word that means to eat and when we say ʻāina we're talking basically about what it is that feeds not just humans but basically everything, and everything is directly dependent and interdependent with the ʻāina" (J. K. K. Osorio 2016a).

An examination of the historical record of hundreds of thousands of pages documenting the lives and thoughts of Kānaka ʻŌiwi from the early nineteenth century well into the twentieth century expands on overly simplistic definitions of aloha ʻāina and further contextualizes it.

> Throughout the thousands of songs, newspaper articles, publications, letters, journals, and legal documents now available, it is clear that the term aloha ʻāina begins its form of meaning as attached to the context into which it was born, one that allowed for cultural sentiment to become well documented in a Hawaiian national context, but also when and how it was popularized. Aloha ʻāina, considered in its many historical contexts, is an expression of love for the mōʻi, land [nation], and people. It is a sentiment that unifies the three parts, intoning the power of this triad and its strength in pride and, therefore, in moments of political resistance. (Sai-Dudoit and Tolentino 2022)

The *Buke Mele Lāhui* (Book of Nationalist Songs) was published in 1895 and contains many mele aloha ʻāina collected from newspapers printed in the 1880s and early 1890s (Testa 2003). Most compositions in the book express patriotism and love of the ʻāina, and some explicitly include the terms aloha ʻāina or the equivalent "aloha i ka ʻāina" in titles and texts. "Kaulana Nā Pua" is perhaps the era's best-known mele aloha ʻāina. It appears in *Buke Mele Lāhui* with the title "Mele Aloha ʻĀina"—the same title used when the newspaper *Hawaii Holomua* originally published the mele just over a month after the overthrow of the monarchy (Stillman 1999; hoʻomanawanui 2005).[10]

The concept of aloha ʻāina reentered the broader public consciousness in the 1970s when an organization known as the Protect Kahoʻolawe ʻOhana (hereafter simply referred to as the ʻOhana) began to challenge the US Navy's use of the island of Kahoʻolawe, located across from the southwest shore of Maui. The US military seized the island for military use after the bombing of Pearl Harbor on December 7, 1941, continued to exert control of the island for decades, and used it for many purposes, including bombing the land for practice. In 1976, members of the ʻOhana filed a lawsuit that sought to end the military's use and control over Kahoʻolawe. In addition to the legal battles waged by the ʻOhana, members of the organization began to stealthily travel to and hide on the island in days leading up to the navy's attempts to use the island for target practice. Their initial efforts to stop the bombing were successful. On January 24, 1976, seven men and two women, later named "the Kahoʻolawe Nine," occupied the island and inspired other occupations.[11]

One year later, on January 24, 1977, five more individuals landed on Kahoʻolawe. Unlike previous occupations, however, their presence did not deter the military from bombing the island. After unsuccessfully lobbying Hawaiʻi politicians to end the bombing, three ʻOhana members—George Helm, Kimo Mitchell, and Bobby Mitchell—traveled to Kahoʻolawe on March 7, 1977, to locate their friends despite the presence of a horrific storm.[12] Bobby Mitchell reportedly lost sight of his friends in the foul weather; Helm and Kimo Mitchell were lost at sea near the small island of Molokini. Bobby returned to Kahoʻolawe and was picked up two days later by the military. It would take another decade and continuous efforts by those opposed to the military's control of the island before President George H. W. Bush instructed his secretary of defense to end the military's use of the island in 1990. In 1994, the US government transferred jurisdiction of the island and its surrounding waters to the State of Hawaiʻi, providing funding for the removal of unexploded munitions and other hazards (Protect Kahoʻolawe ʻOhana n.d.).

The landing of the Kahoʻolawe Nine was of such significance to the Hawaiian music community that the June 1976 issue of *Haʻilono Mele*—the newsletter of the Hawaiian Music Foundation—featured a picture of the Kahoʻolawe Nine on its cover. George Helm was the featured artist for that issue of the newsletter, and the feature written about him by Kimo Turner filled nearly two full pages (Turner 1976). *Haʻilono Mele* also featured a full-page requiem for Helm in its June 1977 issue (Haugen 1977).

While he did not release any commercial recordings during his lifetime, Helm was a gifted and respected musician best known for his distinctive falsetto voice. A bootleg cassette recording of one of his performances at the Gold Coin Restaurant on Oʻahu became the source of a remastered CD of selected songs after Hana Ola Records purchased the rights to the recording from the restaurant owner and came to a royalty agreement with Helm's family (Cord International 1996).[13] Forty years after Helm's disappearance, his younger brother Adolph explained how Helm had been able to win over people who had considered him a troublemaker because of his activism: "How do you draw people to listen to you? To me, it was his music. He then took the opportunity to educate people. I think that's how people were able to gravitate

Musical performance at the Protect Kahoʻolawe rally held at ʻIolani Palace on January 16, 1977. *Left to right*: George Helm, Walter Ritte, Liko Martin, Harry Mitchell. Photo credit: Ian Lind

toward him" (Adolph Helm in Uechi 2017). George Helm addressed the issue of being a Hawaiian music artist and activist and the criticism that embodying both sometimes attracts: "I reject the contention that Hawaiian musicians should only stick to music. There is no dichotomy in my mind between my music and my life and my involvements. Many people in their contention that Hawaiian musicians should just stick to music are talking about the image of the musicians. Image, after all, is a cosmetic, it's make-up, it's a device which when one recognizes how ugly one is, one uses. I am not so concerned with my image as a musician as I am with the ideas that I am expressing" (George Helm in Turner 1976).

One of the most enduring and endearing mele aloha ʻāina of this time was written by Harry Kūnihi Mitchell of Keʻanae, Maui, father of Kimo Mitchell, for the men and women of the Protect Kahoʻolawe ʻOhana. He invokes older names for Kahoʻolawe and praises the original Kahoʻolawe Nine. Mitchell also uses the aloha ʻāina themes of alu like (working together), restoring pono (that which is proper), i mua (progress, move forward), and lanakila (victory).

MELE O KAHOʻOLAWE

Harry Kūnihi Mitchell

FIRST VERSE

Aloha kuʻu moku ʻo Kahoʻolawe	Beloved is my island Kahoʻolawe
Mai kinohi kou inoa ʻo Kanaloa	Whose original name was Kanaloa
Kohemālamalama	Also known as the shining vagina
Lau kanaka ʻole	Unpopulated
Hiki mai nā pua	Until you were invaded by nine young men
E hoʻomalu mai	Who granted you peace

SECOND VERSE

Alu like kākou Lāhui Hawaiʻi	Let us work together as the Hawaiian nation
Mai ka lā hiki mai i ka lā kau aʻe	From sunrise to sunset
Kū paʻa a hahai a hoʻikaika nā kānaka	Stand together and follow, be strong young people
Kau liʻi mākou	We are few in numbers
Nui ke aloha no ka ʻāina	But our love for the land is great

THIRD VERSE

Hanohano nā pua o Hawaiʻi nei	We honor the young people of Hawaiʻi
No ke kaua kauholo me ka aupuni	For their battle with the government
Paʻa pū ka manaʻo o no ka pono o ka ʻāina	With solidarity of thought to bring prosperity to the land
I mua nā pua, lanakila Kahoʻolawe	Go forth, young people, and bring victory to Kahoʻolawe[14]

The final line of the second verse and the third line of the third verse express aloha for the ʻāina, remaining attentive to its needs and not simply what it provides. Aloha ʻāina and its underlying concepts were the subjects of contentious academic debates in the 1990s that pitted Kanaka ʻŌiwi scholar Haunani Kay Trask against nonnative scholars. Those scholars embraced the then-trendy anthropological theories of the "invention of tradition," which posits that "traditions which appear or claim to be old are often quite recent in origin and sometimes invented" (Hobsbawm and Ranger 1983). They argued that Kānaka ʻŌiwi were attempting to "invoke a mythic past to legitimize and promote solidarity in the present" in their arguments to end the US military's use of Kahoʻolawe as a site to practice bombing (Linnekin 1983). Trask noted that the cultural value of caring for the land was a historical practice that continues into the present. She emphasized the complicity of Western scholars, most notably anthropologists, in refuting the authenticity of contemporary cultural practices to bolster the military's argument and desire to maintain control of Kahoʻolawe (Trask 1991). Sadly, many academics continue to use their positions and influence in ways that empower and perpetuate colonial and military enterprises.

A more recent example of the state's refusal to acknowledge and honor the historical basis of contemporary Kānaka ʻŌiwi spiritual practices occurred in 2019 when it ordered the dismantling of an ahu (altar) that kiaʻi had constructed at the Hale Kū Kiaʻi Mauna and the TMT construction site. Officers removed religious offerings and instructed individuals who had placed them to remove them within thirty days, or the offerings would be forfeited or destroyed. This removal was a significant event for many reasons. An ahu is "a Hawaiian altar, shrine, or cairn utilized for spiritual and ceremonial purposes in both the past and the present" (Hawaiʻinuiākea School of Hawaiian Knowledge n.d.). They are made by stacking rocks in various shapes without cement or similar materials. Ahu more than fifty years old may be protected under state and federal historic preservation laws, but newer structures are not. Regardless, "modern ahu are considered as authentic as the ancient structures, being part of a living Hawaiian culture that still continues today" (Hawaiʻinuiākea School of Hawaiian Knowledge n.d.). Emalani Case was in Aotearoa when these events occurred: "I read the news and cried. [In fact, the weight of that memory still makes me cry.] 'Why are we not allowed to age?' I thought. 'Why are our structures, created in this moment in time, not allowed to grow old?'" (2021). Kanaka ʻŌiwi scholar and kiaʻi David Uahihea Maile provides a lucid answer: "Although the state constitution claims to protect Native Hawaiian customary and traditional cultural practices, including religion, with an attempt to eliminate Kānaka Maoli relations with Mauna a Wākea by desecrating and destroying religious offerings, it instead has demonstrated it will remove hoʻokupu (religious offerings) and ahu to assist astronomy industry development and to secure settler capital" (Maile 2021).

In recent years, the term Aloha ʻĀina ʻOiaʻiʻo (a true lover of the land) has become prominent during Kānaka ʻŌiwi interventions that seek to address historical and contemporary wrongs committed by the US, state, and county governments, private companies, institutions, and organizations. *Ke Aloha ʻOiaʻiʻo* was also the name of a short-lived (1896–1897) pro-monarchy and pro-Kānaka newspaper published by Kanaka ʻŌiwi patriot Robert L. Wilcox (Chapin 1996).[15] Kaʻeo notes the extent to which individuals self-identified as

Aloha ʻĀina ʻOiaʻiʻo during that time: "Those words, aloha ʻāina ʻoiaʻiʻo, were famous words that were spoken during the time of the so-called overthrow and the purported, so-called annexation of the Hawaiian Islands when are people called out to identify who we were as Kanaka Aloha ʻOiaʻiʻo—the true lovers of the land—the meaning of patriotism. But think about how we said what a patriot was. A true patriot was, in fact, that you love the land itself" (2019).

The phrases aloha ʻāina and aloha ʻāina ʻoiaʻiʻo and the ideas they embody are common in contemporary mele composed for Maunakea, its protectors, and other cases where Kānaka ʻŌiwi contest control of or access to Hawaiian lands.

These practices reflect the realization of kiaʻi that they are not simply protecting land with their efforts to prevent further desecration of Maunakea—they are protecting a beloved kupuna. This practice is reflected in a well-known ʻōlelo noʻeau, "E kolo ana nō ke ewe i ke ewe" (The rootlet will creep toward the rootlets). Pukui interprets this ʻōlelo noʻeau to mean "Of the same origin, kinfolk will seek out and love each other" (1983). This saying explains the unprecedented number of Kānaka ʻŌiwi and allies who rallied to protect Maunakea and the bonds within the Kānaka ʻŌiwi community that came together for the cause. History does indeed repeat itself, as the practices of haku mele and musical performance are called on to serve the lāhui and remind us of their power to reconnect Kānaka ʻŌiwi to the practices of their ancestors.

MELE, THE MAUNA, AND MOʻOKŪʻAUHAU CONSCIOUSNESS

Kānaka ʻŌiwi's relationship with their past is not static and is aptly described in the well-known saying "I ka wā ma mua, ka wā ma hope" (In the past is the future). My translation is simplistic and literal; Hawaiian scholars have unpacked this simple phrase's various layers of thought. In *Native Lands, Foreign Desires*, Lilikalā Kameʻeleihiwa examines the spatial and temporal meanings of ma mua and ma hope to explain their relationship with the past and physical space: "Interestingly, in Hawaiian, the past is referred to as ka wā mamua, or 'the time in front or before.'[16] Whereas the future, when thought of at all, is ka wā mahope, or 'the time which comes after or behind.' It is as if the Hawaiian stands firmly in the present, with his back to the future and his eyes fixed upon the past, seeking historical answers for present-day dilemmas. Such an orientation is to the Hawaiian an eminently practical one, for the future is always unknown, whereas the past is rich in glory and knowledge" (Kameʻeleihiwa 1992).

Ka wā ma mua "stretches all the way back to pō [night/darkness] and ao [the emergence of light] that begin the epic Kumulipo" (Wilson-Hokowhitu 2019).

Ka wā ma hope, the future, remains the great unknown for which Kānaka'Ōiwi prepare. Silva refers to this epistemological position as "mo'okū'auhau consciousness." She observes this position in the writings of eighteenth century Kanaka 'Ōiwi scholars Joseph Ho'ona'auao Kānepu'u and Poepoe. This observation expands the thought of ka wā ma hope even further to show the implications of present-day decisions on future kānaka: "Kānepu'u and Poepoe [among many others] thought about the Kānaka descendants of the twenty-first century, and they wrote with us in mind. They drew on their ancestral knowledge and accepted and carried out the kuleana to record it so that Kānaka in their own time(s) as well as in the distant future would benefit from it" (Silva 2017).

Hōkūlani Holt recounts a conversation with kia'i leader Kaho'okahi Kanuha (Kanaka 'Ōiwi) on the mauna during the standoff. They talked about the establishment of the Pūnana Leo Hawaiian language immersion preschools and Papahana Kaiapuni Hawai'i immersion schools, of which Kanuha is a graduate. While Holt does not explicitly use the term "mo'okū'auhau consciousness," her description of decisions made over thirty years ago is exemplary of mo'okū'auhau consciousness and how the foresight of those who founded these schools ultimately manifests in and impacts the current movement to protect Maunakea.

> One day upon the mauna, I was having lunch, and Kaho'okahi Kanuha
> sat next to me. He was eating, and I turned to him and said, "You know
> you are what we planned for thirty years ago." And he looked at me, and
> he said, "What do you mean?" I said, "When the Pūnana Leo was started,
> when Hawaiian language immersion schools started, when we decided our
> children must go to college, when we made sure that Hawaiian culture was
> part of our children's education. The plan was in thirty years ago, and you are
> the outcome of that plan." He turned to me and said, "Don't you love it when
> a plan comes together?" "Yes, I do." Then he said, "Thank you for thinking
> ahead." And I think that is what has happened. People like Kaho'okahi are
> adding a page where they're in a position and educated in cultural knowledge
> and to be able to take that into all aspects of our community, not least of
> which is political. (Holt 2020)

Many kia'i, like Kainani Kahaunaele, Ānuenue Pūnua, and others, brought their keiki (children) to the mauna. Keiki assumed kuleana (responsibilities) to assist around the encampment in various ways, and many witnessed the arrests of kūpuna on July 17, 2019. The parents of these keiki demonstrated the mo'okū'auhau consciousness shown by their ancestors by preparing their children to carry out their responsibilities as Aloha 'Āina 'Oia'i'o for future generations while assuring that their safety and well-being were always at the forefront.

In 2021, Kamanamaikalani Beamer (Kanaka ʻŌiwi) was appointed as the inaugural Dana Naone Hall Endowed Chair in Hawaiian Studies, Literature, and the Environment at the Kamakakūokalani Center for Hawaiian Studies at the University of Hawaiʻi at Mānoa. He is a member of the famed Beamer family, which includes some of the most revered composers and performers in the annals of Hawaiian music. Residing in the Waimea area on the slopes of Maunakea, as many of his ancestors did, Beamer displays moʻokūʻauhau consciousness while reflecting on Kānaka ʻŌiwi's genealogical connection to the land and his responsibilities to his descendants: "I knew at that point [when TMT passed its last legal hurdle in the Hawaiʻi Supreme Court] that for the future of my children and grandchildren, they deserve to see plateaus of Maunakea that are undeveloped. And I think what we gain is the world's future students and intellectuals. People want to learn about what we're doing and how we're organizing, and our knowledge systems and perspectives on stewardship and aloha ʻāina as a result because our ʻāina is our ancestor. I mean, that's essentially what we're saying: she has limits; she has rights" (2020).

Not every kiaʻi arrived on the mauna with a strong sense of connection to it. Isaac Maluhia Castillo was raised on the mainland but currently resides in Hawaiʻi. He knew little of his Hawaiian ancestry until reconnecting with his biological father, a Kanaka ʻŌiwi, on Hawaiʻi Island approximately three years before the confrontations between kiaʻi and law enforcement in July 2019.

> And then when they're [kiaʻi on the mauna] saying things like "you're genetically related to this ʻāina and this mountain." I'm waking up every day, I unzip my tent and look at it. And if you do that every day and sit on a lava field, it's going to affect the way you perceive yourself and the rest of your world. So I definitely think it's changed my appreciation for this place, not just as an island or something, but as an actual home, how it relates to me, and how I'm a part of it. It deserves to be respected and protected, and how it's not just about Hawaiians doing that but everybody participating in whatever way they can. (Castillo 2020)

Lehua Kalima-Alvarez (Kanaka ʻŌiwi) grew up in Keaukaha, near Hilo on Hawaiʻi mokupuni. She attended Kamehameha Schools, where she formed the musical group Nā Leo Pilimehana with her classmates Nālani Jenkins (Choy) and Angela Morales. They have performed and recorded together for over forty years and won many Nā Hōkū Hanohano Awards. As a solo artist, Kalima-Alvarez has won multiple Nā Hōkū Hanohano Awards, including wins as a composer in the prestigious Song of the Year category. While she does not possess a deep knowledge of her genealogical ties to Maunakea, she does articulate her intimate relationship to the mauna growing up near the shores of Keaukaha.

> I grew up staring at it [Maunakea] every morning. We had a pretty clear view of it from Keaukaha. You go jump in the ocean, and, in Keaukaha, that's your view—you see the mauna. We take it for granted, obviously, but it was always there, and it felt like a guardian in a sense. I realize now that we're trying to become the guardians of the mauna, but there is this definite role that it played in just feeling like everything is fine. Even when you would see storms, where they all came from the north, and Hilo would get nothing. When [hurricanes] 'Iwa and 'Iniki hit Hawai'i, there were blue skies in Hilo. So my connection is just living on the land, being a part of it, and drinking the water every day. It came from Maunakea, and we swam in the water every day. All of those [freshwater] ponds in Keaukaha come up from the waters from Maunakea. It's a part of you. (Kalima-Alvarez 2020)

Regardless of the extent of their knowledge of their ancestral connections to Maunakea, kia'i like Case, Ka'eo, Holt, Kanuha, Beamer, Castillo, Kalima, and many others have demonstrated a fierce love of place that embodies their mo'okū'auhau consciousness and inherent responsibilities to their ancestors and descendants alike.

NĀ MELE ALOHA 'ĀINA HOU: NEW SONGS OF FIERCE LOVE FOR MAUNAKEA

Kainani Kahaunaele was present on July 17, 2019, for the arrest of kūpuna by state law enforcement officers. While she contributed in other ways and was always ready to offer kōkua (assistance), she recognizes that one of her primary roles and contributions was to perform music for the kūpuna and those in the kūpuna tent.

> As a songwriter, I want to be inspired. I want to put out great mele, and I know that what was happening on Maunakea was going to be something that would be a long haul, and my primary role up on the mauna was to make music. Yeah, I'll help here, help there. But I just check in, say my alohas, and go straight to the mics. And so knowing the role of the mele, knowing the function, how it affected people, how it made the kūpuna happy, the kūpuna tent, how it helped me, and how it helped me realize again my contribution through delivering mele up there. (Kahaunaele 2020a)

Several other individuals had already composed and shared their mele on Facebook since the beginning of the confrontation with law enforcement that week. Kahaunaele wrote her mele "Aloha ʻĀina ʻOiaʻiʻo" in a single sitting a few days after the arrests, wanting the song to be short and memorable: "When I wrote ʻAloha ʻĀina ʻOiaʻiʻo,' I wanted it to be learner friendly or singer friendly. I wanted it to be easy and put into the home, and I wanted it to be sung by ʻohana, schools, hālau [schools where hula is taught], not necessarily a performance or a solo thing. It took a while. I did it in one sitting, but because I wanted it to be short. I had to think really hard how to express the idea concisely, something uplifting. So even though it's short and simple, it was hard" (2020a).

While there are many approaches to haku mele, Hawaiian poetry is often characterized as terse. "In practice, a composer attempts to distill a composition by using the minimal number of words required to express the composer's thoughts" (Donaghy 2010), so Kahaunaele's measured approach is not surprising. In his examination of compositions by famed haku mele Helen Desha Beamer (1882–1952), John Charlot suggests that Beamer restricted her word choice in her mele because of the gradual loss of the Hawaiian language and the inability of the audiences of her time to understand less common words. He also cites Western society's disapproval of sexual expression and proposes that these sensibilities influenced her compositional process (Charlot 2008). I interviewed Beamer's grandson Mahiʻai Beamer in 2008; his cousin Gaye Beamer was also present. Both disagreed with Charlot's conclusion. They believe that their grandmother used whatever words most accurately expressed her poetic ideas and did not consider the audience's ability or inability to understand the language. Charlot has acknowledged the Beamer family's objections to his interpretation, emphasizing that he based his interpretation on his examination of Beamer's compositions. He adds that his interpretation of the text "has no more authority than its arguments" and concludes that "no one can enter into an artist's soul" (Charlot 2008). We are fortunate that Kahauanele and other composers of mele for Maunakea and the kiaʻi have clearly articulated their compositional intent.

With the composition completed and several of her musical companions scheduled to return to Honolulu, Kahaunaele arranged an impromptu recording session using a borrowed sound system in her garage in Wainaku, just outside Hilo. She posted her first video recording of "Aloha ʻĀina ʻOiaʻiʻo" on Facebook on the evening of July 23, 2019. Lee Ann Ānuenue Pūnua, Kahaunaele's daughter Kaniaulono Hāpai, Halehaku Seabury, and Emma Coloma-Nakano joined Kahaunaele in the recorded performance (Kahaunaele 2020b).[17]

ALOHA ʻĀINA ʻOIAʻIʻO

Kainani Kahaunaele

FIRST VERSE

E welo mau nō kuʻu aloha	My love will always prevail
No kuʻu ʻāina ʻo Hawaiʻi	For my homeland of Hawaiʻi
ʻOni a paʻa me ka lōkahi	Standing firm in unity
Aloha ʻāina ʻoiaʻiʻo	I am truly of my beloved land
Aloha ʻāina ʻoiaʻiʻo	I am truly of my beloved land

SECOND VERSE

Huliāmahi, e kuʻu lāhui	Rise up, my people
I ka poli o Maunakea	Be embraced by Maunakea
Mai ʻō a ʻō a puni ka honua	From all around the world
Kūpaʻa mau, e nā Hawaiʻi	We remain steadfast, Hawaiʻi
Kūpaʻa mau, e nā Hawaiʻi	We remain steadfast, Hawaiʻi
I ola ē nā kini ē	So that our people live
I ola ē nā kini ē	So that our people live
Ola!	Live![18]

"Aloha ʻĀina ʻOiaʻiʻo" uses words common in mele aloha ʻāina—ʻoni a paʻa or ʻonipaʻa (to remain firm), huliamahi (to rise and join in unity), kūpaʻa mau (to remain steadfast), mai ʻō a ʻō a puni ka honua (to call out to people around the world), and ola (to live). These words and those of many of the mele composed for this movement are now embodied: to rise, stand, and fight for the ʻāina. Aloha ʻāina is not simply a mindset or a philosophy; it must be followed by action. The final two lines of the second verse, warning kiaʻi to remain steadfast and vigilant, demonstrate Kahaunaele's moʻokūʻauhau consciousness.

With the line "kūpaʻa mau e nā Hawaiʻi," Kahaunaele warns that kiaʻi must remain vigilant as challenges and aggressions confront current and future Aloha ʻĀina ʻOiaʻiʻo. Her composition and recorded performance serve multiple functions: to inspire today's kiaʻi and Aloha ʻĀina, educate the broader public about the issues on the mauna, and document for future generations the struggle undertaken for their benefit. The challenges were many and inspired artists like Heoli Osorio to make sure future generations could experience these challenges through mele.

And so I think she [Maunakea] offered a lot of us that opportunity. Then, of course, all the ʻeha [pain] that surrounded some of the events that happened there and then all the joy and triumph. All of us artists who are up there know

Kainani Kahaunaele with daughter Kaniaulono Hāpai, performing near the site of Puʻuhuluhulu University. Photo credit: Kapulani Landgraf

that all our favorite of most important songs and moʻolelo come from those times of ʻeha and triumph. And so the only way we can continue this like brilliant moʻokūʻauhau is to sit your butt down and compose a song for us and then for our future generations so that they have a feeling of what it was like; they know what it felt like, you know—they get a little piece of it. (2020)

Singer and composer Josh Tatofi shares a similar sentiment with his mele "For the Lāhui" (cocomposed with Kumu Hinaleimoana Wong-Kalu). Of Tongan descent but Hawaiʻi-born, Tatofi speaks to the significance of Maunakea beyond Hawaiʻi to other areas of the Pacific: "The way I relate to it is that it's like the mother. It's at the pinnacle for all natives here in Hawaiʻi. When we look at the mauna, it's not just Maunakea ʻBig Mountain,' known around the world. It's deeper for us. We see the mauna stands for the significance of us Indigenous people of the Pacific. And when she gets harmed, we take it on a personal level. We all go into warrior mode because it's all in our koko [blood]" (2020).

Tatofi quickly rose to prominence in the Hawaiʻi music industry in 2018 and 2019 and was in Hilo visiting friends when the confrontations began in July

Josh Tatofi performing for kūpuna on the Ala Kūpuna. Photo credit: Emma Coloma-Nakano

2019. Feeling helpless, he turned to a friend from Maui, singer and kumu hula Nāpua Greig, who encouraged him to compose and record a mele to express what he was feeling and share it with the world. He then turned to another long-time friend, community activist and haku mele Hinaleimoana Wong-Kalu, to set his thoughts in ʻōlelo Hawaiʻi. She asked him what he wanted the mele to say, and he explained his feelings.

> I don't want to go too kaona [to include a lot of hidden meanings]. I don't want to go into the metaphoric speaking like many mele Hawaiʻi do. Of course, she's [Wong-Kalu] into the poetry so heavy, but I wanted to get more literal because I want to go straight to the point. I just wanted to get straight to the point about being bold and steadfast, standing our ground, and believe and fight the good fight. I just wanted it to be straightforward, and so that's when it started to flow with the words, change words here and there, maybe for like forty-five minutes. I want to say within maybe an hour, "For the Lāhui" was created. (Tatofi 2020)

While the title is in English, the text of "For the Lāhui" is in ʻōlelo Hawaiʻi. It contains a single verse, a chorus consisting of three short lines, with the final line being performed twice:

FOR THE LĀHUI

Josh Tatofi and Hinaleimoana Wong-Kalu

FIRST VERSE

E welo mau loa kuʻu hae aloha	May my beloved flag wave evermore
I ka nuʻu o ka lewa lani lā	In the highest of the heavens and under no other
A e maluhia no nā kau a kau	In solemnity for all time to come
Eō Hawaiʻi kuʻu ʻāina aloha	Oh Hawaiʻi my beloved land

CHORUS

E kuʻu lāhui ē, wiwoʻole ē	To you my nation, my people, be fearless and bold
Kū Kānaka ē, ōnipaʻa mau	Stand in dignity as Kānaka and be steadfast and resilient always
Ua mau ke ea o ka ʻāina i ka pono	The essence, vitality, and freedom of our land and people prevail through justice, truth, and the dignity and honor of our nation (repeat)

As with Kahaunaele's composition "Aloha ʻĀina ʻOiaʻiʻo," "For the Lāhui" touches on themes common in many mele aloha ʻāina. The sight of the hae Hawaiʻi (Hawaiian flag) fluttering high above in the first verse establishes a strong visual element characteristic of many mele. The mele also recalls one of the most striking visual features of the puʻuhonua (place of refuge) at Puʻuhuluhulu: a hae Hawaiʻi fluttering at the hill's summit. This symbol was frequently present in photographs and videos posted on social media throughout the standoff on the Maunakea Access Road. The remainder of the mele uses references common in mele aloha ʻāina: the desire for maluhia (peace), Hawaiʻi as ʻāina aloha (beloved land), wiwoʻole (fearlessness), kū kanaka (standing up as Kānaka ʻŌiwi), and kūpaʻa (steadfastness). The final two lines are a single repeated thought: "Ua mau ke ea o ka ʻāina i ka pono." This phrase was first uttered by Kauikeaouli (Kamehameha III) after Great Britain returned control of Hawaiʻi to the monarch several months after a rogue British captain's takeover of the Hawaiian Kingdom in 1843. The phrase is commonly translated as "the life of the land is preserved in righteousness," though many other possible interpretations and translations exist. The translation Wong-Kalu provides for this line—"For the freedom of our land remains always in the truth of our people"—is certainly as valid as any and reflects her recognition of moʻokūʻauhau consciousness.

HŌʻULUʻULU MANAʻO (SUMMARY)

In this chapter, I examine the genealogical connection between Kānaka ʻŌiwi and ʻāina, the importance of this connection in regards to the protective actions of kiaʻi on Maunakea, and the extent to which this connection is documented in mele and moʻolelo.

Numerous acts and demonstrations of aloha ʻāina are documented in mele and moʻolelo. I compare the actions of kiaʻi and the expressions of aloha ʻāina found in the new compositions written for them and Maunakea with the efforts of Iosepa Nāwahī. During Nāwahī's time in the legislature, he was a tireless defender of Hawaiian rights and the ʻāina and a skeptic of any legislation that could result in greater foreign control or interference in Hawaiian matters. For example, during the legislative session of 1876, Hawaiʻi legislators debated a bill allowing the kingdom to borrow the sum of $1,000,000. Nāwahī believed that incurring this debt would lead to the inevitable surrender of Hawaiian lands and delivered an impassioned speech against the bill during the 1876 legislative session. In his speech before the legislature, he addressed the United States' failed attempt to gain control over Puʻuloa (now known as Pearl Harbor). He compared the proposed legislation to the Trojan horse in Virgil's *Aeneid*.

> Eia wale nō kaʻu e noi aku iā ʻoukou, e kiola loa aku kākou i kēia lio i loko o ke kai, a i ʻole ia, i loko o ka lua pele o Kīlauea. ʻO kākou, ʻo nā kānaka Hawaiʻi, ka poʻe nona ka ʻāina a kākou e haʻanou nei, mea aʻe no ka ʻāina, mea iho no ka ʻāina. ʻĀnō, ʻo ka wā kūpono kēia e hana ai kākou i nā mea e pono ai ko kākou aupuni, a e mau ai hoʻi ke kūʻokoʻa ʻana o ko kākou ʻāina i aloha nui ʻia.[19] (Joseph Nāwahī in Sheldon, Like, and Prendergast 1996)

> This is all that I am saying to you, let us throw this horse into the sea, or else, in the caldera at Kīlauea. We, the Hawaiian people, the people whose lands we boast about, speak up for the land, speak for the land. Right now, this is the appropriate time for us to do the right things for our nation and perpetuate our beloved land's independence.

Nāwahī's fears and those of other Kānaka ʻŌiwi did come true. In 1887, when the Kingdom of Hawaiʻi and the United States renewed the Treaty of Reciprocity, originally signed in 1876, it contained a provision that gave the US control of

Puʻuloa to establish a naval base. Ultimately, Nāwahī's efforts failed and the bill was passed, contributing to the further erosion of native control over Hawaiian lands he had predicted.

In December of 1892, barely a month before the overthrow of the monarchy, Nāwahī's opponents and those of the queen attempted to prevent him from reaching Honolulu in time for the start of the legislative session. They arranged for the steamship *Kīnaʻu* to leave Hilo earlier than scheduled, stranding him there. Nāwahī and his supporters located some whaling skiffs and, under cover of darkness, paddled across the treacherous Alenuihānā channel to Hāna, Maui. From Maui, Nāwahī was able to board another vessel and arrive in time for the start of the legislative session (Sheldon, Like, and Prendergast 1996; Williams 2010).

Like Nāwahī—an Aloha ʻĀina of his era—and the defenders of Kahoʻolawe, the kiaʻi of Maunakea have traversed dangerous waters, putting their lives, health, and much more at risk in defense of their beloved ancestor. Nāwahī was not thinking backward with his statement and concerns about the kingdom taking on tremendous debt (worth approximately $27,000,000 in 2022). He was looking forward and seeing the potential consequences of approving that bill, and ultimately his fears came true.

Looking back at events such as these is not "living in the past"—a criticism frequently leveled at Kānaka ʻŌiwi and other Indigenous peoples. Kānaka ʻŌiwi have been asked to "let go of the past" regarding historical wrongs committed against them and allow TMT to be built. In a listserv post to his colleagues, University of Hawaiʻi at Mānoa physics professor John Learned argued, "In no way should we go back a few centuries to a stone age culture, with a few (illegitimate) Kahunas telling everyone how to behave" (HNN Staff 2019). His racist, settler-colonial, and patronizing statement ignores that Polynesia navigated and populated the breadth of the largest body of water on Earth centuries before Westerners did using only highly developed skill at observing and understanding their world and the sky. They faced the same challenges Nāwahī did during his courageous journey from Hilo to Maui. Many have stated that opposition to TMT's construction is about more than just TMT—it is about historical wrongs committed against Kānaka ʻŌiwi that have yet to be made right. That is only partially correct; it is also about who will decide on present and future uses of lands intended to benefit Kānaka ʻŌiwi. Nāwahī's metaphoric use of the Trojan horse regarding the debt bill is applicable here. If built, TMT could be the harbinger of further degradation of Kānaka ʻŌiwi agency and ability to decide appropriate uses for these lands—not just Maunakea. Kānaka ʻŌiwi and their allies must continue to heed the final words uttered by

Nāwahī to his wife Emma on his deathbed: "E hoʻomalu i ke kūpaʻa no ka ʻāina" (Continue to be steadfast in your love for the land).

NOTES

1. Hawaiʻi Island is sometimes known as the "Big Island"—a term that many residents and particularly those who speak Hawaiian reject. It is sometimes referred to as moku o Keawe (the island of the chief Keawe) or, as I have done here, Hawaiʻi mokupuni (Hawaiʻi Island).

2. Oliveira provides an excellent analysis of these differences and maps genealogical connections in several mele koʻihonua in *Ancestral Places* (Oliveira 2014).

3. ʻŌlelo noʻeau are proverbial sayings commonly rich in metaphoric expressions. A collection of such sayings can be found in *ʻŌlelo Noʻeau: Hawaiian Proverbs & Poetical Sayings* (Pukui 1983).

4. Makekau-Whittaker notes that "He kauā hoʻokō no ka lāhui" was a term of self-identification used by Hawaiian monarchy loyalist Iosepa Nāwahī at the end of one of his newspaper articles.

5. Kimura related the story behind his composition of "Kulaiwi" to me during my time as his student at UH Hilo in the 1990s.

6. hoʻomanawanui related to me that she prefers not to capitalize the first letters of her names. She cited being influenced by poet e. e. cummings in elementary school and in college by bell hooks, who was explicit in her political rendering of her name (hoʻomanawanui 2022).

7. These exchanges are discussed in greater detail later in this chapter.

8. For additional examples of the historical nature of aloha ʻāina, see Basham (2002), E. Case (2021), hoʻomanawanui (2005), J. H. Osorio (2021), Silva (2004), Stillman (1999), and Trask (1991).

9. Kāinga is found in several Polynesian languages: "Kāinga basically means kin, relatives, or land. In some places in Polynesia, kāinga means family or kin, and in other places it means land" (Kaʻili n.d.).

10. "Kaulana Nā Pua" is discussed in greater detail in chapter 6.

11. The Kahoʻolawe Nine were Emmitt Aluli, Kimo Aluli, George Helm, Ian Lind, Ellen Miles, Stephen Morse, Gail Kawaipuna Prejean, Walter Ritte, and Karla Villalba. The roots of the Protect Kahoʻolawe ʻOhana can be found in the formation of Hui Alaloa on Molokaʻi, of which Helm was a cofounder. It fought to protect traditional access rights to natural resources threatened by private land owners on Molokaʻi.

12. Kimo and Bobby Mitchell were unrelated.

13. This recording is still available commercially on CD and by digital download. It was awarded the 1997 Nā Hōkū Hanohano Award for its liner notes.

In 2009, the Hawaiʻi Academy of Recording Arts posthumously honored Helm with its Lifetime Achievement Award for his music and activism.

14. The text of this mele was copied from https://www.huapala.org/Me/Mele _O_Kahoolawe.html. I corrected some errors in its orthographic presentation and made minor changes to the translation for readability.

15. Wilcox was also known by the transliterated name "Wilikoki." He and his acts in support of the queen are well documented in mele.

16. The orthography of the Hawaiian language has evolved over the years. Words that previously were joined, such as mamua and mahope, are most often written as two separate words today—ma mua and ma hope.

17. https://www.facebook.com/kainani/videos/10216772505938035/.

18. Kahaunaele provided the text and translation of this mele.

19. The original text did not include the ʻokina and kahakō. The text was modernized to include these when it was prepared for reprinting by the Hale Kuamoʻo at University of Hawaiʻi Hilo in 1996.

FOUR

—∿—

KAPU ALOHA

Embodied, Composed, and Performed

That was the most important thing, that kapu aloha was a real thing. We began to see it working. We began to see it as not just a bunch of hot-headed Hawaiians throwing stones at people and, you know, fighting amongst each other either. Everybody was together I remember the first time I went up there and going to Puʻuhuluhulu. My sister [Nohea Chun] just introduced me to everybody and go play music and listen to the stories and listen to the classes and see the people, volunteering, and everybody working without being asked. This is what we know weʻve been capable of, but we just really had an opportunity to do it. (Kalima-Alvarez 2020)

In this chapter, I discuss kapu aloha, its practice by kiaʻi and their supporters to protect Maunakea from further desecration, and how it inspired compositional processes and musical performances on and about Maunakea. In practice, kapu aloha embodies cultural values that long predate the term. Kapu aloha is also a strategic approach to applying these values in the face of threats of aggression and violence by settler-colonizers and their descendants who represent domestic and foreign governmental, scientific, and economic interests on Maunakea. The embodiment of these values—expressed by the nonviolent resistance of kiaʻi in words and action on the mauna—inspired an outpouring of creativity on the part of composers and performers of Hawaiian music. In most cases, these poetic expressions reflected the principles of kapu aloha through words, embodying them through the mana (power) inherent to vocalization.[1] I examine Lee Ann Ānuenue Pūnuaʻs composition "Lei Ana Maunakea I Ka ʻOhu" and how kapu aloha is embedded in it, discussing other elements of Hawaiian poetry.

THE EMERGENCE OF KAPU ALOHA ON THE MAUNA

The term kapu aloha came into the public consciousness with the movement to protect Maunakea around 2017 because kiaʻi and supporters used it frequently. Although I spent eighteen years in Hilo as a student and later as faculty in Hawaiian Studies at University of Hawaiʻi Hilo from 1994 to 2012, I had neither seen nor heard the term until the 2015 confrontations over the construction of TMT. I questioned the historical use of kapu aloha. My first reaction to hearing the term—like many—was to search online Hawaiian dictionaries, newspaper archives, and other documents to locate previous examples of its use. I found none. However, the term continued to be used, and its use increased. I recognized that many people using it and teaching its principles on Maunakea were among the most respected Hawaiian cultural practitioners, educators, and leaders of the time. I noted its use among young and emerging leaders in the Kānaka ʻŌiwi community on the mauna. I also recalled debates in the 1990s over Western academic concepts such as the "invention of tradition" that questioned and sometimes directly challenged the authenticity of contemporary Hawaiian cultural practices and the legitimacy of deeply held beliefs about relationships with the land (Trask 1991; Linnekin 1991; Keesing 1989). I began to question whether skepticism about the term, including mine, was justified. To explore the possible origins of or reasons for this skepticism, one must consider the modern movements to revitalize Hawaiian cultural practices that began over fifty years ago.

The Second Hawaiian Renaissance began in the 1960s and 1970s. It included efforts to revitalize many significant cultural practices such as Pan-Pacific navigation by the stars in waʻa kaulua (double-hulled canoes), hula, music, lāʻau lapaʻau (traditional medicines and healing), kapa (clothing made of bark cloth) making, ʻōlelo Hawaiʻi, and other practices. These efforts relied on historical knowledge preserved in writings, recordings, examples of material culture, and those still engaged in these practices and speaking ʻōlelo Hawaiʻi. Efforts to revitalize ʻōlelo Hawaiʻi relied heavily on archives of written materials exceeding one million printed texts and more than 125,000 Hawaiian language newspapers published between 1834 and 1948.[2]

Efforts to revitalize ʻōlelo Hawaiʻi as the language of the home, community, and education began with a small group of young scholars at the University of Hawaiʻi at Mānoa in the early 1970s under the direction of Larry Kimura. Kimura and his students launched the *Ka Leo Hawaiʻi* radio program broadcast on KCCN radio in Honolulu in February 1972. The program was conducted

entirely in ʻōlelo Hawaiʻi and included in person discussions with and tele-
phone calls from Hawaiian mānaleo (native speakers of Hawaiian). The program also featured live and recorded performances of Hawaiian music and
skits. Kimura and his students continued to produce this weekly program on
KCCN until he returned to his home island of Hawaiʻi in 1989, where he began
teaching in the Hawaiian studies program at the University of Hawaiʻi at Hilo.
Many of the guests on *Ka Leo Hawaiʻi* were mānaleo who grew up speaking
ʻōlelo Hawaiʻi. These recorded programs became a valuable repository of linguistic and cultural material that influenced and supported the development
of teaching materials for language and cultural education for decades. Kimura
explains: "When I started teaching Hawaiian at the University of Hawaiʻi at
Mānoa in the fall of 1972, I would sometimes play segments of audio recordings
of native Hawaiian speakers—mānaleo—that I had from the Bishop Museum
or from interviews with speakers I had conducted myself so that my students
could hear the natural sound and expression of the language by native speakers,
most of whom were in their senior years of life. I emphasized the importance
for new speakers learning Hawaiian to be as close as possible to native fluency
in maintaining Hawaiian into the future" (2019).

These textual and aural archival materials were born of the desire to model
standards of language excellence by expressing language like older mānaleo.
As Wong has argued, "In the case of Hawaiian, standards are set for evaluating
communicative competence based on literature produced for the most part in
the 19th century" (1999). Wong did not include in his writing—though he was
undoubtedly aware of—the reliance of many Hawaiian language programs,
including those at UH Hilo and UH Mānoa, on recordings of native speakers
born in the late nineteenth and early twentieth centuries. Many such individuals were still alive when Kimura and his students produced *Ka Leo Hawaiʻi*, and
some appeared as guests on the program. The recordings provide significant
insights into grammar, word use, and embedded cultural knowledge and enable
researchers and teachers to examine pronunciation and prosodic elements of
language absent in texts.

I argue that reliance on historical materials to revitalize the Hawaiian language and the reification of mānaleo contributed to the skepticism displayed
on the emergence of kapu aloha. Because skeptics could not locate the term
kapu aloha in older sources, some chose to doubt or deny its historicity and,
therefore, its authenticity. Wong explains possible reasons for accepting some
new terms when native speakers create them and dismissing or criticizing the
innovations of nonnative speakers.

One way of rationalizing this apparent contradiction is to claim that there is a difference between changes that were made by native speakers at a time when the language was still the dominant medium of communication in the community and changes made by second-language learners or even native speakers at a time of overwhelming English influence. The former is accepted as "natural" change, whereas the latter is considered to be somehow "unnatural" and thus unacceptable. Given that native [Hawaiian] epistemology includes a prescriptive adherence to correctness, it is not surprising that some segments of the community would believe strongly in maintaining the purity of the language and would disdain a reconstruction of the language as illegitimate. (1999)

In the 1990s, former Kamehameha Schools trustee Lokelani Lindsey pursued educational policies prescribing a Hawaiian linguistic "purity" at the school. Those policies required Hawaiian language teachers at Kamehameha Schools to teach only "traditional" Hawaiian words, like those found in the Pukui-Elbert *Hawaiian Dictionary* (1986). Ironically, Lindsey did not speak Hawaiian, and critics gleefully pointed out that her name could not be considered—by her standards—a traditional word as it includes the transliterated word "loke" (for the introduced rose flower). Likewise, some criticized the Kōmike Huaʻōlelo Hou (Hawaiian Lexicon Committee) at UH Hilo's Hale Kuamoʻo Hawaiian Language Center for its approach to coining new Hawaiian words. According to Wong, the purpose of these words is to represent "concepts the Hawaiian language community previously found no need to express" (Wong 1999).

Lindsey's mandate explicitly excluded words from the *Māmaka Kaiao* dictionary (Kōmike Huaʻōlelo 2003) in Hawaiian language instruction at Kamehameha Schools. She also challenged Kamehameha's use of the pepeke system, developed by two faculty members of Ka Haka ʻUla O Keʻelikōlani at UH Hilo, which forms the basis of the *Nā Kai ʻEwalu* (Kamanā and Wilson 1990) textbook many Hawaiian language programs use to teach Hawaiian (Wong 1999). I agree that the Kōmike Huaʻōlelo has earned some criticism, but I disagree with those who contend that its work is a "bastardization" of the language. Much of the committee's work benefits Hawaiian medium education (Hawaiian immersion) schools that operate throughout the state and educate students from preschool through college.

The *Māmaka Kaiao* dictionary can be found online (www.wehewehe.org) and may be purchased as a book (Kōmike Huaʻōlelo 2003). Some subjects taught in Hawaiian medium schools require a lexicon that did not exist twenty years ago, much less a century or two ago. These subjects require new words for technology, mathematics, physics, science, sports, and many other disciplines.

Lacking a specific lexicon to express ideas in Hawaiian, schools would need to either use English for specific terms in an otherwise immersive context or to revert to teaching subjects entirely in English. This limitation contradicts the desire to teach students in a Hawaiian language environment and expand Hawaiian language use into modern contexts. The committee's mission is to create words "the Hawaiian language community previously found no need to express" and identify the need for new words in contexts that did not exist when the Hawaiian language newspapers and Hawaiian-English dictionary were published.

The approaches to creating a lexicon are open to challenge and criticism, and as Wong declares, "such criticism comes with the territory" (1999). In the case of kapu aloha, it was an expression born from the circumstances on Maunakea by those deeply involved in defending the sanctity of the mauna. The conflict provided context by which kapu aloha could function and flourish. The term did not require the official sanction of the Kōmike Huaʻōlelo or any other authority but was effectively sanctioned by those who utilized it when needed in real-world circumstances. Directly translating the term to "nonviolent direct action" would be inappropriate and exclude the complex Hawaiian cultural precepts embodied in kapu aloha. I cannot predict whether or not kapu aloha will find its way into future published dictionaries, but it has clearly found its place in Hawaiʻi's everyday vocabulary.

Herbert Kretzmer, lyricist for "Les Misérables," states, "Words have resonance within a culture; they have submarine strengths and meaning" (quoted in Lahr 2013). The Hawaiian language carries mana (power)—"the meanings had power and explained the universe" (Elbert and Māhoe 1970). Once vocalized, a speaker cannot rescind words, and neither remorse nor apology can prevent the consequences of the utterance. Several ʻōlelo noʻeau (proverbial Hawaiian sayings) express the importance of the Hawaiian language. Perhaps the most widely known and frequently cited is "I ka ʻōlelo nō ke ola; I ka ʻōlelo nō ka make" (In the language there is life; in the language there is death) (Pukui 1983). Would the actions of kiaʻi on the mauna have been less impactful if the term kapu aloha had not identified the behaviors of the kiaʻi, explained their purpose, and connected them to a greater understanding of its tenets? I argue that their actions would not have been as impactful. As Emalani Case explains, "Puʻuhonua o Puʻuhuluhulu has become a place of safety for kiaʻi of every background, Kānaka Maoli and non-Hawaiians included. It has become a place of gathering, a place of prayer and ceremony, a place of learning and sharing, and a place of recommitting to the protection of not just the mauna but all lands and waters. It has become a place where the values of kapu aloha and aloha ʻāina have not only guided those present at the sanctuary but have also permeated surrounding communities and even other nations around the world" (2021).[3]

When kiaʻi spoke and heard the term kapu aloha, it carried the mana (power) inherent to any verbal expression in ʻōlelo Hawaiʻi. Its vocalization reminded them of the reason why they were standing on the mountain and the potential consequences of failure to adhere to its tenets. It was apparent that their adherence to kapu aloha also impacted many law enforcement officers, who experienced its power. It became clear to university and state leaders that kiaʻi would not give them a reason to escalate the confrontation. The resonance and the mana of kapu aloha focused attention on the goals, behavior, and actions of the kiaʻi on Maunakea and their supporters worldwide. The invocation of kapu aloha created a shared, supportive space for kiaʻi, empowered and guarded by the mana of the ʻōlelo, as they faced the threat of violence and made their collective stand to protect Maunakea.

DEFINING KAPU ALOHA

Kapu aloha is not easily defined, and individuals who practiced it on the mauna have offered many different definitions. First, however, I examine the depth and breadth of the two words that comprise the concept. I then briefly discuss the practice of combining two terms to create a singular meaning.

In 1986, the Hawaiʻi State Legislature passed an "Aloha Spirit" bill signed into law by then-governor George Ariyoshi. The writings of respected kupuna Pīlahi Paki famously offer an acronym with each letter in "aloha" as a Hawaiian word. Legislators included her interpretation of aloha in the state law:

A – Akahai – meaning kindness to be expressed with a feeling of tenderness.
L – Lōkahi – meaning unity to be expressed with a feeling of harmony.
O – ʻOluʻolu – meaning agreeable to be expressed with a feeling of pleasantness.
H – Haʻahaʻa – meaning humility to be expressed with a feeling of modesty.
A – Ahonui – meaning patience to be applied with perseverance.

While this acronym is sometimes referred to as a definition of aloha, Paki created a philosophical treatise that identifies specific Hawaiian terms expressed through language and action. Kumu hula (hula master/instructor/ source of knowledge) Olana Ai posits, "Aloha is the intelligence with which we meet life"—a definition that supports Paki's acronym (quoted in Meyer 2003). Embodiment is a crucial concept here—we meet life through our thoughts, words, and behaviors. Each of the five terms that Paki lists includes an English word that approximates the meaning of the Hawaiian word and is followed by "expressed" or "applied." These characteristics cannot remain dormant within the individual; they must be embodied, expressed, and practiced.

The Pukui/Elbert *Hawaiian Dictionary* lists over thirty English terms with far-ranging meanings found in a Hawaiian conceptualization of aloha. The dictionary glosses kapu as "taboo, prohibition; special privilege or exemption from ordinary taboo; sacredness; prohibited, forbidden; sacred, holy, consecrated" and more. When combined, these two words—kapu and aloha—express Hawaiian cultural values that are more than simply their sum. Similarly, in his discussion of Indigenous poetry in Canada, Armand Garnet Ruffo (Anishinaabe/Ojibwe) observes, "Sometimes two ordinary words placed unexpectedly side by side can energize each other, much like two colours placed side by side can vibrate" (Ruffo in McLeod 2014). I encountered an example of this kind of word pairing in a conversation with Hawaiian composer and educator Ileialoha Beniamina (Kanaka ʻŌiwi) from the island of Niʻihau in 2009. I asked her to translate a few words from her composition "Pua ʻAla Aumoe" whose meaning eluded me: ʻōlino haʻa mai ana. The combination of ʻōlina and haʻa confounded me. She replied, "ʻAʻohe ona unuhi. Nui ka poʻe i nīnau iaʻu—he aha kēlā laina?" (It cannot be translated. There are plenty of people who have asked me—what does that line mean?). She spent the next five minutes explaining her intended meaning to me—in ʻōlelo Hawaiʻi—and included her interpretation of the metaphor's meaning. Her explanation did not correspond to the definitions found in the Hawaiian dictionary (Beniamina 2009).

In an interview recorded on Maunakea a few months after the arrests of kūpuna, Maui-based educator and kumu hula Hōkūlani Holt offered her definition of kapu aloha: "Kapu aloha is always thinking about others, thinking about place, thinking about relationships and how to best have that happen, and to keep yourself in that disciplining of thinking that what I want is not the most important thing if it does not align with these ways of behaving well with each other and with the place that we are in. So that is, at its simplest level, how we want people to be here" (Holt and Kanahele 2019).

In the same interview, Hilo-based educator and kumu hula Pualani Kanahele (Kanaka ʻŌiwi) supported and expanded on Holt's definition of kapu aloha: "Kapu aloha has two English definitions that are usually used. One word is prohibited and the other word is sacred. In the case of kapu aloha, it means both, and the idea of the way you behave should be sacred to not only yourself but the people around you. Prohibited because you're prohibited to act in a certain way. The aloha part has many different meanings; one of them the greater meanings that everybody uses of aloha is love. You can use love in many different ways and may love as many different levels of acceptance" (Holt and Kanahele 2019).

Each kiaʻi would likely offer a different definition of kapu aloha—each deeply personal and philosophical. Still, most would echo Holt and Kanahele's significant themes and sentiments. Their status as leaders of the Maunakea movement and as respected kūpuna and educators certainly lends weight and authority to their words.

Lee Ann Ānuenue Pūnua, Chad Takatsugi, and Zachary Alakaʻi Lum were among the first haku mele to call on the Hawaiian music community to compose new mele to honor Maunakea and its many kiaʻi and to use this medium to educate the community about the movement. Lum and Takatsugi also organized and produced the *Kūhaʻo Maunakea* compilation, released in September 2020. I asked Lum, as a scholar, composer, and performer of Hawaiian music, how he perceives and interprets concerns about the antiquity and authenticity of kapu aloha.

> We had these conversations, too, especially when the term started to become really prominent and especially when it came off the mauna because there is a definite power to the term. But you and I both agree that the name of it seems problematic at first. It's not just a kapu like "against the law." It means, "No, you really shouldn't do that." So, when you attach it to aloha, there is a lot at stake if you do not aloha in this situation. And I think that's the messaging that the term kapu aloha delivers to a much wider audience. But I think eventually we'll all get to the point where if there needs to be the use of the word kapu in order for aloha to proliferate, then I think that alone is the thing that is old, right? (2020)

Amy Kuʻuleialoha Stillman (Kanaka ʻŌiwi) is a professor of American studies at the University of Michigan, a haku mele, and a multi-Grammy Award-winning producer of Hawaiian music. She has been the most prolific and respected scholar of Hawaiian music over the past thirty years. While maintaining her Hawaiʻi connections, Stillman witnessed the confrontations on Maunakea from afar—in Michigan. She offers her thoughts on the discourse surrounding the use of kapu aloha on the mauna.

> I think a big part of our problem lies in this belief that is not insurmountable—the power of binary dichotomies. So people are vested with measuring authoritativeness or the authenticity or the antiquity of something. It's only partly about the measurement, but more so, it's about weaponizing the power behind the measurement. It's a way of ending up with a cultural formation that is essentialized and frozen in time. It is possible to

trace, to say, okay, this concept has morphed over time. And that's the same thing with kapu aloha. I'd like to think that there's a way to pry people's thinking open. Yes, culture can morph as long as nobody is trying to present something as ancient. (Stillman 2020)

Stillman's thinking greatly influenced my own as my concerns over the term kapu aloha began to fade, and I began to use it more myself. I was grateful that throughout encounters between kia'i and law enforcement in the months that followed, attitudes against and concerns about kapu aloha seemed to diminish and the term become more widely embraced.

EMBODYING KAPU ALOHA

Hāwane Rios began training in chant, hula, and other Hawaiian arts under her mother's tutelage at a young age. This training inspired her interest in Hawaiian language composition and vocal performance. She, her mother, and other family members have long opposed the desecration of Maunakea in both word and action. I asked her about her understanding of kapu aloha and its origins.

Kapu aloha was introduced to me years ago by Aunty Pua Kanahele. It was conduct and discipline, and it was for the first twenty-four-hour vigil that I ever did in my life. I was really, really young, but it was on the hour every hour pule. And I remember I slept through some of it, but she said we're going to leave all of our pilikia [problems] outside, and we're going to bring our highest self to this moment. So our conduct, our discipline, and our best selves were brought forward because that's what the pule deserves and with the ceremony deserves. . . . And so she said this is what we know as kapu aloha, it's my mom and my mom learned this from Auntie Pua. I saw how much criticism was going around on Facebook about this term, like saying, you know, things like "I can't find this anywhere in the nūpepa kahiko [old newspapers]. Why are we introducing something new? This is like a new age thing?" But what I would hope that people would remember is that we are living people, and our culture evolves just like how in our language all throughout the nūpepa kahiko. There are words that they made up that were English, and they put it into Hawaiian because we were in a space of needing to evolve for survival. So our language evolved. (Rios 2020)

Heoli Osorio was present at the kia'i encampment as the numbers of kia'i and law enforcement personnel increased leading up to the arrest of kūpuna. She was also one of the eight kia'i who chained themselves to a cattle guard that ran across the access road on Monday, July 15, 2019. One of her duties was to train fellow kiaʻi in nonviolent direct action. She explains how kapu aloha became a significant part of their strategy to confront law enforcement: "In the State of Hawaiʻi, noncompliance does not count as resisting arrest, right? So how do we prepare people not to escalate their charges? How do we prepare them to take arrest in ways that are safe?" (J. H. Osorio 2020). While some question the antiquity of kapu aloha, Osorio addresses the social issues and attitudes she believes contribute to skepticism about the term.

> I think I understand why some people on the outside take issue with the phrase. When you are there day in and day out, you're learning from the folks who are running protocol. You're learning from the folks who are running the front line. As a united core, we had a very strict and intimate understanding of what kapu aloha meant to us on the mountain, and it wasn't just like being passive. Nothing about kapu aloha is being passive. It's about being disciplined. It's about being able to take violence that's coming at you and not return it, not react to it, and that's hard. And so one of the things we train people in doing is understanding was that like kapu aloha doesn't mean you're not emotional. It doesn't mean that you're not feeling all these things at once. It means you understand where your breaking point is. And when you come up against that breaking point, you remove yourself, right? So kapu aloha is this. (2020)

Noe Noe Wong-Wilson was one of the primary spokespeople for those on the Ala Kūpuna. She also heard criticisms and questions regarding the antiquity of the term. She acknowledges that while the combination of words "kapu aloha" may be a modern innovation, the concept certainly is not.

> I laugh when I see that because—I have to tell you this—the language is a living language. When and how we compound words is appropriate for the time and the space. Right? The concept of kapu aloha, though, should not be foreign to any of us because we see it play out in contemporary times, and we saw it in our history, in all the moʻolelo that we know. We see that as well in the stories about the fierce warrior-like moves, right? We know that Kamehameha, as an example, people like the military still study his war tactics as written by Kekūhaupiʻo.[4] So we know that he was a fierce warrior, and they had all these brilliant formations, but he's also known for his love for his people on his ʻāina. So, maybe they didn't use the term kapu aloha, but it's the same thing but manifested in today's world. (Wong-Wilson 2022)

Kapu aloha helped define interpersonal relations among the kiaʻi as they prepared for confrontations with law enforcement. Its embodiment was evident during interactions with law enforcement, state, and university officials.

While some questions and doubts regarding the antiquity or appropriateness of the term may remain, its effectiveness in bringing focus to kiaʻi's purpose and defending against the intimidation techniques and violence that threatened them is undeniable.

THE EMBODIED POETICS OF KAPU ALOHA

Many haku mele were present on the mauna during the standoff between kiaʻi and law enforcement and when the kūpuna were arrested. Many more witnessed the arrests live as they were streamed on various social media sites or watched recordings later. Whether one observed the arrests in person or online, the events that played out that day were both alarming and inspiring. The dignity the kūpuna displayed inspired many of us to document what we had witnessed in mele and their acts were indicative of embodying kapu aloha. Not only did haku mele document the sights and emotions of what they had witnessed, but they also recognized these demonstrations of kapu aloha and embraced the concept in their compositions. I have examined dozens of Hawaiian language compositions written for Maunakea in the time leading up to and following the arrests and have located no lyrics that express anger or hostility to law enforcement, the state government, or pro-TMT forces. Instead, compositions praise Maunakea and its significance to Kānaka ʻŌiwi, honor the efforts and sacrifices of the kiaʻi, and espouse the virtues of kapu aloha and aloha ʻāina.

Noenoe Silva describes four broad categories of Hawaiian literature: mele (poetry, song), moʻolelo (prose), pule (prayer), and moʻokūʻauhau (genealogy), adding that "these are not completely distinct categories because many moʻolelo contain mele" (2014). Mele can also contain genealogical information. As a form of literature, interpreting mele depends on specialized knowledge and experience that Jonathan Culler calls "literary competence" (2002). He expands on this idea: "A poetics describing literary competence would focus on the conventions that make possible literary structure and meaning: what are the codes or systems of convention that enable readers to identify literary genres, recognize plots, create 'characters' out of the scattered details provided in the text, identify themes in literary works, and pursue the kind of symbolic interpretation that allows us to gauge the significance of poems and stories" (Culler 1997).

There are two Western philosophical approaches to poetic analysis: a hermeneutic approach that seeks to find meaning in texts and a poetics approach that aims to interrogate the effects of texts on the reader and how those effects are achieved (Culler 1997). Hawaiian poetry is rich in figures of speech and structural poetic devices, which serve as mnemonic devices that, for centuries, have assisted in the accurate transmission of mele and the valuable knowledge contained within them. Modern haku mele maintain these practices in their works and have largely eschewed the most well-known elements of English poetry, such as line-terminal rhyming. However, these Western epistemological approaches do not entirely encompass Indigenous poetics, as Gail MacKay (Anishinaabe-Métis) explains: "Indigenous poetics reach beyond Western literary theoretical orientations to bring Indigeneity to the forefront of all factors being considered. Indigenous identity of authors and audiences, the contexts of Indigenous cultural survival in various eras and regions, the foundation of Indigenous philosophy in language structure and discourse patterns, tropes, symbols, metaphors, and methods" (2014).

It is difficult to make these Western philosophical terms—hermeneutics and poetics—directly correspond to Hawaiian concepts. In Hawaiian, the words themselves can be referred to as the ʻōlelo mele (words of the song) but are usually simply referred to as mele. While metaphors and other figures of speech are common in mele, there is no older term for particular devices. Figures of speech such as metonymy, personification, simile, and synecdoche exist in mele; I often hear them identified collectively as metaphors. Kimura coined the term kūhōʻailona (to stand as a sign or symbol) for metaphor in his master's thesis, and kaona refers to the hidden or layered meaning of mele (2002).[5] Although there is a common misconception that correctly interpreting the metaphors in Hawaiian poetry leads to understanding the mele's underlying kaona (hidden or veiled meanings), this is not true. The kaona is sometimes absent from the text—contextual—and therefore inaccessible to readers. As such, the kaona of a mele is only known to the composer and those with whom the composer has shared this information.

Lee Ann Ānuenue Pūnua (Kanaka ʻŌiwi) is a kiaʻi, educator, and haku mele who hails from Oʻahu. Her first composition, "Pua ʻAʻaliʻi," was recorded and released by the Hawaiian band Hoʻokena in 1999 and awarded the Haku Mele Award for best new Hawaiian language composition in the 2000 Nā Hōkū Hanohano Awards. She describes the experience of asking a friend of her family, esteemed Hawaiian language and cultural resource Patience Nāmaka Bacon, to paka (review, offer suggestions to improve) "Pua ʻAʻaliʻi" and offer thoughts and suggestions to improve it. During their discussion, they whittled twenty lines of poetry down to eight. Bacon emphasized to Pūnua the importance of Hawaiian cultural knowledge to haku mele. Pūnua describes part of her four-hour-long conversation with Bacon and the importance of completing specific thoughts or expressions: "I think I was talking about 'ke ʻimi nei,' meaning,

'I'm looking for something,' and I can't even remember what it was. She just showed you those things, you know. [Pūnua paraphrasing Bacon] 'Yeah, lots of Hawaiian mele have them.[6] But those people have written songs all their life, right?' So she was to put it right like that. If you don't know how to close your mele, we're going to be searching forever" (Pūnua 2020).

Bacon emphasized using positive words in composition, much as Jean Ileialoha Beniamina (Kanaka ʻŌiwi) did when I interviewed her in 2009. Beniamina was a native speaker of ʻŌlelo Hawaiʻi from Niʻihau and a revered haku mele. She shared with me her experiences in the 1980s with a young Kanaka ʻŌiwi physician who had recently graduated from medical school and was working with other medical school graduates to evaluate serious health issues in the Niʻihau community. After observing the eating habits of community members, he predicted that if they continued eating as they did, most would experience serious health problems by the time they reached forty years of age. He solicited Beniamina's help to compose a mele to communicate his concerns to the community and shared a draft of his English language song with her. The physician's thoughts focused on the adverse outcomes he believed would befall members of the Niʻihau community if they continued to practice what he characterized as unhealthy lifestyles. Beniamina found his perspective to be inappropriate to include in a mele: "My mother began to read his thoughts, looking at his words. She looked at Hiram and said, because you're here, darling, you will change this, yeah? The flowers won't be dying. The flowers will be blooming. Yeah? Healing the Hawaiian nation and people. And the land will not be barren. Because of your knowledge, it will flourish"[7] (Beniamina 2009).

This conversation led to Beniamina composing "Hoʻōla Lāhui Hawaiʻi," for which she was honored with the Haku Mele Award at the 1987 Nā Hōkū Hanohano Awards. In this composition, she takes the dire situation that the young physician predicted and reorients it to reflect a positive perspective and outlook in which native Hawaiians flourish by adopting healthy lifestyles. Hoʻōla Lāhui Hawaiʻi also became the name of a health organization on Kauaʻi "dedicated to improving the health of our community through our clinical care and innovative integration of our Hawaiian values" (Hoʻōla Lāhui Hawaiʻi 2009).

Larry Kimura emphasized the importance of avoiding negative expressions when I was a student in his haku mele class at UH Hilo in the 1990s and many more times when I asked him for assistance in reviewing and correcting issues of grammar or thought. He emphasized the importance of approaching expression through the language in a manner consistent with a Hawaiian worldview.

Pono kākou i loko o kēia hoʻāla, hoʻōla ʻōlelo hou e haku ma ke kumu mai he Hawaiʻi ka manaʻo. Mai lawe kahiki. Kēlā ʻano unuhi hāiki, ʻaʻole. That's the way the cookie crumbles. Pēlā e heleleʻi ai ke kuki? ʻAʻole. He lawe kahiki kēlā ʻano. Pono mai ke kumu mai, he Hawaiʻi a e puka he māpunaʻōlelo Hawaiʻi ke ʻano. (Kimura quoted in Donaghy 2010)

In this time of language revitalization, we need to compose with a foundation of Hawaiian thought. Don't take things from foreign places. That kind of narrow translation is wrong. That's the way the cookie crumbles? Pēlā e heleleʻi ai ke kuki? No, that is borrowing from foreign sources. It must be done from the source and must be expressed in a Hawaiian manner.

The examples above clarify contemporary haku mele issues, including for those who composed mele for the kiaʻi and Maunakea. Hawaiian epistemology that "includes a prescriptive adherence to correctness," as Wong discusses, is not a barrier to learners. It ensures that the mele we compose will continue to be performed and recorded for future generations. These concerns address both hermeneutic elements that reflect the meaning and interpretation of the text and poetic elements that impact the reader. In the examples provided in the following section, I examine both, including passages in which both approaches are relevant. As Katarina Teaiwa (Banaban, I-Kiribati, African American) has noted, "to truly acknowledge diverse ontological realities, we need to acknowledge that in Indigenous epistemologies and ontologies, poetics are never just poetics" (2014).

"LEI ANA MAUNA KEA I KA ʻOHU"

Pūnua shares her initial inspiration for writing "Lei Ana Maunakea I Ka ʻOhu" (Maunakea sits adorned in the mists) and the intent behind some of the expressions in it: "We were driving away from the road on that afternoon, and there was a layer on mauna—he ʻohu [a mist]. I remember thinking that's so appropriate, especially with our kūpuna—that was our Hulu Kūpuna [revered and cherished elders] that were standing there. Also, one of the girls in our crew is [named] Leiʻohu, and another one of our crew members is [named] Keʻala. So this is dedicated to them and to that day. I wanted to honor our kūpuna" (Pūnua 2020).

Pūnua completed her mele quickly and shared a video of her performing it on Facebook on Monday, July 22, 2019—just five days after the arrests of the kūpuna. Although this was the first public performance of "Lei Ana Maunakea I Ka ʻOhu," Pūnua notes in the recorded introduction and explanation that precede the performance that she has not yet given her mele a title. She

Left to right: Koʻiahi Pūnua, Kūlaʻilaʻi Pūnua, Ānuenue Pūnua, and Maʻaloa Pūnua. The dark maroon flowers behind them are those of the ʻaʻaliʻi plant mentioned in "Lei Ana Maunakea I Ka ʻOhu." Photo credit: Koʻiahi Pūnua

appears tired, her skin reddened by the sun. Her voice cracks with emotion as she speaks—all the result of long hours in the often harsh environment of Puʻuhuluhulu, traveling back and forth between that location and her housing on the west side of Hawaiʻi Island and eventually returning to her home on Oʻahu. She acknowledges the inspiration of fellow haku mele Chad Takatsugi and Zachary Lum for "putting out the call" to others to document the previous week's events in mele and share them with the world. What follows is her response to their call.

LEI ANA MAUNAKEA I KA ʻOHU

Composed by Lee Ann Ānuenue Pūnua

PAUKŪ ʻEKAHI	FIRST VERSE
Lei ana Maunakea i ka ʻohu	Maunakea sits adorned in the mists
ʻOhuʻohu i ka uʻi o nā pua	Abundant with its beautiful children

Nā pua hoʻoheno o ka ʻāina   The beloved children of the land
Honi mai ke ʻala o ke aloha   Embraced in the fragrance of aloha
Honi mai ke ʻala o ke aloha   Embraced in the fragrance of aloha

HUI   CHORUS
Noenoe mai nā pua   The mists greet the children
E luana i ka leo kūpaʻa   Who graciously sit firm on their word
Me he lei ʻaʻaliʻi i ke anu   Like steadfast lei ʻaʻaliʻi in the cold
Hiwahiwa i ka lei lanakila   Our precious lei of victory
Hiwahiwa i ka lei lanakila   Our precious lei of victory

PAUKŪ ʻELUA   SECOND VERSE
Paʻē mai ana ka leo hoʻokahi   The resounding voice was heard
E kū like i ke alo o ka Mauna   To stand in the presence of the
                                      mountain
Ea mai ana nā mamo o Hāloa   Descendants of Hāloa answered
Mālama i ke kapu aloha   Maintaining the kapu of aloha
Mālama i ke kapu aloha   Maintaining the kapu of aloha[8]

"Lei Ana Maunakea I Ka ʻOhu" contains many rich metaphoric expressions that entice the senses. Visual imagery is a common and effective tool in all Hawaiian literary forms, including mele (John Charlot quoted in Donaghy 2010). Pūnua utilizes this element of Hawaiian poetry, describing the mist encircling the mountain as a lei that embraces it. This expression is a common Hawaiian metaphor for clouds surrounding mountains and seas surrounding islands. kuʻualoha hoʻomanawanui has observed that the lei is "one of the most important cultural and poetic metaphors for Hawaiians." She notes that the term haku describes a technique to make certain kinds of lei and to compose mele because both weave together different elements into a unified whole (hoʻomanawanui 2005). Both are also among the most precious gifts anyone can create and give.

Pūnua documents her view as she descends from the kiaʻi encampment to the town of Waimea and includes the name of Maunakea itself to identify the mele's location for the listener. In my 2008 discussion with haku mele, singer, and kumu hula Kealiʻi Reichel (Kanaka ʻŌiwi), Reichel explained the significance of determining where the events of a mele occur. We discussed Kaumakaiwa Kanakaʻole's use of the place name Haleakalā in Kanakaʻole's composition "Lani Kau Keha": "That sets the place, and for me, chants and songs for me always have to set something right away. I have to be taken to that spot or shown that image almost right away. And so that kind of helped because I know what Haleakalā looks like" (Reichel in Donaghy 2010).

The vocal performance of mele provides the opportunity for listeners who have never visited a particular location to experience it in their mind's eye. Charlot notes that "hearing about the wahi pana [storied places] merely whetted one's appetite to visit them oneself, and one's own experience of the place would be a part of one's chant in its praise" (2005). As the *Ad Herennium* and its interpreters note, "One critical feature of a memory image is that it be striking, indeed, idiosyncratic enough to be clearly recalled" (Parshall 1999). Helen Roberts documented and recorded performances of many older mele in the early 1900s. She praises the ability of Hawaiian composers to convey images through the language: "To the Hawaiian mind, the chief charm of the singing or chanting lay in the words, for their obvious meaning in many cases consisted of exquisite imagery, of word painting succeeding word painting, describing the beauties of natural scenery, used in a profusion bewildering to one accustomed to the restraints of most of our modern poetry" (Roberts 1967).

Pūnua invokes the sense of smell in the first verse, albeit metaphorically. Line three states, "Honi mai ke ʻala o ke aloha" (embraced in the fragrance of aloha). Aloha is an emotional state that—as I have posited—becomes embodied through one's behavior. Aloha does not carry a scent, but Pūnua's metaphoric expression affirms the presence of aloha around us and our ability to sense it, much as our olfactory system can detect scents. During my 2008 conversation with Reichel, we discussed Beniamina's composition "Pua ʻAla Aumoe," and he explained the importance of the sense of smell: "Fragrance is important to us [Kānaka ʻŌiwi], and maybe I'm getting off into a tangent, but you know fragrance to me is like Godliness—it changes your thought process almost instantly. . . . it's like when you walk into a room, and someone has pīkake [Indian jasmine] on, almost right away you go [takes a deep breath through the nose] kind of thing because it changes your whole mind, it alters your thinking of them" (Reichel in Donaghy 2010).

There are many other examples of this metaphoric use (expressing aloha or another emotion as a fragrance). For example, he inoa ʻaʻala (a fragrant name) describes someone famous or revered. The ʻōlelo noʻeau "He aikāne, he pūnana na ke onaona" poetically refers to "a friend, a nest of fragrance" (Pukui 1983). Pūnua's expression is consistent with a Hawaiian epistemology and easily interpreted by those proficient in ʻōlelo Hawaiʻi. Through this expression, aloha transcends the emotional realm. Those on the mauna could feel and experience its presence as one would experience a scent.

Pūnua also uses linked assonance—a common Hawaiian poetic device—in the first verse.[9] She uses the word ʻohu (mist) at the end of the first line and begins the second line with ʻohuʻohu (adorned with numerous flowers or lei).

The end of the second line contains the words nā pua, which repeat at the beginning of the next line. She translates nā pua (literally "the flowers") as "the children"—another common Hawaiian metaphoric expression. While Pūnua's children and the children of many kiaʻi were present on the mauna during the arrests of kūpuna, Pūnua deepens her metaphoric use. She uses nā pua to represent all kiaʻi present as keiki o ka ʻāina (children of the land), not simply referring to kamaliʻi (youngsters).

Pūnua references the names of several individuals in this mele. She includes the first names of Noenoe (Wong-Wilson) and Luana (Busby), who were among the thirty-eight kūpuna arrested on July 17, 2019. She mentions two members of her ʻohana waʻa (canoe family) from the voyaging canoe Makaliʻi—Leiʻohu (Santos-Colburn) and Keʻala (Kahuanui)—and kiaʻi leaders Kahoʻokahi (Kanuha) and Lanakila (Mangauil). While she honors these individuals by mentioning them, their names are also utilized for their meanings within the context of the poetic expression of the text. Pūnua does not always use the complete first names of individuals; she uses ʻohu for Leiʻohu Santos-Colburn and hoʻokahi for Kahoʻokahi Kanuha. Nevertheless, those familiar with the haku mele will recognize the names and identities of some of the individuals.

The first line of the second verse entices the listener's sense of hearing. Pūnua translates this line, "Paʻē mai ana ka leo hoʻokahi," as "The resounding voice was heard." Pūnua explained the second part of this line, "Ka leo hoʻokahi," means "a single voice," adding that this expression represents the early call made by her friend and daughter's former preschool teacher, Kahoʻokahi Kanuha, for Kānaka ʻŌiwi and their allies to defend Maunakea. This phrase could easily be interpreted by those who understand Hawaiian to represent the combined voices of the kiaʻi on the mauna, expressing a unified thought. This was my first impression, and such an interpretation is certainly valid. According to Pūnua, "I wrote it with the manaʻo [thought] that everyone answered his [Kanuha's] call. Paying homage to his particular leo kahea [call]. But that is the beauty of ʻōlelo Hawaiʻi—many layers of understanding" (2021).

In the third line, the kiaʻi respond: "Ea mai ana nā mamo o Hāloa" (Descendants of Hāloa answered). Hāloa is a well-known metaphoric reference to the shared ancestor of Kānaka ʻŌiwi—Hāloa (or Hāloalaukapalili). Ea has multiple meanings, including sovereignty, independence, breath, and air. Pūnua uses Pukui and Elbert's third gloss of the word: "to rise, go up, raise, become erect" (Pukui and Elbert 1986). While Pūnua translates ea as "answered," it does not simply mean that there has been a verbal reply from those called but that supporters have responded by rising and traveling to defend Maunakea.

Their response is embodied. The mele ends with her call for kiaʻi to "Mālama i ke kapu aloha" (maintain the kapu of aloha), a call that is repeated. I do not believe it is coincidence that Pūnua chose to repeat this line.[10] Knowing the mana inherent to any vocalization, repetition emphasizes and amplifies the thought. In doing so, she reminds kiaʻi that they must maintain and embody the tenets of kapu aloha as they gather and prepare for the inevitable confrontation with law enforcement. Finally, it brings appropriate closure to the mele, as Bacon taught Pūnua.

HŌʻULUʻULU MANAʻO (SUMMARY)

In this chapter, I explore the meaning and interpretations of the term kapu aloha—a term significant and invaluable to the movement to protect Maunakea. I note that while some individuals have expressed concerns about the antiquity and perceived authenticity of kapu aloha, its practice by kiaʻi and supporters proved to be an effective strategy against pro-TMT forces, including the State of Hawaiʻi and its law enforcement agencies. It was also an effective social practice that united Kānaka ʻŌiwi and their allies to address current and future challenges to pursuing Indigenous rights and self-determination. As a concept and embodied practice, kapu aloha became a subject within mele, such as Pūnua's "Lei Ana Maunakea I Ka ʻOhu." It became a principle for composers such as Pūnua and me, facilitating our adherence to the idea that mele should remain positive and avoid negative expression. In the living, vibrant culture of which ʻōlelo Hawaiʻi is a critical and central part, the creation of new terms is akin to the creation of new mele, both inspired by and founded on the kahua paʻa (foundation) of ʻike kūpuna (ancestral knowledge).[11]

Kapu aloha must be not only embraced by the individual but also embodied and performed. Stephanie Nohelani Teves (Kanaka ʻŌiwi) notes that "aloha is a performance, negotiated at the intersection of ancestral knowledge and outsider expectations, manifest in the daily contradictions and complexities of Kanaka Maoli indigeneity" (2018). I will not mislead the reader into believing that kiaʻi and their supporters followed the tenets of kapu aloha without exception. There were undoubtedly encounters before, during, and after the arrests of kūpuna where some fell short of the behavior they expected of themselves and each other. These encounters more frequently played out on social media and in the press.

As challenging as it was for many kiaʻi and their supporters to maintain the practice, and as contested as the term became beyond the mauna, the invocation of kapu aloha was successful. Lum observes:

From a logistical standpoint, the call to have everyone silent means there would be no physical engagement with enforcement. I'll never forget images that I've seen of the officers or the sheriffs or whoever; they were at the knees of the kūpuna, crying because they realized that aloha is the thing that will change the world. And Kahoʻokahi called it. He said it all the time, too. Aloha eventually becomes the thing that changes the officers, and it breaks the binary between us and you, but it's like we're all aloha right here. So, you do your job. And there's just something so beautiful about it, and I always come back to, you know, the stories about Pīlahi Paki saying that the world will look to aloha one day, and it will see that as the answer, I guess. Aloha is aloha. I mean, for now, aloha won Maunakea. It was the kūpuna, and it was the commitment of all of these key people. But at the end of the day, it was their aloha that won because there could have easily been a fight there, and people could have been hurt. But the fact that it didn't happen was, I think, a turning point. And I think that's why we "won." That's the beautiful part about it. (2020)

I was among those who fell short of expectations. A few days after the arrests of the thirty-eight kūpuna, I began to compose a mele to honor Maunakea and its kiaʻi. It is entitled "Lei Ana Maunakea I Ke Aloha ʻOiaʻiʻo" (Maunakea wears genuine love as a lei). Overcome by emotion, I briefly forgot the wisdom of my mentors Kimura and Beniamina in the first draft. I included a verse that portrayed pro-TMT individuals and organizations in an unflattering albeit abstract and metaphoric manner. After completing the lyrics, I reconsidered the wisdom of having negative expressions in the mele. I called my friend and frequent musical collaborator, Kenneth Makuakāne, the Kahu (minister) at Kawaiahaʻo Church on Oʻahu. We discussed my composition, and he echoed my concerns about including negative expressions. He suggested that sharing, recording, or performing them would be inappropriate. I returned to the compositional process, focused on the tenets of kapu aloha, and completed the lyrics in a way that removed these negative expressions.

As noted earlier in this chapter, during her conversation with Pūnua, Bacon emphasized the importance of properly closing a mele in a good and positive manner, just as someone who creates a lei would want to have a lei completed in a good way. While that act concludes the process of creating the lei, the lei's life and usefulness continue. A lei is to be shared, worn, and visible for all to see. One wears kapu aloha like a lei for that reason. It needs to be more than a symbol and must become an extension of the wearer—it has to be embodied. Kapu aloha, refined and honed under the duress experienced by kiaʻi on the mauna, is now the lei that adorns not just the mountain but the lāhui (nation) as it moves forward on issues as pressing as those faced on the mauna.

NOTES

1. Individuals have varying levels of power or authority based on their genealogy or achieved place in society. Each vocalization—as spoken or sung—carries that mana with it.

2. The extent and significance of Hawaiian archives is well documented. See Arista (2018), hoʻomanawanui (2017), Nogelmeier (2003), J. H. Osorio (2021), and Silva (2004).

3. Defining nonviolent direct action is beyond the scope of this book. I refer the reader to the Center for Peacemaking at Marquette University: https://www.marquette.edu/peacemaking/nonviolence.php.

4. Kekūhaupiʻo trained Kamehameha to prepare him for combat and later became his advisor and bodyguard.

5. hoʻomanawanui also discusses these poetic devices in *Voices of Fire: Reweaving the Literary Lei of Pele and Hiʻiaka* (2014).

6. Pūnua refers to the embedded cultural knowledge found in words or phrases that go beyond a literal translation.

7. Benimina switched between Hawaiian and English during this part of our conversation. For clarity, I provide my translation of her Hawaiian with her paraphrasing of her mother's English when speaking to the physician.

8. Pūnua provided the lyrics and translation of this mele.

9. Larry Kimura refers to this Hawaiian poetic device as kuʻina kani like (joining device of similar sounds) in his master's thesis that identifies and names a myriad of devices common in Hawaiian poetry (2002).

10. I learned from Kimura during my time as his student at UH Hilo that he coined the term pīnaʻi (to repeat or echo) for this kind of repetition of thought in mele.

11. There are precedents for negative sentiments in mele in appropriate contexts. However, as hoʻomanawanui notes, "it seems to be very specific in a way that it has a genre specification, humor is attached, and wouldn't be part of any other mele that otherwise had positive sentiments in it" (hoʻomanawanui 2023). I have composed several such mele myself, all of which include the humorous aspects she speaks of. Takatsugi discusses his affinity for the practice of hakukole (to defame or ridicule in poetic or figurative language) in chapter 5.

FIVE

—ɯ—

PAIO NO KA PONO Ē

Music and Conflict

I think it is pretty remarkable that, at least on *Kūhaʻo Maunakea*, I can only think of one line out of the entire project that actually refers to opposition. Instead, every mele is about the true motivation of our lāhui. So it's interesting to acknowledge that it was all really about aloha ʻāina. Was it about fighting or battle or struggle? This is really the waiwai [value] of haku mele if you understand the context: the struggle is what triggered this ancestral response. To actually reflect that every mele is rooted in a positive force, it demonstrates the motivation behind our people uniting together and standing for aloha ʻāina. I love when a mele is used to take jabs at people. I mean, I'm fascinated with the practice of hakukole.[1] I love looking into that kind of stuff, and I've done a couple of them on my own. The most incredible part about this is that as much as it was a struggle and challenge, we've achieved huge milestones in this whole journey of seeing the unification of our lāhui in ways that we had never seen before. It's not our anger towards somebody that's going to make us puka [to emerge] through to our unification, but it's us coming together that's going to carry us forward. (Takatsugi 2020)

In this chapter, I discuss the role that music plays in conflict and the potential resolution of conflict. There is a rich body of literature theorizing conflict, its sources, and possible solutions and a growing body of literature on the role that music can play in these solutions. I describe several encounters on Hawaiʻi mokupuni before and after the months-long standoff on the Maunakea Access Road and the establishment of the kūpuna encampment in 2019. I focus on those who composed, performed, and recorded music to support the efforts to protect Maunakea during the most contentious period of aggression against the kia'i: the weeks before and months following the arrest of kūpuna in July 2019. I also provide a historical overview of music's role in politics and conflict and examine the role of traditional media and social media in these encounters.

In the days and weeks that followed the arrest of kūpuna at the kia'i encampment in July 2019, the number of law enforcement officers rose, as did the number of kia'i.[2] While negotiations between law enforcement and kia'i continued without resolution, tensions on both sides escalated. Kia'i on the mauna and supporters watching the confrontation via social media sites began to compose and record new mele as expressions of support and in defense of the sanctity of the mauna. Some shared their work on Facebook, hoping that the performances would bolster the spirits of kia'i and support for their efforts. Among the early creatives whose work was shared were Del Beazley ("Rize"), Ānuenue Pūnua ("Lei Ana Maunakea I Ka 'Ohu"), Lehua Kalima-Alvarez ("Ka Nani A'o Maunakea"), Josh Tatofi ("For the Lāhui"), and Zachary Lum ("Nā Pu'uwai Haokila"). The mele I composed with my colleague Robin Leihuanani Keali'inohomoku, "Lei Ana Maunakea I Ke Aloha 'Oi'a'i'o," was recorded by her and released about a week later.[3] Shortly after that, I began to scour Facebook, YouTube, and other sources for mele written for the mauna. I located a list created by Malia Nobrega-Olivera and, with her permission, combined it with a list I had compiled. By July 2020, I had identified sixty-two compositions, including some songs written for Maunakea predating the arrests. Still, most were composed and released in the days leading up to and the months following the arrests.[4]

This chapter's Hawaiian title is a line from the mele "E Nā Kini," written by Ernest Kala and John Pūnua.[5] The Hawaiian lyrics state, "Paio no ka pono ē, e nā kini o ka 'āina," presenting a call for the multitudes of the 'āina to rise up and fight for their rights. It includes the famous words uttered by Kamehameha at the battle at Kepaniwai on Maui in 1790: "I mua e nā pōki'i a e inu i ka wai 'awa'awa" (Move forward, my younger siblings, and drink the bitter waters).

POLITICS, CONFLICT, AND MUSIC ON THE MAUNA

Chad Takatsugi (Kanaka 'Ōiwi), a founding member of the popular Hawaiian music group 'Ale'a, released his debut solo recording, "Ahuwale," to widespread acclaim in 2015. He was recognized with four Nā Hōkū Hanohano Awards (Hawaiian music album of the year, liner notes, Haku Mele Award, and Hawaiian Language Performance Award) in 2016. He describes the days leading up to his post calling on haku mele and what triggered and inspired his compositional instincts.

I felt very very compelled to focus on Maunakea, so I jotted some stuff down, with some of it making it into the final product. Some of it didn't, but it wasn't until we got back and then that Wednesday happened, right and then, you know, it's all over the news. It's all over the radio, and I remember thinking to myself, there's something different about this time, and then I'm not really sure what it is. So that night, I finished it up and put the melody to it, and that's when I made the video. I wanted it to be a vehicle for me to say there are many ways to support. Donate to KĀHEA.[6] That was really what my cause was. But the mele was definitely intentional, my intentional way of saying this battle is going to rage everywhere—it'll be on the mauna, but it's also going to be in our own spaces, and we have to find our ways to fight that battle and my particular contribution was a testament to that. (Takatsugi 2020)

Before the release of *Kūhaʻo Maunakea* CD, Pūnua reflected on the events she witnessed on the day the kūpuna were arrested that inspired her creativity: "I witnessed grace, strength, wisdom, and courage in the eyes of our kūpuna who stood steadfast to protect our Maunakea. As I stood behind the kūpuna patiently waiting their turn to be arrested, Kainani [Kahaunaele], Mahina [Paishon-Duarte], and I filled the air with mele aloha ʻāina, witnessing the power of music. In some of the tensest moments in that tent, we witnessed how a simple line like ʻnani pua ʻaʻala, onaona i ka ihu' [beautiful, fragrant flower] could calm the crowd at that moment" (2020).

Conflict and its causes and potential solutions have been the subject of extensive scholarly inquiry because conflict has been a significant part of human history. In their review of conflict literature, John Wall and Ronda Callister compare conflict to the common cold: "We all know what it is, but objectively analyzing it can prove difficult, as can identifying the causes and understanding the effects. And most difficult is discovering a cure" (1995). While economic disparity is often cited as a primary cause of conflict, research has shown that it is not always conflict's primary source and that other factors must be considered, including cultural and intercultural ones. As Stephen Fox writes: "Conflict requires interdependence, in that two or more parties share interest in something, whether land, resources, customers, or recognition. Without overlap of interests, there is no conflict, so conflict and competition require a relationship of some sort. Human conflict happens in cultural or intercultural contexts, following culturally determined patterns and processes. Conflicts may arise over tangible issues, as when a finite resource or location is at stake, or over intangibles like religion. The crucial requirement is that people perceive that a conflict is occurring" (2019).

Regardless of the roots of conflict, "inequality is legitimized in one way or another; that the inequality comes with a degree of power and repression that are simply too great to overcome; or that various obstacles are preventing collective action" (Cramer 2005). Such is the case with the conflict over Maunakea and the proposed construction of TMT. Still, the roots of this conflict are much more profound and are also reflective of the disempowerment experienced by Kānaka ʻŌiwi in their homeland: "The sorrow-laden, everlasting conflict between the beauty and power of our homeland and our culture, and the forced Americanization that all Hawaiians endure leaves our people in a state of continual despair, a kind of unfocused yearning for another world forever out of reach. In response to this, many of our writers now reflect a new consciousness which sovereignty has helped to shape, namely, that we are indigenous to Hawaii and what we do is very much a part of being indigenous, even if it is vastly different from what we did in the past" (Trask 1999).

Trask speaks eloquently about the disproportionate power wielded by non-Indigenous academics and their potential social and political impacts on Kānaka ʻŌiwi: "Of course, the claim to knowledge by anthropologists is their academic training applied to the field. Native nationalists' claim to knowledge is their life experience as Natives. The problem is more serious than epistemology, however. In a colonial world, the work of anthropologists and other Western-trained 'experts' is used to disparage and exploit Natives. What Linnekin or Keesing or any other anthropologist writes about Hawaiians has more potential power than what Hawaiians write about themselves" (1991).

In his testimony to a contested case hearings officer, renowned Hawaiian composer, singer, and scholar Jonathan Kay Kamakawiwoʻole Osorio (hereafter Jon Osorio) noted his ancestral connections to Hawaiʻi mokupuni on both his mother's and father's sides, his ʻohana. He spoke of his long-standing opposition to the project. He demonstrated his moʻokūʻauhau consciousness by framing the conflict between kiaʻi and pro-TMT forces to include unresolved historical issues, present issues, and the uncertainty of the future that the conflict's outcome would shape: "I do not believe that the struggle over the future of Mauna Kea is a conflict between Hawaiians and non-Hawaiians, nor is it a clash between western science and Hawaiian cultural beliefs. This conflict is actually between people who see the history and future of Hawaiʻi very differently from one another, and the issue is about how we manage resources and how we align our laws, our economy and the values of a whole, yet diverse society in Hawaiʻi in order to connect a ruptured past, contentious present and very uncertain future" (J. K. K. Osorio 2016b).

Andre Perez holding a koʻi
(adze) on Maunakea. Photo
credit: Andre Perez

While explaining the usual causes and processes of conflicts, such examina-
tions are often predicated on identifying a resolution to the conflict. The literature on conflict that proposes approaches to resolution is also extensive and
beyond the scope of this book. Instead, I briefly address a Kānaka ʻŌiwi form
of conflict resolution within the ʻohana (family) that was periodically raised as
a means of resolving the conflict: hoʻoponopono. Pukui notes, "*Hoʻoponopono*
is getting the family together to find out what is wrong. Maybe to find out why
someone is sick or the cause of a family quarrel. Then, with discussion and
repentance and restitution and forgiveness—and always with prayer—to set
right what was wrong" (1972). The practice and context of hoʻoponopono have
been changed or recentered in modern times not only to include someone from
outside the immediate family conducting the hoʻoponopono but also to achieve
resolution between unrelated individuals and even businesses and organizations (Myron B. Thompson School of Social Work n.d.).[7]

I asked both Andre Perez and Noe Noe Wong-Wilson if hoʻoponopono had been discussed as a possible means of resolving the dispute over Maunakea. Perez noted that while there were attempts to negotiate with the state, kiaʻi leaders did not consider hoʻoponopono for several reasons: "It was our understanding that hoʻoponopono is usually conducted within the family context and depends on if you want to maintain the relationship or not. We felt that it wasn't appropriate with the state" (Perez 2022). He added that when a third party attempted to fulfill the role of negotiator, "We were already at the stage of no compromise while they [the third party] were trying to negotiate a compromise on both sides." Indeed, with neither side willing to budge on the fundamental issue of whether or not TMT would be built on Maunakea's summit, such processes would likely have been futile. As Wong-Wilson noted, "there were efforts to bring parties to the table to meet face-to-face, talk story, but I don't consider it hoʻoponopono while we continued to be assaulted by law enforcement" (2022).[8]

Music has long served many different roles in conflict and even war, and the language of music is rife with metaphoric borrowings: "The language of music is profoundly informed by the metaphors of conflict, offering a lexical setting for understanding the place of music in conflict" (O'Connell 2010). If one examines the conversations with kiaʻi found throughout this book, one sees that the vocabulary of conflict and war is quite common.

Mele written about times of conflict in Hawaiʻi are usually composed during the era of the events they document. Examples include "Kaulana Nā Pua" (discussed in chap. 6), written less than two months after the overthrow of the Hawaiian Kingdom in 1893. "Kū Haʻaheo e Kuʻu Hawaiʻi" was written in 2007 amid multiple social and political issues that Hinaleimoana Wong-Kalu and her students encountered (discussed in chap. 6). Mele like "Aloha ʻĀina ʻOiaʻiʻo" (chap. 3), "Lei Ana Maunakea I Ka ʻOhu" (chap. 4), and "For the Lāhui" (chap. 3) were written during the time of the confrontations on the Ala Kūpuna. I examine one mele written "out of its time": Palani Vaughan's "Ka Māmakakaua" (Vaughan 1977).

Palani Vaughan was a composer and singer who gained popularity in the early years of the Second Hawaiian Renaissance, first with the musical group Sunday Mānoa and later as a solo artist and with his group The King's Men. Vaughan and his group wore attire reminiscent of that worn in the royal court, and Vaughan sported mutton chops similar to those worn by King David Kalākaua. His recordings primarily feature older mele written in or associated with the monarchial era, particularly the reign of King David Kalākaua, and new compositions with similar themes. "Ka Māmakakaua" is one such song.

"Ka Māmakakaua" was inspired by events in 1887, when a haole (foreign, white) militia coerced Kalākaua to sign a new constitution, nicknamed "The Bayonet Constitution," that forced him to transfer many of his powers to the legislature. "Ka Māmakakaua" refers to Kānaka Maoli who took up arms against and supported the return of Kalākaua's royal powers. Ultimately, the actions of the king's supporters failed.[9] The term māmakakaua is comprised of two words—māmaka (to bear or carry on the shoulders) and kaua (war). This term was commonly used in the late nineteenth century to describe individuals loyal to the Hawaiian Kingdom and its monarchs.

KA MĀMAKAKAUA[10]

Composed by Palani Vaughan

PAUKŪ ʻEKAHI	FIRST VERSE
Ua ala a kūʻē! Kūʻē! Kūʻē!	They arose and revolted! Revolted! Revolted!
Ka māmakakaua hanohano! Kūʻē!	That glorious company of warriors! Revolted!
Ua ala a kūʻē! Kūʻē! Kūʻē!	They arose and revolted! Revolted! Revolted!
Ka māmakakaua Loialiki! Kūʻē!	The Loyalist company of warriors! Revolted!
Kūʻē! Kūʻē!	Revolted! Revolted

PAUKŪ ʻELUA	SECOND VERSE
Ka māmakakaua!	The company of warriors!
(Nā Loialiki koa)!	Courageous Loyalists!
Kipū Lani!	Loyal to the chief!
(Ka māmakakaua)!	The company of warriors!
Ka māmakakaua!	The company of warriors!
(Kūpaʻa ma hope)!	Standing firmly behind!
Kūpaʻa ma hope!	Standing firmly behind!
(O ka ʻāina)!	The land!
Ua ala a kūʻē! Kūʻē!	They arose and revolted! Revolted!

PAUKŪ ʻEKOLU	EKOLU VERSE
Ka pūkaua koa!	The brave war leader!
(ʻO Wilikoki wiwoʻole)!	Fearless Robert Wilcox!
Me Lopaka Poe!	With Robert Boyd!
(A me nā koa Loialiki)!	And the Loyalist warriors!
Ka māmakakaua! (I hōʻikaika hoʻi)!	The company of warriors! Strove, indeed!

E hoʻihoʻi i nā pono! (O Kalākaua)!	To restore the rights of Kalākaua
Nā Loialiki! Kūʻē! Kūʻē!	The Loyalists! Revolted! Revolted!

PAUKŪ ʻEHĀ	FOURTH VERSE
Ka māmakakaua!	The company of warriors!
(Me nā pālule ʻula)!	With red shirts
Ma loko a ka pā!	Inside the grounds!
(O Hale Aliʻi ʻIolani)!	Of ʻIolani Palace!
Ka māmakakaua!	The company of warriors!
(I paio wiwoʻole)!	Who fought bravely!
Kūʻē i ka ʻenemi! (O Ka Mōʻi)!	Against the enemy of the King!
I ke aupuni hoʻohuli!	Against the revolutionary government!

PAUKŪ ʻELIMA	FIFTH VERSE
Ka māmakakaua!	The company of warriors!
(ʻOiai ua pohō)!	Though they failed
Kūʻē i ka ʻenemi!	Against the enemy!
(O ka lāhui o Hawaiʻi)!	Of the Hawaiian nation!
Ka māmakakaua!	The company of warriors!
(ʻAʻole poina ʻia)!	Not forgotten!
ʻAʻole poina ʻia!	Not forgotten!
(No ko lākou wiwoʻole)!	For their bravery!
Aloha no nā Loialiki ē!	Great love for the Loyalists!

PAUKŪ ʻEONO	SIXTH VERSE
Ua ala a kūʻē!	They arose and revolted!
(Ka māmakakaua)!	The company of warriors!
Kipū Lani ē! (Nā Loialiki koa)!	Loyal to the King! The brave Loyalists!
Kūpaʻa ma hope o ka ʻāina!	Standing firmly behind the land!
Aloha ʻāina hoʻi ē!	Patriots, indeed!
Aloha ʻāina hoʻi ē!	Patriots, indeed![11]

Vaughan's composition invokes common themes and words heard in other compositions of the time and in compositions for Maunakea. Vaughan uses the cry of kūʻē (resist!) repeatedly, sometimes in succession, and adds the familiar exhortation to kūpaʻa mahope o ka ʻāina (be steadfast for the land). He describes the māmakakaua as wiwoʻole (fearless) and uses phonetic transcriptions of the English words "loyalist" (loialiki) and "enemy" (ʻenemi), which was a common practice during that time. He also uses phonetic transcriptions for the names of two well-known Hawaiian patriots of the time, Wilikoki (Robert Wilcox) and Lopaka Poe (Robert Boyd), explicitly identifying them as Aloha ʻĀina. Vaughan does not restrict his references to the king and his supporters but entices the visual senses of the listener by including the name of 'Iolani Palace, built by Kalākaua in 1882, and describing the attire worn by the māmakakaua as nā pālule 'ula (the red shirts).

Vaughan's recording of "Ka Māmakakaua" appears on the LP *Iā 'Oe E Ka Lā*, volume 3, the third of the four volumes he recorded. It was released in 1977.[12] While other albums in this series celebrate specific milestones, such as the hundredth anniversary of Kalākaua's coronation, the celebration held on his fiftieth birthday, and the hundredth anniversary of his worldwide travels, this third volume honors the "footprints" of the Renaissance Monarch.[13] The recording features a percussive introduction with Vaughan and members of The King's Own reciting the opening verse. The tempo is brisk—approximately 170 beats per minute—and the listener can imagine a group of soldiers marching in cadence to its rhythm. Guitars become audible about eight seconds in. The performance includes some call-and-response vocal passages reminiscent of the vocalization one might encounter during a military exercise. Vaughan can be heard singing alone while other musicians (or perhaps Vaughan himself in overdubs) perform the call-and-response passages and harmonies throughout the performance. The performance begins to fade at 2:27 and ends at 2:37.

Vaughan recorded four albums honoring the anniversary of significant milestones in Kalākaua's life and reign. Through his rerecordings of songs written by Kalākaua and new compositions in the 1970s, Vaughan brought to life an era in which aloha 'āina and Hawaiian resistance against colonizer desires and aggressions were alive and part of everyday life. This four-volume series' thematic nature and extent capture the era's spirit. When hearing Vaughan live or watching video-recorded performances, listeners could experience the sights and sounds of that crucial time in Hawai'i's history.[14]

The thematic nature of the *Iā 'Oe E Ka Lā* albums created a model for future endeavors of musical aloha 'āina and activism. Noting the shared thematic characteristics of Vaughan's *Iā 'Oe E Ka Lā* series and *Kūha'o Maunakea*, I asked the producers of *Kūha'o Maunakea*, Chad Takatsugi and Zachary Lum, if the *Iā 'Oe E Ka Lā* recordings influenced it. Takatsugi replied that while they did not consciously reproduce Vaughan's approach, "the whole premise of *Kūha'o Maunakea* was to replicate the historical record-keeping qualities of mele that our kūpuna established" (Takatsugi 2020).

There are examples elsewhere in the Pacific of musical performance playing a significant role in resolving conflicts. Brian Diettrich examines two musical examples from Chuuk State in the Federated States of Micronesia that demonstrate the role of music in restoring and maintaining cohesion in society. Both examples are representative of a broad category of traditional music known as kéélún lóómw (and as kéénún nóómw in Chuuk Lagoon), a musical genre that "extends from the cultural past and is socially valued in the present" (Diettrich 2017). His first example, "Wélúmetaw," retells a story of a past conflict and resolution between residents of the Pollap and Tamatam—islands sharing a lagoon. The second example, "Worofes," was described to Diettrich as a form of conflict resolution between chiefs and populace "by taking an elaborate and imagined sea journey in order to mediate conflict through traditional moral authority, contemplation, and ideas of diplomacy" (2017). In both circumstances, the conflict was between two Indigenous groups of the area and not with settler-colonizers or colonizer-established governments, as in Hawaiʻi with the dispute over Maunakea and the Tāngata Whenua at Ihumātao.

CATTLE GUARDS AND KŪPUNA TENTS

On the evening of Sunday, July 14, 2019, the kiaʻi gathered in the kūpuna tent and prepared for confrontation with law enforcement officials the following day, with the expectation that many would be arrested. Depending on strategies learned from their nonviolent direct-action training, they identified individuals ready and willing to be arrested, those who were willing (if necessary) but preferred not to be arrested, and those who, for personal or strategic reasons, needed to avoid situations that could subject them to arrest. Each group then gathered to discuss their strategy for the next day. Kaleikoa Kaʻeo and Walter Ritte were among those deemed "arrestable" and led the group that planned to chain itself to the cattle guard.

In the early morning of Monday, July 15, 2019, eight kiaʻi awoke at their encampment on Maunakea Access Road, just above the Daniel K. Inouye Highway. They walked several hundred feet ma uka (upland) of the encampment. They prepared to chain themselves to the cattle guard grate that crossed the Maunakea Access Road to prevent heavy construction vehicles from driving through this strategically important point on the road. At approximately four a.m., group members arrived at the cattle guard and began securing themselves to the cattle guard and each other. One kiaʻi, Kamuela Pāka, took his position in the ample space underneath the cattle guard and, from that position, was chained to Mahiʻai Dochen. Kaleikoa Kaʻeo was chained to "Uncle" Walter Ritte, Noe Goodyear-Kaʻōpua to her kāne (husband), ʻĪmaikalani Winchester, and Heoli Osorio to Malia Hulleman (now Osorio).[15] With temperatures in the forties, the Mauna Medic Healers were concerned about the possibility of the group developing hypothermia before temperatures rose after sunrise and about heatstroke should those chained to the grate continue to lie on the road for more than a few hours into the day.[16] Heoli Osorio describes the situation.

> I always imagined that the closer you get to sunrise, it's going to get warmer, but it doesn't get warmer; it gets colder. This is something I learned on the first night because I slept on a cot. I didn't sleep in a tent. I was out in the open, but the temperature drops like five or six, maybe seven degrees. So we're freezing. We're trying to stay warm; they're trying to take care of us. And then, at a certain point, our medic tells us okay, in the next hour we shift from trying to make sure you don't get hypothermia to trying to make sure you don't get heatstroke. So this is the most ridiculous thing I've ever experienced. But eventually, you know, we're okay, people are feeding us, they're taking very good care of us. (2020)

Law enforcement officers arrived at the cattle guard shortly after the eight kiaʻi were chained and ordered them to release themselves from the cattle guard or face arrest. When the kiaʻi refused, the officer in charge, not knowing all of their names, called a description of each kiaʻi and what they were wearing and declared them under arrest. Osorio continues:

> As the sun came up, I start to feel like we should like sing. So one of my favorite songs growing up—not growing up but in the last few years—was taught to me by my grandfather and my grandfather's sister, and it's "Song for Hilo." And the way that I was taught about the song, my dad always told me that the song is about two lovers who are constantly going off into the forest and making love, but they always return before morning before the sun rises. But then one day they fall asleep, and they wake up, and the sun has risen above them, and now like their whole pilina [relationship] with each other has changed because they have like made light together. And so I was thinking about this song, and I was thinking about this woman I was chained to and also the six other people. We were making daylight with each other; we were going to watch the sunrise together. And so I sang the song "Ua Like Nō A Like." I sang the song to Malia and everyone else who was there, and that's the first song that was sung on the cattle guard. I forgot to tell this part of the story, but that was probably one of the most profound moments on the mauna for me because that's when my pilina to the mountain changed, and my pilina to Malia changed, and my feeling is everyone else who was there on that cattle guards changed. (2020)

After dawn, others in the encampment became aware of what was happening above their position on the access road. Among the kūpuna who made their way to the cattle guard was Heoli Osorio's father, Jon.

Jon Osorio and daughter Jamaica Heolimeleikalani Osorio singing on Maunakea. Photo credit: Malia Osorio

When my dad came up at whatever time he came, he looked really sad and kind of scared, and he asked me, "What can I do for you?" Any time I've been in pain or like physical or emotional pain, my dad's always sung for me. You know, when I got my tonsils or my appendix taken out, my dad brought his guitar and sang for me. When my heart was broken, my dad sang for me. When I got my ala niho [a tattoo] done, my dad brought his guitar and sang to me. And it's always made me feel better, but I also know it makes me feel better because he can do something for me. So I looked at him, and I said, "Can you sing for me and my friends?" Someone ran down the mountain, got him a guitar, and that's when he started playing for us. (2020)[17]

Jon Osorio played and sang the mele "Puʻu Waʻawaʻa," the Beatles' "In My Life," his composition "Hawaiian Eyes," and other songs. Those chained to the cattle guard, the medics, and others gathered around the cattle guard sang along.[18] As the standoff continued, a tent was moved over those chained to the cattle guard to provide protection from the sun. Little known to those chained to the cattle guard, a large crowd was assembling at the encampment. Live video streams had broadcast their actions and images of Jon Osorio and others singing as his daughter and her companions remained chained to the cattle guard.

In midafternoon, law enforcement officers informed the kiaʻi that there would be no attempt to transport any equipment up the mountain that day. They informed those arrested in the early morning that they were no longer arrested and were free to go and that no further actions would be taken. The kiaʻi unchanged themselves from the cattle guard and returned to the Puʻuhonua. They found that its population had substantially increased since their departure early that morning. Later that day, kiaʻi near the Ala Kūpuna noticed activity near the cattle guard and found that construction had begun on a gate over the cattle guard in an attempt by the state to gain control over this important strategic location on the road. Feeling betrayed by assurances they had been given earlier by law enforcement officers who had "unarrested" those on the cattle guard, kiaʻi began negotiations with law enforcement. Unable to negotiate a solution acceptable to both sides, kiaʻi dug in and organized for the long struggle ahead. This included establishing a kitchen and arranging a kūpuna kōkua (support people for the kūpuna) team. Around this time, regular musical performances featuring many different genres of music began on the Ala Kūpuna.

Older and contemporary forms of Hawaiian music, including chant, hula, "island music," and reggae were among the more frequently heard genres of music on the mauna.[19] Punahele (Kanaka Maoli) is a composer and recording artist of rap music who hails from the west side of Oʻahu and has long been active on social issues in his community.[20] He was present on the mauna in the days leading up to the arrest of the kūpuna on July 17, 2019, and left the mauna infrequently for the remainder of the year. Punahele and Kaʻikena Scanlan (Kanaka Maoli) were among those who composed and performed in more contemporary music styles such as rap, hip-hop, and reggae on the mauna. While Punahele did not go to the mauna to perform, he, like many, was called on to do so and obliged. Punahele discusses the influence his experiences had on him and his compositional process.

> When I was on the mauna, I had no intentions of performing at all—just being a kiaʻi to the best of my ability. I felt like it was finally my time to do more for the lāhui at that point, and I was dedicated just to being there to protect the mauna and focusing on that. . . . In those early days, from like the thirteenth to the seventeenth [of July 2019], I probably wrote fifteen songs in those three or four days. There was times when there was only like four

people on one side of the road. I remember it like it was yesterday. There was me, Lanakila [Mangauil], Kaʻikena Scanlon, and Hāwane Rios—just us four on the road against all these cops at one point. And they'd all laugh and look at me and Kaʻikena because they were trying to keep it more traditional and I was like, "What?" We're like, "We got this kūʻē [resistance] stuff, me and Kaʻikena." There were times where it's kind of like really traumatic, kind of a war-like situation. I remember just feeling discouraged, feeling angry, feeling full of rage, feeling sad. I walked straight across the highway, feeling defeated. And I wrote. I sat on this one rock, right below Puʻuhuluhulu, and I wrote like six songs in one sitting within about three hours. I wrote about forty-four songs in total in my six months there, but like fifteen to twenty was within the first week. (Punahele 2022)

There were no genre boundaries that music for Maunakea could not cross. While heavy metal music may not come to mind when considering the genres of music performed in Hawaiʻi, a robust underground community of performers and fans has existed since at least the early 1970s. Conflict, opposition, chaos, rebellion, and injustice are common themes in heavy metal lyrics (Weinstein 2000). Sandy Essman (Kanaka ʻŌiwi) and Gerard Gonsalves are members of the Honolulu-based heavy metal group Storm. While they did not perform on the mauna, Gonsalves and Essman tried to find ways to contribute to efforts there. Essman is also a practitioner of lomilomi (a type of massage) and went to the Ala Kūpuna in September 2019 to provide lomilomi to the kūpuna. Essman noted the importance of solidarity within the kiaʻi during the conflict with the state, university, and law enforcement and wanted her composition for the mauna to reflect this value.

We lost so many of the cultural ties that connected us to the earth, so to speak. But going back to the mauna and hearing all the protocol, it literally brought me to tears; you have to feel the mana [spiritual power] that's out there in the group. They impressed upon us the kapu aloha that they need to carry, and they gave a kuleana to each and every person that was up there because without that solidarity and if you have some little faction over here or one eruption over here, you're going to bring that whole group down. It brought me to write the lyrics [of her composition "Ka Mauna A Wākea"]. I didn't want to write something to bash; that would be bad, that's not what I want. I just wanted to have you know that you just need to come together as one entity and fight. The point was to bring the lāhui together in solidarity as one to fight for the land and our culture. It was pride—enough already. You know, I saw it in a way that's not bashing. But just to bring a sense of pride in the lāhui. (Essman 2020)

Gonsalves composed the music to which Essman wrote lyrics for "Ka Mauna A Wākea." Gonsalves notes that while he is not Hawaiian, his long awareness of issues facing the Hawaiian community and the Kānaka ʻŌiwi presence in the band compelled him to address the confrontation on Maunakea through musical composition and performance.

> I'm not Hawaiian. My daughter is Hawaiian. I'm born and raised here, a fourth-generation descendant of Portuguese immigrants. I grew up in the Hawaiian Renaissance era with all that music and rejuvenation of Hawaiian culture and music; I was aware of all of that. Though I'm not Hawaiian, because I was born and raised here, my parents were born and raised here, and my grandparents were born and raised here. I've always had this connection. Sandy and the other two members of our band, Brian [Spalding] and Darren [Soliven], they're Hawaiian, too. We've felt like we should write something for the mauna. It's basically about standing together in kapu aloha. It's a fight, but it's more about rallying and standing together and fighting this injustice. (Gonsalves 2020)

The acceptance and appreciation of kūpuna and kiaʻi were evident on the mauna, regardless of the performers' musical genre, talent, industry awards, or nationality. Music served as food for the soul of kiaʻi between periods of conflict with law enforcement, who undoubtedly enjoyed the performances as well.

THE BATTLE WILL BE STREAMED

Many deeply personal encounters and experiences on the mauna remain out of the public consciousness. I have some of my own that stay between myself and Maunakea and individuals with whom I spoke. Many kiaʻi shared personal memories with me, some of which are included within these pages with the sharers' permission. However, it is unlikely that any significant interaction between kiaʻi, law enforcement, and other representatives of the state or university was not recorded or streamed. Many events that occurred at the kiaʻi encampment between kiaʻi and supporters were also recorded or streamed and can still be found and viewed on social media sites such as Facebook and YouTube.

The internet and social media sites have been a double-edged sword for Indigenous communities worldwide. Hawaiʻi is no exception, and interactions on social media were a significant part of the multisited nature of contact zones in which the struggle for Maunakea took place and continues to occur. Bronwyn

Carlson (Aboriginal) argues that communications on social media are the norm and not an aberration in Indigenous communities. She observes that social media is a new frontier where "Aboriginal people, like many others, are busy seeking new ways of representing and identifying ourselves to each other—and others—in a global amphitheater" (Carlson 2013). But as Frazer, Carlson, and Farrelly have noted, "research documents how the internet has facilitated the extension of racist discourse, the settler 'logic of Indigenous elimination,' and the coordination of white supremacist and anti-Indigenous hate groups" (2022). Similarly, Kānaka ʻŌiwi have endured racial stereotyping and racist attacks on social media sites, as they have elsewhere, whenever and wherever they have stood up to systematic settler-colonial oppressive acts and attitudes.

Social media sites have also been "sites of immense Indigenous creativity, imagination, and agency—the production of ideas, practices, and relations that work against, below and outside settler power relations" (Frazer, Carlson, and Farrelly 2022). Social media allowed kiaʻi to quickly respond to and disprove allegations such as those made by Governor Ige when he characterized the encampment as an "unsafe situation" without having visited it (Dayton and Gomes 2019).[21] Kiaʻi present on the Ala Kūpuna could quickly share videos and photos of the well-organized, clean encampment. These activities and others are characteristic of what Wilson, Carlson, and Sciascia have labeled "the Indigenous reterritorialization" of social media (Wilson et al. 2017).

Lum notes Lee Ann Ānuenue Pūnua's sharing her composition "Lei Maunakea I Ka ʻOhu" and her call for other composers and performers to share their work in solidarity with kiaʻi. This call and the resultant actions represent one example of the Indigenous reterritorialization of social media, as described by Wilson, Carlson, and Sciascia, in the context of the struggle for Maunakea:

> I think Ānuenue [Pūnua] is a great example with the "E Kanikapila Kākou" ["Let the instruments sound"] challenge. There are all of these other opportunities, whether because people are staying home or because they are feeling a need to say something via mele. Social media becomes this opportunity for people to say whatever they like, and then sometimes that's good. We were talking about mele and being able to control the things that come out. There's an opportunity for it to catch fire because it's really good and really inspirational, and then there's opportunity to catch fire because there's outrage. (Lum 2020)

Mainstream media kept the public informed of events as they unfolded on the mauna. Jaz Kaiwikoʻo Yglesias (Kanaka ʻŌiwi) and Kaʻea Lyons (Kanaka ʻŌiwi), a husband and wife team at KAPA radio on Hawaiʻi mokupuni, contributed to this effort by focusing on Maunakea in mainstream media, talking about current events during their morning radio program, and playing mele written and recorded for the kiaʻi and the mauna as they were released. Several years before the arrests, Yglesias and Lyons were approached by a private nonprofit organization to create an ad highlighting the importance of Maunakea and the aquifers located around it. This educational piece was later combined into a commercial with a voice-over featuring Hawaiian recording artists using the slogan "We Are Maunakea," which became popular among kiaʻi and supporters.

> YGLESIAS: This is where Jason Momoa comes in. I had just finished doing a post where he had worn a shirt with "We Are Maunakea" on his chest. I said, "Let's call up as many musicians as we can and do this commercial, where it's not an anti-TMT but a pro-Hawaiʻi, promoting that we [Kānaka ʻŌiwi] were already navigators and such." So each commercial started, at our suggestion, with "Aloha mai kākou. This is Kaumakaiwa Kanakaʻole. We are Maunakea." So we started running that commercial, got a bunch of sponsors, and started this big promotion.
>
> LYONS: Then we added its scientific dialogue, and two people provided facts that we are working with.
>
> YGLESIAS: We kind of made the commercial sound like a rebuttal to that TMT commercial, explaining what it could do to our aquifers and things like that. But it was without being negative at all. (Yglesias and Lyons 2020)

Yglesias and Lyons recall receiving an email from a listener who claimed to be an advertiser on KAPA radio informing them that they would cease advertising on the station because of the on-air activism.[22] However, after consulting with their superiors at Pacific Media Group (the owners of KAPA and other radio stations), they were allowed to continue to feature music written in support of the kiaʻi and Maunakea, as well as report on significant happenings on the Ala Kūpuna. Yglesias and Lyons also received messages from artists of many different genres of music who wanted to record in Yglesias' and Lyons' recording studio. They sought to have their music for Maunakea played on the radio to demonstrate their support for the kiaʻi and Maunakea (Yglesias and Lyons 2020).

Social and traditional media provided kiaʻi an immeasurably effective vehicle to refute inaccurate allegations by Ige and other pro-TMT individuals and focus on issues important to kiaʻi and their supporters. Unfortunately, this capability was sorely lacking during earlier confrontations between Kānaka ʻŌiwi and the government, such as those that occurred in the 1970s over issues like the eviction of Kānaka ʻŌiwi from ancestral lands from Kalama Valley and Waiāhole/Waikāne on Oʻahu and the US Navy's bombing of the island of Kahoʻolawe. The latter's implications still reverberate today.

THE BATTLE OVER THE SACRED

Settler-colonizer invocations of the false construct of authenticity are no more evident than in the state and university denying the sacredness of Maunakea, and the examples noted in this book were not their first attempts to contest Kānaka ʻŌiwi assertions of ʻāina's sacredness. In the 1970s, the US Navy, supported by writings of non-Kānaka Maoli academics, attempted to deny the sacredness of the island of Kahoʻolawe to continue using it as a bombing range. This battle over the island's sacredness raged in the halls of government, the court of public opinion, and academic circles that pitted white academics against Kanaka ʻŌiwi scholar Haunani-Kay Trask (Trask 1991, Linnekin 1991, Keesing 1991, Hanson 1991). Trask noted that one of the academics involved in the exchanges that had occurred for several years in academic journals had failed to include the scholarship of a single Kanaka ʻŌiwi scholar in his work, relying primarily on the writings of one white scholar: "Beyond his poverty of sources, there is Keesing's willful ignorance of solid evidence from Native forms of history-genealogy which reveal that in pre-haole Hawaiʻi our people looked on land as a mother, enjoyed a familial relationship with her and other living things, and practiced an economically wise, spiritually based ethic of caring for the land, called *malama ʻaina*" (Trask 1991).

The conflict over ending the navy's control over and bombing of the island was costly, with the loss of two Kānaka ʻŌiwi lives—George Helm and Kimo Mitchell. Maunakea is more than a reminder of a genealogical connection; it is a physical presence that forces those in its presence to alter their behavior.

> What I'm talking about are places that, when you have a connection to them, they physically and spiritually shape you and teach you. And how do you know they're doing that? When you change your conduct, your behavior in their presence. It's likened to when you're in church or a holy place, and your whole demeanor changes when you enter. You stand and interact in a manner in which your elders would be proud of you and every Hawaiian value and tradition you ever learned or practiced is what guides and leads you. That to me, signifies being in the presence of the sacred—when you are on a place where generally speaking, the majority of the people assembled there understand that it's living and breathing and an extension of themselves. When you say that you are standing in the wao akua [realm of the gods], you

hear the nature deities speak to you through the elements, where you learn something at that spot from beyond the human realm. It is the place where your conduct totally changes and shifts because you know it's expected not just by others at your side, but by the place itself. That to me is sacred. Sacred is when we go up that mountain and when we are chanting these chants and we are singing these songs, we know that they hear us. There is no doubt, because the mountain changes as well. (P. Case 2020)

David Aiona Chang (Kanaka ʻŌiwi) is a historian of Indigenous people, colonialism, borders, and migration at the University of Minnesota. Chang visited the mauna and spent time there during the standoff between the kiaʻi and law enforcement. He notes how engaging with the performance of mele and hula during protocol connected him to the sacred elements of mauna: "The most powerful experience for me was going up to the mauna a couple of times, staying up there, running support in any way that I could. But most the most powerful experience was taking part in protocol three times a day, or four times a day when you count dawn, singing mele along with doing hula with the kiaʻi and everybody up there to support and to experience those songs, some of them old, some of them new, in a way that's proper and is powerful and is sacred and is political" (Chang 2020).

Chang speaks to the contentious issue of sacredness on the mauna and in confrontations between Kānaka ʻŌiwi and a government that imposes its own narrow view of authenticity and sacredness to justify its control of ʻāina, denying the historical and genealogical basis for Kanaka ʻŌiwi assertions of the mauna's sacredness.

This [Maunakea] is a site, the kapu of which is recognized in mele that are old and recognized and that we sing again today. The mauna and the lāhui are genealogically tied to the akua [gods] and to kūpuna going back all the way to Wākea and Hāloa. So these connections are very strong. And so that sacredness is, therefore, originary, but the sacred is also being reaffirmed. Every day and every moment and every kiaʻi and every supporter was up there is participating in the sacredness, which is not just ancient but is also contemporary, and I think that needs to be recognized. (Chang 2020)

Kenneth Makuakāne is a renowned composer, singer, guitarist, and producer of Hawaiian music who is currently the Kahu (minister) of Kawaiahaʻo Church on Oʻahu, which was established in 1820 and is the oldest Christian church in Hawaiʻi. He is a renowned composer, performer, engineer, and producer of Hawaiian music, with over twenty Nā Hōkū Hanohano Awards to his credit. Makuakāne's parents were Christian ministers on Hawaiʻi Island at the

'Opihikao Church in Puna.[23] He speaks to the spiritual aspects of Maunakea and the personal connection to it that inspired and empowered him to express his Hawaiianness and spirituality through the composition of mele.

> We sometimes overuse the word "sacred," but it is a pretty good word for
> it. It tells me how special something is because it's given to me without
> asking for anything in return. That, to me, is sacred, and I think that's what
> began—not the songwriting process, but the journey of my soul process. I
> could never have done that unless I first began with Maunakea because that
> was the essence that opened me up to the spiritual world within me. Because
> I used to think I was a physical being with a soul until I finally saw this,
> and I realize now I am a soul that uses a physical being. And how do I move
> forward in it is always to look back at those things that inspire me? Those are
> sacred things to me because those are the things that constantly give without
> asking for anything. In addition, Ke Akua is the creator of all life. In ka buke
> mua a Mose, i kapa 'ia Kinohi [the first book of Moses, called 'Genesis']
> after Ke Akua [God] brought something into being each day, he said, "Pēlā
> 'i'o nō" [that is right, that is certainly it]. Everything that has been brought
> into existence's certainly made right by Ke Akua. Therefore everything
> *is* [interviewee's emphasis] sacred because it was brought into being by
> Ke Akua. So, in the final analysis, there is the sacred and then there is the
> desecration of the sacred. (Makuakāne 2020)

The destruction of the two ahu on Maunakea (discussed in chap. 3) is an example of the state government's unwillingness to accept Kānaka Maoli epistemologies and cosmologies regarding sacredness. If something is not old and is made by present-day Kānaka 'Ōiwi, the government reasons, it cannot be sacred. Like the Western academic ideas of the invention of tradition brought forward in the 1980s and contested by Indigenous peoples, denial of the sacredness of these places and structures and their desecration and destruction must end.[24]

HŌʻULUʻULU MANAʻO (SUMMARY)

In this chapter, I discuss the role music plays in conflict and the potential resolution of conflict. I examine portions of the rich body of literature theorizing conflict, its sources, and possible solutions and a growing body of literature on the role that music can play in these solutions. In the case of the construction of TMT on Maunakea, there is little hope for compromise as there truly is none to be found on the fundamental issue of TMT being built or not. The state and TMT officials offer financial remuneration and concessions on other matters, such as establishing an "independent" board to oversee the lands knowing that the state will continue to control the selection of its representatives. There is also the possibility of a future legislature abolishing the board and returning direct control of these lands to the state or university.[25]

I have frequently seen social media posts and read letters to the editor from individuals complaining about the lack of aloha demonstrated by kiaʻi and Maunakea supporters and supporters of other issues that affect Kānaka ʻŌiwi and their rights. I have seen and heard some version of, "Where's the aloha? Isn't Hawaiʻi supposed to be the ʻAloha State'?" Kumu Hula and Hawaiian practitioner Charles Kaʻupu offers a response to this privileged attitude.

> We're like any other people on the face of this earth. Ours are specific because of where we are. We are a reflection of our world. Since our world is beautiful more than not, that's who we are. But that doesn't mean we're a welcome mat, that you can step all over us when you come here and expect us to be nice, and then ask us, "Where's the aloha?" Aloha went out the door when you decided to step on my face. A lot of people hear so much about this thing called aloha, and they expect it. That's their free pass. But it's not that way. . . . It's not something you can buy. It doesn't come with money. It comes with giving from the heart. (2011)

Teves notes the irony of demanding aloha from Kānaka ʻŌiwi such as kiaʻi and their supporters while they continue to be threatened by the state, university, and law enforcement: "As a seminal Hawaiian concept of love and inclusion, aloha, ironically, serves to obscure troubling lived realities that Kānaka Maoli experience, such as increasing poverty, houselessness, low educational attainment, and overall poor health" (2018). Until these and other issues are resolved, any call for aloha by settler-colonizers and the state government is as ludicrous as it is disingenuous. The aloha of kiaʻi is directed precisely where it should and needs to be—to the mauna and those who have banded together to defend it.

NOTES

1. Hakukole is a type of mele that defames or ridicules its subject using poetic or figurative language.

2. Kahoʻokahi Kanuha estimates that more than two thousand people assembled at the Maunakea Access Road within a week of the arrests of kūpuna on July 17, 2019 (Andone, Jorgensen, and Sandoval 2019). Perez estimates that there were eighty to one hundred law enforcement personnel there at that time (Perez 2023). By December 20, 2019, the State of Hawaiʻi Attorney General's

Office estimated the cost of law enforcement activities on Maunakea up to that point to be \$12.2 million (KHON2 News 2019).

3. https://www.youtube.com/watch?v=dl6J_nljNjo.

4. This list is available at https://docs.google.com/spreadsheets/d/1n628TQV m6xrNX7HX_QNhhWoJcob8yH_vEd8ly1bI6-s/edit#gid=0.

5. Kala and John Pūnua are often credited as cocomposers. Ānuenue Pūnua related that an uncle told her Kala composed the lyrics and John Pūnua the music (2023).

6. KĀHEA is an acronym for Ka (the) Hawaiian-Environmental Alliance, a 501(c)3 nonprofit led by Kānaka ʻŌiwi. Kāhea translates to "the call." Its mission is to support and enable the power of community through collective action. It and other such organizations provided logistical and financial support for kiaʻi during the standoff with law enforcement.

7. I do not include in this statement about recentering the modern misappropriation of the term hoʻoponopono by non-Kānaka ʻŌiwi practitioners who apply it to practices more closely resembling new age mysticism than they do hoʻoponopono.

8. During an email exchange, hoʻomanawanui communicated additional concerns about this request. The first was that moʻokūʻauhau consciousness is partially about looking back to see how the ancestors of today's Kānaka ʻŌiwi resolved such conflicts and applying their methods to contemporary circumstances in the appropriate contexts.

9. For a comprehensive discussion of The Bayonet Constitution and a critique of previous scholarship and depictions of the events, see Jon Osorio's *Dismembering Lāhui: A History of the Hawaiian Nation to 1887* (2002).

10. The structure of "Ka Māmakakaua" is slightly different than a standard mele hula kuʻi (strophic song), and contains some harmonic and melodic variation not typically found in those kinds of mele. But as it does not feature a clearly defined hui (chorus), I have simply assigned verse numbers to each passage.

11. The lyrics and translation of this mele are found in the liner notes of the original LP release of *Iā ʻOe E Ka Lā*, vol. 3 (Vaughan 1977). I have updated some orthographic elements to current standards.

12. In 2022, Mountain Apple Company began to rerelease Vaughan's *Iā ʻOe E Ka Lā* on digital formats. They are all currently available via online streaming services.

13. Kalākaua's era is now commonly referred to as the First Hawaiian Renaissance for his efforts to revitalize Hawaiian arts and practices such as the hula. He was also known for his acceptance and support of the ʻukulele in Hawaiian performance. The "footprints" reference is the translation of a line in a chant composed for Kalākaua: "Aloha aʻe ana mākou i ke au wāwae o ka lani"

(We will fondly remember the footprints of the King) found in the CD *Nā Leo Hawaiʻi Kahiko* (Bishop Museum 1997).

14. Vaughan died in 2016 at the age of seventy-two.

15. Goodyear-Kaʻōpua composed a poetic account of her experience at the cattle guard in Goodyear-Kaʻōpua 2020.

16. The Mauna Medic Healers Hui is "a group of healers dedicated to protecting the Protectors of Mauna a Wakea" (Mauna Medic Healers n.d.).

17. I am grateful to an anonymous reader of an early draft who noted the spontaneous nature of these performances. Indeed, not all musical performances on the mauna were planned in advance; some were driven by circumstance and cultural propriety. I plan to explore this aspect of the performances in future writings.

18. Jon Osorio is currently dean of Hawaiʻinuiākea School of Hawaiian Knowledge at UH Mānoa. He is also a composer, singer, and recording artist who formed the duo Jon and Randy with Randy Borden in the 1970s. Jon and Randy was one of the more influential groups during the early years of what is now known as the Second Hawaiian Renaissance. Their popular song "Hawaiian Soul" was written for Aloha ʻĀina George Helm, who was lost at sea during the efforts to cease bombing on Kahoʻolawe and return the island to the Hawaiian people (Haugen 1977).

19. Island music is a broad genre of contemporary music that is mostly sung in English and borrows musical elements from reggae, hip-hop, rap, and other genres of popular music. For more on the influence of rap and reggae on the contemporary music of Hawaiʻi, see Akindes (2001), hoʻomanawanui (2006), Kale (2017), and Weintraub (1998).

20. Punahele requested that his stage name alone be used in this book, as it is common practice among rap performers.

21. Governor Ige visited the kiaʻi encampment three days later and spoke to the kiaʻi leadership on July 23, 2022 (*Star-Advertiser* Staff 2022).

22. Neither Yglesias nor Lyons could remember whether the writer of the email was actually an advertiser or not.

23. Makuakāne and I have been musical collaborators for nearly twenty years. Several of our compositions have been written to honor Maunakea and the kiaʻi who protect it.

24. One of the most absurd displays of this kind of ethnocentric denial of Kānaka ʻŌiwi epistemologies occurred when then-Maui County mayor Alan Arakawa defended the removal and crushing of many large boulders from the stream near Kepaniwai Park in ʻĪao—the site of a famous battle between the forces of Kamehameha I and Maui forces led by Kalanikūpule. Many warriors on both sides died at this location. This is the battle described at the beginning of this chapter, where Kamehameha commanded his warriors: ""i mua e nā

pōkiʻi a inu i ka wai ʻawaʻawa, ʻaʻohe hope e hoʻi mai ai" (Move forward, my young brothers, and drink of the bitter waters. There is no turning back). The boulders were displaced during a severe flood, removed from the valley by the county, and crushed elsewhere. Arakawa proclaimed that "there is no such thing as sacred rocks" and publicly questioned the motivation of Kānaka ʻŌiwi who were upset by this irresponsible action (Pignataro 2017).

25. In early 2023, the Hawaiʻi State Legislature established a new, independent board—the Mauna Kea Stewardship Oversight Authority (MKSOA)—though the scope of its authority is currently being debated. More details of this board are found in the conclusion.

SIX

—ᨳ—

KŪ HAʻAHEO E KUʻU HAWAIʻI

The Birth of an Anthem

I was at home, and I remember playing YouTube on my computer and just
having something on for sound in the background, and I was walking around
the house doing my thing. All of a sudden, I heard "Kū Haʻaheo."[1] I was
like—that's not my kids. Yeah, that's not my students because I can tell who
I taught, and I can tell who learned it from somebody else who listened to my
kids. That was my defining moment. I went back to the computer, scrolled
back, and I watched Lanakila [Mangauil]. Lanakila wore tapa cloths, and it
reminded me so much of myself, because for many years I, too, have worn
tapa cloth and went to those kinds of events. And I'm always down for a good
protest, you know. That was a defining moment. Then I said, okay, I have
to pay attention now, and I'm going to have to make it up to the mountain.
(Wong-Kalu 2020)

On October 7, 2014, representatives of the TMT consortium, government,
university, and other dignitaries gathered below the summit of Maunakea at
the site chosen for the construction of TMT.[2] Shortly after the ceremony began,
Lanakila Mangauil—a long-time kiaʻi of Maunakea and opponent of astronomical development on the mauna—appeared from just above the ceremony's location. He was draped in a kīhei (ceremonial shawl) and shouted at the attendees in Hawaiian. He proclaimed, "Hewa loa!" (completely wrong, immoral)
as he took a position directly in front of the attendees. He reminded those in
attendance of Maunakea's significance, accused Hawaiʻi County's mayor and
other officials of lying about the proceedings, and compared those involved in
the construction of TMT to snakes. When officials at the event failed to provide
satisfactory and truthful answers to his questions, he repeated his cry, "Hewa
loa!" After lecturing the attendees for several more minutes, he stepped back.

Kahu Danny Akaka then stepped forward to provide a Christian blessing to the ceremony. As Akaka proceeded with the blessing, Mangauil began chanting his pule (prayer) to the mauna and stood quietly again as Akaka completed his ceremony. When Akaka spoke of his hopes that the construction of TMT would benefit the mauna and the culture, Mangauil and others immediately challenged his contention. Whose culture? Whose benefit? Mangauil challenged the TMT consortium representatives from Japan and informed them that Maunakea is just as important and sacred to Hawaiians as Mount Fuji is to the Japanese. He also reminded them of the historical ties between Japan and the Hawaiian Kingdom.

Shortly after, Mangauil called to other kiaʻi waiting off to the side, who moved toward the ceremony area. Some adorned themselves with lei; others carried stalks of the lāʻī (ti-leaf plant), kāhili (ceremonial standards, often symbolizing royalty), or signs bearing messages of aloha ʻāina. As they proceeded, they sang the chorus of "Kū Haʻaheo e Kuʻu Hawaiʻi," a mele of aloha ʻāina and kūʻē composed by Hinaleimoana Wong-Kalu. The kiaʻi repeated the mele's chorus several times before Mangauil led the group in a performance of "E Iho Ana O Luna," an older mele oli (text to be performed in a chanted style) that foretells a time when those in power will fall and pono will be restored.

E IHO ANA O LUNA

E iho ana ʻo luna	That which is above shall be brought down
E piʻi ana ʻo lalo	That which is below shall be lifted up
E hui ana nā moku	The islands shall be united
E kū ana ka paia	The walls shall stand upright

The action of the kiaʻi ended with impassioned speeches by Mangauil and Waimea-native Hāwane Rios, followed by embraces between many participants, including Mangauil and Akaka, before the confrontation and ceremony ended.[3]

In this chapter, I examine anthems and other musical compositions identified as "anthemic." I define anthemic compositions as those that function similarly to anthems in a nation or society and evoke the same feelings and emotions as anthems but lack official sanction or standing. I discuss their role in society and how they espouse the collective values and aspirations of the people who perform them. I provide a history of anthems and anthemic compositions in Hawaiʻi, French Polynesia, and Aotearoa. Finally, I analyze Hinaleimo-ana Wong-Kaluʻs (Kanaka ʻŌiwi/Tongan) composition "Kū Haʻaheo e Kuʻu Hawaiʻi" and the mele she used as a model for it: "Kaulana Nā Pua."

I also utilize Maria Isabel Mayo-Harpʻs study and analysis of anthems that appeared during the emergence of Spanish American nations in the nineteenth century and her discussion of the functions of national anthems.[4] She identifies three different functions of national anthems: (1) to define the members of the nation, (2) to crystallize the idea of national identity, and (3) to motivate collective action (Mayo-Harp 1994). While her examination focuses explicitly on national anthems, I argue that these functions apply to the anthemic compositions examined in this chapter.

OF ANTHEMS AND ANTHEMIC COMPOSITIONS
IN HAWAIʻI AND THE PACIFIC

Lyrically and musically, anthems resonate with communities of common nationality, ethnicity, location, ideology, and interests. J. Martin Daughtry observes that national anthems are songs that speak to "the ideologies and collective self-images of the nations to which they are attached . . . anthems are used to generate a collective sentiment among those who sing them" (2003). He adds that "ideologies and collective self-images are subject to the conflicting and ever-changing interpretations of groups and individuals within nations and as such are always conditional, contestable, and fluid" (Daughtry 2003).

The creation or designation of a new anthem often receives official sanction from a government or other political entity. Such was the case when post-Soviet Russia proposed to replace its anthem—written in the nineteenth century and lacking lyrics—with one featuring the music of the former Soviet Unionʻs anthem and new lyrics. Russiaʻs new anthem, "Unbreakable Union," had both supporters and detractors but was ratified on New Yearʻs Day in 2001 (Daughtry 2003). On the other hand, "God Save the King" has never been officially designated through legislation or decree as the anthem of Great Britain.[5] Instead, it has become an anthem through customary use and performance at royal ceremonies and sporting events.

Sometimes anthems are written to coalesce a group with shared attributes, strengthen their bonds, address mutual concerns, and express solidarity of thought and action. Such is the case with the four songs that have served as the Hawaiian Kingdomʻs national anthems. The British anthem "God Save the King" served as its anthem until 1860, when King Kamehameha IV (Alexander

Liholiho) announced a competition to create a new anthem for the kingdom. The King's edict was that composition use the melody of "God Save the King" but be written in the Hawaiian language. *Ka Nupepa Kuokoa* published an announcement of this competition in its December 16, 1862, issue.

"E Ola Ke Ali'i Ke Akua," a composition by Prince William Charles Lunalilo (who later became King Lunalilo), was selected as the new anthem. *Ka Nupepa Kuokoa* published Lunalilo's composition in its February 8, 1862, issue. The newspaper also published a summary of the competition's prior announcement, rules, adjudication criteria, a statement from the committee regarding the adjudication process, and a letter of gratitude from Lunalilo. The committee noted that while it had received many entries containing excellent thoughts, they had not matched the melody of "God Save the King." Lunalilo indicated he had not expected his composition to be chosen as he had just begun learning haku mele (Ka Nupepa Kuokoa 1862).[6]

E OLA KE ALI'I KE AKUA

William Charles Lunalilo

PAUKŪ 'EKAHI
Ke Akua Mana Mau
Ho'omaika'i, pōmaika'i
I ka mō'ī
Kou lima mana mau
Mālama kia'i mai
Ko mākou nei mō'ī
E ola ē

FIRST VERSE
Eternal, mighty God
Bless us from your bright abode
Our sovereign king
May your all powerful arm
Ward from our sire all harm
Let no vile foe alarm
Long may he reign

PAUKŪ 'ELUA
Ka inoa kamaha'o
Lei nani o mākou
E ola ē
Kou 'eheu uhi mai
Pale nā 'ino ē
Ka mākou pule nō
E ola ē

SECOND VERSE
Royal distinguished name
Our beauteous diadem
Long life be yours
Thy wing spread over our land
From every foe defend
To you our prayers ascend
Long live our king

PAUKŪ 'EKOLU
I mua ou mākou
Ke ali'i o nā Ali'i
E aloha mai

THIRD VERSE
Before Thee
King of Kings
Of Whom all nature sings

E mau ke ea e	Our prayer we bring
O ke aupuni nei	Oh, let our kingdom live
E ola mau mākou	Life, peace and union give
Me ka mōʻī	Let all Thy care receive
	Bless Thou our king

While not a direct translation of "God Save the King," "E Ola Ka Mōʻī I Ke Akua" retains more than the melody of its British progenitor; it also mirrors many of the sentiments contained in its text. Its words include a plea to God to protect the monarch and grant long life, followed by expressions of admiration and praise for his power and authority and his role in defending his subjects. "E Ola Ke Aliʻi Ke Akua" remained the kingdom's anthem until 1866, when it was replaced by then-Princess Liliʻuokalani's composition "He Mele Lāhui Hawaiʻi." Kamehameha V (Lot Kapuāiwa) tasked Liliʻuokalani with composing a new national anthem so that Hawaiʻi's anthem would not express the same patriotic themes as other nations' anthems. He noted that the music of "E Ola Ke Aliʻi Ke Akua" was also not of Hawaiʻi.

> In the early years of the reign of Kamehameha, he brought to my notice the fact that the Hawaiian people had no national air. Each nation, he said, but ours had its statement of patriotism and love of country in its own music; but we were using for that purpose on state occasions the time-honored British anthem, "God Save the King." This he desired me to supplant by one of my own composition. In one week's time, I notified the king that I had completed my task. The Princess Victoria had been the leader of the choir of the Kawaiahao church; but upon her death on May 29, 1866, I assumed the leadership. It was in this building and by that choir that I first introduced the "Hawaiian National Anthem." The king was present for the purpose of criticising my new composition of both words and music, and was liberal in his commendations to me on my success. He admired not only the beauty of the music, but spoke enthusiastically of the appropriate words, so well adapted to the air and to the purpose for which they were written. (Liliʻuokalani 1898)

HE MELE LĀHUI HAWAIʻI

Liliʻuokalani

PAUKŪ ʻEKAHI	FIRST VERSE
Maliu mai iā mākou	Almighty Father bend thine ear
E hāliu aku nei	And listen to a nation's prayer

Queen Liliʻuokalani. Photo credit: Wikipedia Commons

Me ka naʻau haʻahaʻa	That lowly bows before thy throne
E mau ka maluhia	And seeks thy fostering care
O nei pae ʻāina	Grant your peace throughout the land
Mai Hawaiʻi a Niʻihau	Over these sunny sea girt isles
Ma lalo o kou malu	Keep the nation's life, oh Lord,
	And on our sovereign smile

HUI

E mau ke ea o ka ʻāina

Ma kou pono mau

A ma kou mana nui

E ola e ola ka mōʻī

CHORUS

Grant your peace throughout the land

Over these sunny isles

Keep the nation's life, oh Lord

And upon our sovereign smile

PAUKŪ ʻELUA

E ka haku mālama mai

I ko mākou nei mōʻī

E mau kona noho ʻana

Maluna o ka noho aliʻi

Hāʻawi mai i ke aloha

SECOND VERSE

Guard him with your tender care

Give him length of years to reign

On the throne his fathers won

Bless the nation once again

Give the king your loving grace

Maloko a kona naʻau	And with wisdom from on high
A ma kou ahonui	Prosperous lead his people on
E ola e ola ka mōʻī	As beneath your watchful eye
Hoʻoho e mau ke	Grant your peace throughout the land
PAUKŪ ʻEKOLU	THIRD VERSE
Ma lalo o kou aloha nui	Bless O Lord our country's chiefs
Nā Liʻi o ke Aupuni	Grant them wisdom so to live
Me nā makaʻāinana	That our people may be saved
Ka lehulehu nō a pau	And to You the glory give
Kiaʻi mai iā lākou	Watch over us day by day
Me ke aloha ahonui	King and people with your love
E ola nō mākou	For our hope is all in You
I kou mana mau	Bless us, You who reign above
E mau ke ea	Grant your peace throughout the land

Like its predecessor, "He Mele Lāhui Hawaiʻi" begins with an appeal to God to protect and deliver peace throughout the Hawaiian archipelago. However, it does not mention the monarch until the second verse. The first verse calls to God and uses poetic Hawaiian less indicative of hīmeni (hymns) and more like older mele. The mele features musical characteristics that Liliʻuokalani, her siblings, and her contemporaries borrowed from Western song forms they likely learned as young students in the Royal School. This style includes the verse/chorus or A/B structure common during this era.

The second verse again asks for God's intervention in bestowing the king a patient and benevolent nature. It utilizes Hawaiian poetic devices and means of expression, such as the Hawaiian concept of naʻau (intestines) as the physical location where aloha resides, rather than means of expressing these characteristics more reflective of a haole (foreign) worldview.[7] In the final verse, Liliʻuokalani mentions the makaʻāinana (people who attend to and work the land) and lehulehu (multitude, populace), asking God to protect the people, monarch, and the land.

The change in focus from the monarch-centric "E Ola Ke Aliʻi Ke Akua" to the broader, citizen-inclusive "He Mele Lāhui Hawaiʻi" is notable. Aliʻi had ruled Hawaiʻi, their status determined through lineage and military victories. After Kamehameha I united the Hawaiian Kingdom, it became an absolute monarchy and remained one until 1840—the year that Kamehameha IV called for the composition of a new anthem based on the music of "God Save the King."[8] In 1840, a new constitution established a legislative body while reserving significant authority for the monarch. This constitution granted the right to vote to some citizens and gave them a more substantial say over their lives and activities through elected representatives. It is perhaps the reason for Liliʻu's broadening of themes to include both citizens and ʻāina in her composition.

"He Mele Lāhui Hawaiʻi" served as the kingdom's anthem until it was replaced in 1876 by "Hawaiʻi Ponoʻī," composed in 1874 by Kalākaua with music by Heinrich Berger, bandmaster of the Royal Hawaiian Band. "Hawaiʻi Ponoʻī" remained the Hawaiian Kingdom's national anthem until 1893, when non-Hawaiian businessmen and politicians overthrew the kingdom with the support of the US government and the presence of US military personnel. It was adopted as Hawaiʻi's state song by Act 301 of the Hawaiʻi State Legislature on June 13, 1967.

Hawaiʻi is not the only Pacific Island group to have borrowed—or had imposed on it—the anthem of former or current colonial powers.[9] "La Marseillaise," the national anthem of France since 1870, was the official anthem of French Polynesia until 1993, when a competition was held to create a new anthem for the islands. "Ia Ora ʻO Tahiti Nui" (Long Live Tahiti Nui) was composed by multiple authors and adopted as French Polynesia's anthem in 1993. Its lyrics are entirely in the Tahitian language, and it is frequently played along with "La Marseillaise" at public events. Likewise, "God Save the King" has been New Zealand's national anthem since the 1800s. "God Defend New Zealand," whose words were written in 1876 by Thomas Bracken with music by Joseph Woods, gained increasing popularity as an expression of New Zealand's colonizer-centric nationalism. "God Defend New Zealand" became New Zealand's second national anthem in 1977 with the blessing of Queen Elizabeth of England. It was declared equal in standing with "God Save the King" and appropriate for any occasion that calls for the performance of the national anthem.

A Māori language version of "God Defend New Zealand," entitled "Aotearoa," was created in 1878. It is not a direct translation of "God Defend New Zealand." The English version was primarily performed at sporting events and other public gatherings, and performances of the Māori version were less common. A New Zealand female vocal duo, String of Pearls, performed the anthem in both English and Māori at sporting events around the country starting in the 1990s but drew no significant reaction from those who attended the events. In 1999, Tangata Whenua singer Hinewehi Mohi performed only the Māori lyrics at a World Cup quarterfinal game in which New Zealand's famed All-Blacks played at Twickenham, near London, England. Her impromptu decision to perform the anthem only in Māori led to outrage in New Zealand, including threats of physical violence against her.[10] Today, it is common for the first verse to be sung in both Māori and English, with the Māori lyrics often performed first. Mohi later produced an anthology titled *Waiata Anthems*, which contains recorded performances of eleven well-known English songs translated into Māori by revered te reo Māori (Māori language) scholar and advocate Sir Tīmoti Kāretu (Creative NZ 2019). Not surprisingly, the compilation opens with a recording of "Aotearoa" by Hātea Kapa Haka and includes performances by popular Māori performers and recording artists such as Stan Walker, Six6o, TEEKS, and Sons of Zion. The release was number one on the New Zealand music charts in September 2019.

The recording and release of *Waiata Anthems* in Aotearoa offer a possible model for connecting those who do not speak Hawaiian with the aspirations of those on the mauna through mele. Recorded over ten weeks in 2019 and releasing her work during Māori Language Week, Mohi worked with the singers to guide their pronunciation and understanding of new Māori lyrics set to the music of popular songs. She notes, "These tracks are well known to people, so they can connect the English words they know to the Māori translation and feel like they're accessing Te Reo Māori through something familiar" (Creative NZ 2019).[11] The results of recent research conducted by Awanui Te Huia (Ngāti Maniapoto) show that Pākehā (those of European descent) who learn te reo Māori are more supportive of Māori and more apt to develop positive attitudes about building intercultural relationships with them than others in the dominant New Zealand culture. "Even though mainstream New Zealand has a dominant discourse that is discriminatory toward Māori . . . there is a minority group of Pākehā (those of predominantly European descent) who are rejecting of such discourses in support of a bicultural relationship" (Te Huia 2016). There is no mention of any role that Māori language music may have played in the attitudes of participants. However, with strong language ties between the Māori language and music performed in it, there is undoubtedly a similar prospect and promise for success in utilizing both the Māori language and music performed in Māori, much as there is for their potential in mitigating conflicts between Kānaka ʻŌiwi and settlers in Hawaiʻi.

Some compositions are so personal that they do not become accepted as a public expression—"there's a personalizing of mele that makes them so personal that they're almost not a collective and shared piece" (Nogelmeier in Donaghy 2010). Other songs achieve anthemic status in their country or community by expressing collective ideas, beliefs, or values; they are often born in times of social and political changes. For example, the World War I-era waiata (Māori song) "Pōkarekare Ana" is often referred to as the unofficial anthem of Aotearoa. Allen Thomas discusses its popularity: "Pokarekare is a curious song because although the Maori language in which it is written is known by only a few, the song has a wide popularity. Although very few individuals could sing the full number of verses or even the first verse in Maori, a majority of New Zealanders believe they know and easily recognise the song, and they value it as a New Zealand heritage item" (Thomas 2007).

"Kaulana Nā Pua" is indisputably a song that has achieved anthemic status in Hawai'i. Written by Ellen Kekoahiwaokalani Wright Prendergast in 1893, "Kaulana Nā Pua" expresses the sentiments of the composer and those shared with her by members of the Royal Hawaiian Band in support of Lili'uokalani and against the annexation of Hawai'i by the United States. It was published on March 23, 1893, as "He Inoa No Nā Keiki O Ka Bana Lāhui," then again on May 10, 1893, as "He Lei No Ka Poe Aloha." It was printed with the title "Mele Aloha Aina" in 1895 in *Mele Lāhui Hawai'i*—a compilation of Hawaiian mele aloha 'āina (patriotic songs). Since then, the mele most often appears or is introduced as "Mele 'Ai Pōhaku" or "Kaulana Nā Pua" (Basham 2002).[12]

Massachusetts-born reverend Lorenzo Lyons composed the hymn-like "Hawai'i Aloha," in which he refers to Hawai'i as ku'u 'āina hānau (my beloved birthplace) and ku'u home kulaiwi (my beloved native homeland).[13] Lyons's expression of love of homeland and aloha 'āina gives voice to the Kānaka 'Ōiwi and those like him who were not born in Hawai'i but wish to express sentiments of belonging and aloha for their home.

Hawai'i was declared the fiftieth state of the United States in 1959. Less than a decade later, substantial political and social changes began to occur in Hawai'i; this era became known as the Hawaiian Renaissance. Kanahele identifies several significant events in the mid-1960s that could be early indicators of the nascent movement. However, "it was not until the early 1970s that the Hawaiian Renaissance really flowered" (Kanahele 1982).

One mele composed, performed, and recorded during this era that has arguably achieved anthemic status is "Hawai'i Loa," commonly known by the first line of its chorus, "All Hawai'i Stand Together." It was composed by Kanaka 'Ōiwi poet Liko Martin and first performed at a rally at 'Iolani Palace in January 1977 (Martin n.d.). "Hawai'i Loa" begins with a verse, chorus, and two additional verses in English. It concludes with a chorus in 'ōlelo Hawai'i that is usually repeated. All verses contain references to places with expressions of aloha 'āina. The English chorus is a call for unity and to join in singing the praises of Hawai'i. The Hawaiian chorus uses many Hawaiian language terms that are common in mele aloha 'āina—kū like (stand together), kūpa'a (be steadfast), lōkahi (unity), 'onipa'a (steadfastness), wiwo 'ole (fearlessness), lanakila (victory), and ola (to live).

"Kaulana Nā Pua," "Hawaiʻi Aloha," and "Hawaiʻi Loa" are all commonly performed today. "Kaulana Nā Pua" was the first song recorded by Project Kuleana in what has become a long-running series of Hawaiian music videos shared on YouTube.[14] Project Kuleana's recording of "Kaulana Nā Pua" features many well-known Hawaiʻi recording artists performing live at locations throughout Hawaiʻi. "Hawaiʻi Loa" was one of two mele (along with "Kū Haʻaheo e Kuʻu Hawaiʻi") performed at the Jam4Maunakea event streamed worldwide from the Ala Kūpuna on August 11, 2019. Project Kuleana also recorded and released "Hawaiʻi Loa" as a music video in 2019. Like their earlier recording of "Kaulana Nā Pua," it featured Hawaiʻi recording artists performing at locations throughout Hawaiʻi. Today, "Hawaiʻi Aloha" is frequently performed throughout Hawaiʻi and in Hawaiian communities abroad. It is commonly performed at the end of events, with audience members joining hands and raising them above their heads during the performance of the last line. Doing so reaffirms their connection through shared love of Hawaiʻi.

KŪ HAʻAHEO E KUʻU HAWAIʻI: THE BIRTH OF AN ANTHEM

Hinaleimoana Wong-Kalu, known in the Hawaiian community as Kumu Hina, is an educator, cultural practitioner, and community leader born in the Nuʻuanu district of Oʻahu. She is a māhū wahine who works as a cultural ambassador at the Council for Native Hawaiian Advancement (CNHA) and serves the Oʻahu and state-wide communities in various capacities.[15] In 2014, Wong-Kalu ran for the Office of Hawaiian Affairs board seat. She was also the subject of a documentary film, "Kumu Hina," released in 2014 and broadcast nationally on PBS (Wong-Kalu 2014).

Wong-Kalu composed "Kū Haʻaheo e Kuʻu Hawaiʻi" in 2007 for her Hālau Lōkahi Public Charter School students. Teachers, students, and parents were often called on to appear and support various Hawaiian issues at the legislature and elsewhere. Issues included genetically modified kalo (taro),[16] the Akaka Bill,[17] conversions of leasehold lands controlled by Hawaiian entities to fee simple ownership by the lessees,[18] and Hawaiian burials.[19] While "Kū Haʻaheo e Kuʻu Hawaiʻi" was not written explicitly for Maunakea, Wong-Kalu understands why the sentiments contained within it resonated with those who had engaged the state and TMT developers over the desecration: "The issue of Maunakea is not unlike many other issues that we have here. Maybe it's different slightly in context. But it really all points to the larger understandings that we as a people are disenfranchised from our land and natural resources and that we experienced great inequities when asserting ourselves for our culture,

Hinaleimoana Wong-Kalu,
composer of "Kū Haʻaheo e
Kuʻu Hawaiʻi." Photo credit:
Hinaleimoana Wong-Kalu.

our language, and our people. And we are the scapegoats for everything that
the current city and state government would have us be a scapegoat for" (2020).

Wong-Kalu did not intend to write an anthem for the movement to protect
Maunakea and other struggles over Hawaiian lands and rights that quickly
followed. However, its themes resonated with the Hawaiian community, much
like the mele that served as a model for her composition: "Kaulana Nā Pua."
"Kaulana Nā Pua" is composed in a strophic format—five verses and no chorus.
Each verse contains four lines and expresses sentiments of aloha ʻāina, kūʻē (opposition) to annexation, and loyalty to the deposed Queen Liliʻuokalani. Unlike "Kaulana Nā Pua," "Kū Haʻaheo e Kuʻu Hawaiʻi" is written in an A/B form,
containing verses and a chorus performed once between each verse. This A/B
form dates back to the 1860s in Hawaiʻi and was frequently employed by members of Nā Lani ʻEhā—royal siblings Kalākaua, Liliʻuokalani, Leleiohoku, and
Likelike. By examining early printed Hawaiian sheet music, ethnomusicologist

Amy Stillman (Kanaka ʻŌiwi) discovered that this form was known as "mele Hawaiʻi" in the nineteenth century—a term that seems to have been later abandoned (Stillman 2005). Each verse of "Kū Haʻaheo e Kuʻu Hawaiʻi" focuses on a particular element: "The first verse speaks to the problem. The second verse speaks to the plea, and the third verse speaks to the plan. Well, you know the plea in the second verse is a call to all the Islands to come help. The third verse talks about that plan—what we're gonna do. We're gonna move forward, and we're going to be brave and fearless, and the last one was the prayer" (Wong-Kalu 2020).

I now examine the text, themes, and use of language of both mele, showing the verses side by side, with translations of each mele below.

Kaulana Nā Pua (Verse 1)	Kū Haʻaheo e Kuʻu Hawaiʻi (Verse 1)
Kaulana nā pua aʻo Hawaiʻi	Kaikoʻo ka moana ka i lana nei Hawaiʻi
Kūpaʻa ma hope o ka ʻāina	Nāueue a halulu ka honua a Haumea
Hiki mai ka ʻelele o ka loko ʻino	Nākulukulu e ka lani kiʻekiʻe kau mai i luna
Palapala ʻānunu me ka pākaha	Auē ke aloha ʻole a ka malihini
Famous are the children of Hawaii	*The sea of Hawaiʻi surges in turmoil*
Ever loyal to the land	*The earth of Haumea rumbles and shakes*
When the evil-hearted messenger comes	*The highest heavens shudder up above*
With his greedy document of extortion[20]	*Alas! Woeful indeed are the heartless foreigners*[21]

The first two lines of "Kaulana Nā Pua" praise "the children of Hawaiʻi," metaphorically represented as flowers. These lines accomplish what Mayo-Harp identifies as the first and most crucial function of anthems: to help define the nation's members (Mayo-Harp 1994). Even those with only a modest ability to speak Hawaiian at the time "Kaulana Nā Pua" was composed, published, and performed would have understood the poetic use of "nā pua o Hawaiʻi" to refer to the people of Hawaiʻi. This reference is widely understood today. Finally, this verse directly addresses the problem: representatives of the illegitimate Provisional Government demanding that the members of the Royal Hawaiian Band sign oaths of allegiance to that government.

While it does not immediately define group members, the first verse of "Kū Haʻaheo e Kuʻu Hawaiʻi" addresses the problems that Kānaka ʻŌiwi have and continue to face. It utilizes figurative language that would be understood by those proficient with ʻōlelo Hawaiʻi: the ocean breaking, the earth shaking, and rumbling in the heavens. The verbal representations of these events entice the senses, a common feature of Hawaiian poetry. They depict elements of the natural world that are seen, heard, and felt. Language like this can also cause the listener to vividly recall their previous encounters with these phenomena. Because of their kinesthetic nature, these representations assist in retaining and recalling the lyrics (Donaghy 2010). The final line laments the sources of these tribulations—"heartless foreigners"—using straightforward language.[22]

Because of its strophic nature, "Kaulana Nā Pua" does not include a chorus, but "Kū Haʻaheo e Kuʻu Hawaiʻi" does. While the chorus in mele is often called the hui, Wong-Kalu uses the term hoʻōho (to call or exclaim) instead.

Hoʻōho:

Kū haʻaheo e kuʻu Hawaiʻi	*Stand tall my Hawaiʻi*
Māmakakaua o kuʻu ʻāina	*Band of warriors of my land*
ʻO ke ehu kakahiaka o nā ʻōiwi	*The new dawn for our people of Hawaiʻi is*
o Hawaiʻi nei	*upon us*
No kuʻu lāhui e hāʻawi pau a i ola mau	*For my nation, I give my all so that our*
	legacy lives on

The chorus of "Kū Haʻaheo e Kuʻu Hawaiʻi" identifies the community members it is intended to address. Wong-Kalu refers to Kānaka ʻŌiwi as māmakakaua (warriors)—those who shoulder the burden of conflict—and calls on all of them to take up the struggle to perpetuate their ancestors' legacies. She again uses visually enticing words such as māmakakaua and ehu kakahiaka (the morning mist or dawn, also metaphorically used to describe youth) to stir emotions and the glories of the ancestors.

Kaulana Nā Pua (Verse 2)	**Kū Haʻaheo e Kuʻu Hawaiʻi (Verse 2)**
Pane mai Hawaiʻi moku o Keawe	ʻAuhea wale ʻoukou pūʻali koa o Keawe
Kōkua nā Hono aʻo Piʻilani	Me ko Kamalālāwalu lā me Kākuhihewa
Kākoʻo mai Kauaʻi o Mano	Alu mai pualu mai me ko Manokalanipō
Paʻapū me ke one Kākuhihewa	Kaʻi mai ana me nā kama a Kahelelani
Hawaii, land of Keawe answers	*Where are you, soldiers of Keawe?*
Piʻilani's bays help	*Along with those of Maui and Oʻahu*
Mano's Kauaʻi lends support	*Unite, join together with those of Kauaʻi*
And so do the sands of Kākuhihewa	*Marching alongside the descendants of Niʻihau*

After calling to all Kānaka ʻŌiwi in the hoʻōho, Wong-Kalu borrows the theme of "Kaulana Nā Pua" with some differences reflecting her experiences as an individual and a member of the Hawaiian community. Prendergast calls the islands by the names of the chief for which each island is arguably best known: Keawe for Hawaiʻi Island, Piʻilani for Maui, Mano (Manokalanipō) for Kauaʻi, and Kākuhihewa for Oʻahu. Wong-Kaluʻs call is directed to these islands' pūʻali koa (soldiers or warriors) to come together with a common purpose. There are two minor differences expressed in Wong-Kaluʻs version—the use of Kamalālāwalu (another great chief of Maui) instead of Piʻilani for Maui and the addition of Niʻihau, which Prendergast does not mention in "Kaulana Nā Pua." However, these differences are insignificant to the overall impact of the verse and its function to instill a sense of collective purpose in performers and listeners. These elements fulfill Mayo-Harp's second function of national anthems: to solidify the idea of national identity and, "more than any other national symbol, concretely appeal to the common characteristics, the shared history, and the passions, emotions, feelings, loyalties, and goals of the collective" (Mayo-Harp 1994).

Kaulana Nā Pua (Verse 3)	Kū Haʻaheo e Kuʻu Hawaiʻi (Verse 3)
ʻAʻole aʻe kau i ka pūlima	E nāue i mua, e nā pōkiʻi, a e inu wai ʻawaʻawa
Ma luna o ka pepa o ka ʻēnemi	E wiwoʻole a hoʻokūpaʻa ʻaʻohe hope e hoʻi mai ai
Hoʻohui ʻāina kūʻai hewa	A naʻi wale nō kākou kaukoe mau i ke ala
I ka pono sivila aʻo ke kanaka	Auē ke aloha ʻole a ka malihini
No one will fix a signature	*Move forward young ones and drink of the bitter waters*
To the paper of the enemy	*Be fearless, steadfast for there is no turning back*
With its sin of annexation	*Let's press onward straight on the path of victory*
And sale of native civil rights	*Alas! Woeful are the heartless foreigners!*

Kaulana Nā Pua (Verse 4)
ʻAʻole mākou aʻe minamina
I ka puʻu kālā o ke aupuni
Ua lawa mākou i ka pōhaku
I ka ʻai kamahaʻo o ka ʻāina
We do not value
The government's sums of money
We are satisfied with the stones
Astonishing food of the land

I have included the third and fourth verses of "Kaulana Nā Pua," as both describe actions taken or to be taken by Kānaka ʻŌiwi in response to the "heartless acts of the foreigners." In these verses, Kānaka 'Ōiwi are urged to reject foreigners' offers and refuse to sign documents that would swear recognition of and allegiance to the illegitimate Provisional Government. Wong-Kalu characterizes the third verse of "Kū Ha'aheo e Ku'u Hawai'i" as "the plan"—the acts Kānaka 'Ōiwi must take to achieve their goals. The first line includes Kamehameha's words to his warriors as they battled Maui forces led by Kalanikūpule, son of Chief Kahekili, at 'Īao (also discussed in chap. 5). This phrase is well known and often used in the Hawaiian community, particularly when facing challenging circumstances. Her use of na'i (conqueror) in the third line also recalls one of Kamehameha I's well-known nicknames, ka na'i aupuni (the conquer of the nation), and implores all those present to persevere in their task. The remainder of her third verse continues with its exhortation for Kānaka 'Ōiwi to fight and achieve victory against those opposed to their ultimate goals.

Kaulana Nā Pua (Verse 5)	Kū Ha'aheo e Ku'u Hawai'i (Verse 4)
Ma hope mākou o Lili'ulani[23]	E lei mau i lei mau kākou, e nā mamo aloha
A loa'a ē ka pono o ka 'āina	I lei wehi 'a'ali'i wehi nani o ku'u 'āina
Ha'ina 'ia mai ana ka puana	Hoe a mau hoe a mau no ka pono sivila
Ka po'e i aloha i ka 'āina	A ho'iho'i hou 'ia mai ke kū'oko'a
We back Lili'ulani	*Be honored always oh beloved descendants of the land*
Who has won the rights of the land	*Let us wear the honored 'a'ali'i of our beloved land*
Tell the story	*Paddle on in our pursuit of civil justice*
Of the people who love their land	*Until our dignity and independence is restored*

In the final verse of "Kaulana Nā Pua," Prendergast reaffirms allegiance to Lili'uokalani and her right to rule Hawai'i. The last two lines bring the mele to a conclusion, as in many Hawaiian compositions, summarizing the overriding theme of the mele: the aloha 'āina felt by Kānaka 'Ōiwi for their homeland. Wong-Kalu implores "nā mamo aloha" (the beloved descendants) to wear the lei made of the flowers of the 'a'ali'i plant—a plant often used metaphorically to express strength and resistance as it resists the strongest winds.[24] In the penultimate line, Wong-Kalu returns to metaphorical expression by using the act of paddling a canoe continuously—symbolic of both moving forward together and the effort expended to reach one's destination.

The final verses of both compositions fulfill the third function identified by Mayo-Harp: to motivate collective action. Both "Kaulana Nā Pua" and "Kū Ha'aheo e Ku'u Hawai'i" embody the struggles, hopes, strength, and determination of Kānaka ʻŌiwi to gain the ability to control their destiny as a people and nation as well as their homeland. Wong-Kalu acknowledges being inspired by "Kaulana Nā Pua" and using it as a model for "Kū Haʻaheo e Kuʻu Hawaiʻi." In doing so, Wong-Kalu connects to the historical roots of Kānaka ʻŌiwi and their challenges over the past two-and-a-half centuries in the face of settler colonialism. She quotes words Kamehameha I uttered during his attempt to bring the islands under a single ruler. Nogelmeier has described this kind of usage as a kuhi (to point): "I appreciate and try and foster in old music is what I call a kuhi, where there's a reference to an outside story. So it enriches this if you know the story. If you don't know the story, this is still a lovely mele, so I like that layering that goes into it" (Nogelmeier in Donaghy 2010). Wong-Kalu also uses figurative language characteristic of old and modern Hawaiian poetry. Some of the knowledge embedded within the language is accessible to proficient Hawaiian speakers, and some is not. Unlike compositions in English and perhaps other cultures where individuality is more highly prized, Wong-Kalu's modeling of her mele after "Kaulana Nā Pua" is acceptable and valued in haku mele. Her approach to composing "Kū Haʻaheo e Kuʻu Hawaiʻi" links this modern composition to those of the past but does so in her unique voice. It has found its way into the vast repository of mele that have been and will continue to be composed as long as Kānaka ʻŌiwi document their lives in mele. Through its lyrical and musical form, it reflects, as noted by Daughtry, "the ideologies and collective self-images" of Kānaka ʻŌiwi and their allies as displayed on Maunakea and in other situations in which their well-being is challenged or their rights are minimized or completely ignored by the settler state and others who seek to usurp them. For these reasons, I argue that "Kū Haʻaheo e Kuʻu Hawaiʻi" has indeed reached an anthemic status and will continue to be performed to communicate a message of solidarity and action whenever circumstances compel it.

> "Kū Haʻaheo" and these other mele that just emerged became such an opportunity for everyone to share voice together, to see and release some of that aloha, but also that angst. Then you know the confrontation that we're feeling, even within our naʻau. Even if you're not on the mauna, you know that living on a daily basis. So I think the mele were such an essential part of galvanizing and expressing the naʻau, the heart, the love, the conflict that each of us were living through, but knowing that we will get through it with aloha for the majesty of Maunakea. (Beamer 2020)

Although it has become a shared expression of Kānaka ʻŌiwi and allies, it is important for those who learn and perform the mele "Kū Haʻaheo" to recognize that it was composed by an individual with specific thoughts and intentions. While Wong-Kalu recognizes and accepts that the impact and use of the mele go beyond her original intent, she has one request for those who learn and use it: "Please don't sing my song if you don't know what it means, because I don't want you to sing the song just to be a bandwagon song. You need to know what it means. And you need to be cognizant of what I'm saying. Because that song is an extension of me" (Wong-Kalu 2020).

JAM4MAUNAKEA: ALL HAWAIʻI (AND BEYOND) STAND TOGETHER

Social media's role on Maunakea is a subject worthy of more extensive research than is possible in this book. Social media platforms such as Facebook, YouTube, and Instagram enabled kiaʻi to broadcast live events from the mauna and relay crucial information to supporters around the globe. This connection was tenuous, as a single data point provided data service for all cell phones at the kiaʻi encampment.[25] A video recording of the 2014 TMT groundbreaking that Mangauil and other kiaʻi interrupted quickly reached the eyes and ears of supporters everywhere (Big Island Video News 2014). Protectors streamed live video from Puʻuhuluhulu, from the earliest confrontations with law enforcement through the arrests of July 17, 2019, and beyond.

On Friday, July 26, 2019— nine days after the arrests of kūpuna—Puʻuhonua o Puʻuhuluhulu, Kanaeokana, and Mana Maoli announced that a live, worldwide event titled Jam4Maunakea would be broadcast from the Ala Kūpuna at eleven a.m. on Sunday, August 11, 2019. It would feature kiaʻi and performers at Puʻuhuluhulu; supporters worldwide would perform along with those on the mauna, record their performances, and submit them for inclusion on a compilation video that editors would splice together at a later date (Puuhonua o Puʻuhuluhulu 2019).

> What we did was we put out there is a couple of phases. So phase one was we put out a promo/practice video of many well-known musicians and Maunakea leaders at the Mauna Kea frontline singing a medley of just the choruses of two songs to be more feasible, especially for non-Hawaiian speakers to learn. And we said everybody, you know, shares this video, and we invite you all to learn one or both of these courses. There's the English chorus, the Hawaiian chorus of "Hawaii Aloha," and the chorus of "Kū Haʻaheo" is in Hawaiian. So two in Hawaiian and one English chorus. Of course, people could learn one or all of them and pre-recorded or live everybody on August 11th at 11 a.m. And a "hana hou" [encore] at

11:11 a.m.[26] Everybody post in support of Maunakea. Use this hashtag [#Jam4Maunakea]. Tag all these pages and all the Maunakea pages: Protect Maunakea Puʻu Huluhulu, Kākoʻo Haleakalā, and Kanaeokana, ʻŌiwi TV. We had no idea what to expect. (Keola Nakanishi in Quiamzon 2020)

Puʻuhonua Puʻuhuluhulu's website provided detailed technical instructions for those who could not be present on the mauna for the event but who wanted to watch and participate. This approach allowed those not attending to contribute video recordings to the final product. Organizers prepared and uploaded a video with recordings and the lyrics of the songs for participants to learn.[27] The key and arrangement were those performed at Puʻuhuluhulu and streamed worldwide. This video would also be used by those watching the streaming performance as they played along from their locations and—for those who chose to—recorded their performances for possible inclusion in the video that Mana Maoli staff would compile later.

On August 11, 2019, my wife, Marie, and I were joined by our friends Halemanu and Lisa Villarimo in the ʻApo Leo Learning Studio at UH Maui College at about ten thirty. I had already prepared the studio's computer, microphone, stands, and DAW (digital audio workstation) to record our performance with the provided audio track and watch the event as it transpired on the mauna. Like many others around the globe, we observed the event's opening, led by Pōmaikaʻi Keawe-Lyman, granddaughter of famed Hawaiian female vocalist Genoa Keawe. She provided instructions to the crowds and those watching the live stream on the technical aspects of the performance. Nearly four minutes into the stream, she led a countdown in Hawaiian, and on its completion, participants began to perform "Kū Haʻaheo." Those of us watching online observed the proceedings on the mauna from various vantage points as those directing the stream provided multiple cameras and frequent cutaways. Views included close-ups of kiaʻi leadership and well-known Hawaiian musicians in the front line and aerial and side views of the multitudes who came to the mountain to participate in the event, many wearing the red shirts emblazoned with yellow lettering and graphics that became synonymous with the movement to protect Maunakea. They performed the chorus of "Kū Haʻaheo e Kuʻu Hawaiʻi" twice (but did not perform the verses), ending the performance by repeating the last line, "No kuʻu lāhui e hāʻawi pau a i ola mau."[28] Our small group sang along with those gathered on the mauna and worldwide, and we recorded our performance with a digital video camera.

Immediately after completing the performance of "Kū Haʻaheo," a trio of musicians with electric amplification—Emma Nakano on upright bass,

Kamakakēhau Fernandez on ʻukulele, and Wailau Ryder on guitar—began to play the introduction of "Hawaiʻi Loa." Shortly after the kāhea (call) of "Hawaiʻi Loa" was made, attendees began to sing it.[29] Prominent Hawaiian musicians in the front row of the recorded performance included Starr Kealaheleokalani Kalāhiki, Kaumakaiwa Kanakaʻole, Hāwane Rios, and Pōmaikaʻi Keawe-Lyman. Kiaʻi leaders Pua Case and Lanakila Mangauil also stood on the front line. Many hae Hawaiʻi (Hawaiian flags) were visible and held high throughout the crowd, with several Kanaka Maoli flags and flags of other nations visible.[30] Kanakaʻole wore a T-shirt bearing the tino rangatiratanga (absolute sovereignty) flag of the Māori people.[31] Our small group, with me on upright bass, Halemanu Villarimo on guitar, and our wives singing, performed along with the kiaʻi on the mauna for the approximately three-and-a-half minutes it took to complete "Hawaiʻi Loa."

Following the performance, Hāwane Rios called out to all the attendees "Kū kiaʻi mauna!" followed by "aloha ʻāina" twice, with attendees echoing each call. She closed with "ʻoiaʻiʻo," her kāhea (call) again echoed by attendees. Finally, all those present raised their hands in the air, forming the mountain-shaped gesture that has become an unspoken symbol of the movement to protect Maunakea. The video closes with a brief speech by Rios' mother, Pua Case.

> ʻO kākou nō ʻo Mauna a Wākea [we are the mountain of Wākea]. We are the hoa ʻāina [friends of the land], the native people of this land; we are the hoa welo like [friends with common ancestry]. We are the Pacific with our Polynesian relatives and cousins. We are the hoa pili [friends bound together]; we are those who stand for our mountains, our lands, our waters, and our lifeways all around the world, and we are the hoa aloha kākou a pau [we are all friends], and we stand to aloha ʻāina, love our lands like no other. We are the pillars from the four cardinal points, and we are the beloved warriors, and we rise like a mighty wave. We are those who stand strong as mountains. We are a rock standing, and we are the water protectors of Mauna A Wākea and all waters of all mountains and right back here again, and we rise like a mighty wave.[32]

On January 13, 2020, just over five months after the performance and recording on the mauna, Mana Maoli released the final edit of the recorded performances, including video submissions from throughout Hawaiʻi and worldwide.[33] The audio tracks of these submissions are mixed into the audio track recorded on the mauna on August 11, 2020. The names of the locations appear as subtitles as the performance proceed, with performers from Aotearoa, Times Square in New York City, Massachusetts, Italy, Virginia, and Ukraine, to name a few. The video also includes performances by many well-known Hawaiian musicians. Significantly, it has people from all walks of life, ages, races, and ethnicities.

> By the end of the video, if you watch the outtakes as well, we featured thousands of kiaʻi, of protectors, across well over 100 locations, different countries, states, and ahupuaʻa. By the end of this video and these kiaʻi or supporters from around the world were featured on the choruses of these two songs. Participants included gatherings of 5,000 or more at the palace in the [San Francisco] Bay area. Gatherings of a thousand or more—there's about a dozen of those are maybe five or ten of those that we know of, and then, of course, you have just a family and a house or just an individual. (Keola Nakanishi in Quiamzon 2020)

Andre Perez, who arrived on the mauna before the arrests of July 17, 2019, and remained there for forty-four days, offers his recollection of the event's significance.

> All I remember is a bunch of smiling faces and everybody singing together. That's the thing, you know, there's music, right? There's just music, which we can articulate that music brings this vibe, brings the feeling, has the lyrics have the sounds and the tones. But then there's Hawaiian music, which I think is a whole other level because you'll play a song that everybody knows. You'll have hundreds of people singing along in unison, and to me, that's the essence of our unity, when we can speak together, sing together, harmonize together. For that particular moment in time, Hawaiian people are one voice. (2020)

The individuals who coordinated and participated in the Jam4Maunakea overcame tremendous logistical and technological challenges to perform, record, and broadcast this event. In doing so, they managed to embrace and extend "the ways in which Indigenous people have utilized digital technologies to revive, repatriate, and transmit musical traditions in complex articulations of Indigeneity" (Hilder 2017). They provided a potent example of the power of digital media through which other Indigenous peoples may transmit such articulations.

HŌʻULUʻULU MANAʻO (SUMMARY)

"Kū Haʻaheo e Kuʻu Hawaiʻi" has undeniably taken its place alongside the anthems and anthemic compositions of Hawaiʻi and the other Pacific Island groups discussed in this chapter. It has achieved the purpose Daughtry identifies for anthems: "to generate a collective sentiment among those who sing them" (2003). It also contains elements that equate to the three functions of anthems identified by Mayo-Harp. While many countries have officially sanctioned anthems to represent the values and unity of their people, it is clear that compositions can achieve anthemic status through the acceptance of the people. "Pōkarekare Ana" has reached an anthem-like status in Aotearoa, as have "Hawai'i Aloha," "Hawai'i Loa," and now "Kū Ha'aheo e Ku'u Hawai'i" in Hawai'i. I do not believe the composers of any of these mele knew that their mele would live on beyond their lifetimes. Such an outcome is certainly one that most composers can aspire to but not anticipate.

I do not believe it is a coincidence that the theme of kū (to stand) is prominent in both "Hawai'i Loa" and "Kū Ha'aheo." Indeed, it appears in English and Hawaiian in their titles. Kū means to stand (among several other meanings) but is also a principal Hawaiian deity. In his seminal text *Kū Kanaka: Stand Tall*, George S. Kanahele notes that

> The attribute or value that Kū personifies is revealed in his name, which means 'upright"—standing tall, as in "Kū Kanaka!" A warrior who is standing tall on the battlefield clearly is being brave in the face of the enemy. Kūkā'ilimoku's presence not only put fear in the hearts of the opposing forces but also inspired the "good guys" with a fighting "go for broke" spirit that would lead them to victory.[34] He gave them not only physical courage but also, more important, moral courage—the feeling of confidence and pride— that is the source of all acts of bravery and valor. (1992)

Many mele have been composed using similar expressions to those found in these mele—love for the 'āina, the ancestor of Kānaka 'Ōiwi, lōkahi (unity), kūpa'a (steadfastness), wiwo'ole (fearlessness), and other prized cultural values. These mele have achieved anthemic status through their acceptance by Kānaka 'Ōiwi and allies because they reflect shared values, reminding them that they have more in common than not. It enables them to find strength by unifying in their shared values and achieving their shared goals. "Kū Ha'aheo e Ku'u Hawai'i," along with its progenitor and predecessors, will undoubtedly be called on again to awaken the indomitable spirit of Hawaiian people in future situations where Kānaka 'Ōiwi and their allies need to turn back the forces of colonization that have flourished in Hawai'i since the establishment of the Hawaiian Kingdom and, in the wake of its contested dismemberment (J. K. K. Osorio 2002), in the era after US annexation and occupation of the 'āina, continuing efforts to summon lāhui through anthemic music.

NOTES

1. While "Kū Haʻaheo e Kuʻu Hawaiʻi" is the complete name of this mele, it is frequent referred to as simply "Kū Haʻaheo."

2. I was not present at this ceremony. The descriptions provided are based on examination and transcription of publicly available video recordings, other cited sources, and depictions of the events as told by participants.

3. David Uahikea Maile notes that when groundbreaking participants left the area, they left behind their chairs. Seeing this, the kiaʻi cleaned up the mess, gathered and stacked the chairs neatly for event staff, and noted the normativity of such actions: "Kanaka Maoli are left to clean the messes made by the astronomy industry and telescope observatories" (Maile 2021).

4. Mayo-Harp identifies these Spanish American countries as Argentina, Bolivia, Chile, Colombia, Costa Rica, Cuba, Dominican Republic, Ecuador, El Salvador, Guatemala, Honduras, Mexico, Nicaragua, Panama, Paraguay, Peru, Uruguay, and Venezuela.

5. "God Save the King" is performed as "God Save the Queen" when the reigning monarch is a female.

6. For all of the anthems presented in this chapter, I add the ʻokina and kahakō that do not appear in the original texts. I also use modern spelling conventions, such as breaking up single words that are printed as two words today.

7. The naʻau is considered the seat of intelligence and emotion in Hawaiian culture. Naʻau aliʻi and ʻōpū aliʻi are terms for royals—and others, for that matter—of a benevolent or generous nature.

8. Kamehameha failed to capture the island of Kauaʻi by military force as he had the other major islands in Hawaiʻi. Kauaʻi forces withstood several attempts by Kamehameha to gain control of the island. Ultimately, Kauaʻi united with the rest of the Hawaiian Kingdom on the death of and through Kamehameha's agreement with its final ruler, Kaumualiʻi, in 1824.

9. It is important to note that except for a five-month-long period known as "The Paulet Affair," Hawaiʻi has never been under British control. In 1843, British naval officer Captain Lord George Paulet of the vessel HMS *Carysfort* exerted control of the Hawaiian Islands without authorization of the British government. The rightful government of the Hawaiiian Kingdom was subsequently restored. The affinity of Hawaiian royals for the British monarchy is well documented, with Hawaiʻi's royals borrowing not only "God Save the King" from the British but also symbols such as its flag, clothing, crown, and other trappings of the monarchy.

10. In July 2008, Mohi was appointed Dame Companion of the New Zealand Order of Merit for her services to the Māori people on the occasion of the celebration of the queen's birthday.

11. There is a legal complexity to this possible solution. A Hawaiian language translation of any copyrighted song would be deemed a derivative work and require explicit permission from the composer or copyright holder. Such works do not fall into the fair use doctrine. I have made several attempts to obtain permission to translate popular songs into Hawaiian, and only once have I received a reply and permission to do so. In another case, I was asked by a friend to translate Rogers and Hammerstein's composition "You"ll Never Walk Alone." The Rogers and Hammerstein estate allowed the translation under the condition that I sign over rights to the translation to the estate—a condition I agreed to.

12. Stillman provides a detailed account of the composition of "Kaulana Nā Pua," a chronology of its many printings, and other pertinent information in "Aloha Aina: New Perspectives on 'Kaulana Na Pua'" (Stillman 1999).

13. The exact date of Lyon's composing "Hawai'i Aloha" is unknown. It is based on the gospel song "I Left It All with Jesus," written by James McGranahan. Kam suggests that "Hawai'i Aloha" was most likely composed after the publication of the hymnal *Gospel Hymns, No. 4 (Words Only)* in 1879, in which "I Left It All with Jesus" was first published (Kam 2017).

14. Project Kuleana's YouTube landing page can be found at https://www.youtube.com/c/ProjectKULEANA.

15. The term māhū identifies a Hawaiian third or "in-between" gender that is difficult to equate to any specific term in English such as LGBTQ+ or transgender. A more nuanced dicussion of the term can be found in Alexis Cheung's interview with Wong-Kalu (Wong-Kalu 2021).

16. In 2007, opposition to the testing and cultivation of genetically modified kalo intensified after years of resistance by Kānaka 'Ōiwi, who, according to Hawaiian cosmology, descended from kalo. The University of Hawai'i responded by agreeing to stop testing and modification of Hawaiian varieties of kalo. In 2009, the state legislature approved a bill that placed a moratorium on further GMO testing of Hawaiian kalo.

17. The Akaka Bill, officially titled Native Hawaiian Government Reorganization Act of 2009, was federal legislation introduced by Hawai'i's late US senator Daniel K. Akaka. It built on previous attempts to gain US federal recognition of Native Hawaiians and establish a relationship similar to what the US has with Native American and Native Alaskans. There were significant differences in this proposed relationship that are too nuanced to discuss here. The legislation failed to gain approval from the US Senate.

18. Since the 1960s, Hawai'i has enacted and enforced laws to compel the sale of leasehold lands—many of which are owned by entities such as the Kamehameha Schools and intended to benefit Kānaka 'Ōiwi—to the leaseholder.

19. Hawaiian burial sites are found throughout the state, particularly in areas that are (or were) largely comprised of sand. Countless burials have been

disturbed, with remains removed and relocated. The Native American Graves Protection and Repatriation Act (NAGPRA), legislation enacted by the State of Hawaiʻi, and the establishment Island Burial have given greater power to individuals and organizations to ensure proper handling of human remains and funary devices; however, they have not completely addressed issues nor prevented mishandling.

20. The lyrics and translation of "Kaulana Nā Pua" appear in *Na Mele o Hawaiʻi Nei* (Elbert and Māhoe 1970).

21. The lyrics and translation of "Kū Haʻaheo e Kuʻu Hawaiʻi" were copied from a document on the OHA website: https://www.oha.org/ku-haaheo.

22. Unless otherwise noted, all lyrics, translations, and background information about this mele comes from a page on the Kamakakoi website on which the mele appears (Wong-Kalu 2016).

23. Sai-Dudoit and Tolentino note that Liliʻuokalani's name does not appear in any handwritten drafts of this mele held by the composer's family. Instead, she uses "mōʻī" (king, queen, sovereign, monarch) (2022).

24. There is an ʻōlelo noʻeau that states "He ʻaaliʻi kū makani au, ʻaʻohe makani nāna e kulaʻi" (I am a wind-resisting ʻaaliʻi, no gale can push me over) (Pukui 1983).

25. On August 12, 2019 (the day after the Jam4Maunakea), I traveled to Puʻuhuluhulu as part of a contigent of University of Hawaiʻi employees who worked in Hawaiian programs throughout the UH system. One of my tasks was to determine possible ways to improve data connectivity to kiaʻi. After extensive research, I learned that additional connectivity was possible only through a single satellite that provided coverage of the area. Kiaʻi leadership had already identified that option.

26. It is quite common, at the end of a musical performance, for the audience to exhuberantly call out "hana hou!" as a request for an encore performance.

27. At the time of this writing, this first video is still available for viewing on YouTube and has been viewed over two hundred thousand times: https://www.youtube.com/watch?v=EDd9xJOQuAk&list=PLTg8V5WvojM7TnGKkzbpH3ei WI56zgsGm.

28. Musicians refer to the practice of repeating the last line or two of a verse or chorus at the conclusion of a performance as tagging. It is common and useful in Hawaiian performances in situtations where the performers are unfamiliar with each other or unrehearsed as it clearly signals the end of the performance.

29. It is common in the performance of mele for a member of the group to kāhea, or "call out," the first word or two of a verse as a reminder to others— sometimes a hula performer—what verse is about to be performed. It is arguably even more common when the musicians do not regularly perform together. It is not uncommon for a hula dancer to kāhea to the musicians.

30. The Kanaka Maoli flag has a controversial history and is not, as some believe, the original flag of the Hawaiian Kingdom (Hawaiian Kingdom 2013).

31. The tino rangatiratanga flag was designed in 1990 and has become known as the Māori flag representing all Tāngata Whenua (Māori people). At the time of the Jam4Maunakea performance, Māori were engaged in a dispute with the New Zealand government over lands at Ihumātao that had been wrongfully confiscated from Tāngata Whenua in the 1800s and were slated for development as an exclusive residential area. Māori groups visited Maunakea to show their support for Kānaka ʻŌiwi, and groups of Kānaka ʻŌiwi appeared at Ihumātao to show support for tāngata whenua.

32. The unedited performance of "Kū Haʻaheo e Kuʻu Hawaiʻi" as it was recorded and shared on July 19, 2019 has garnered nearly 165,000 views and can be viewed at https://www.youtube.com/watch?v=iwRnQQn6m2E.

33. The final, edited version of this video has received over 125,000 views. It can be watched at https://www.youtube.com/watch?v=k1Ul5xp4PTg.

34. Kūkāʻilimoku is often described as a god of war. Kamehameha attended to Kūkāʻilimoku after the death of Kalaniʻōpuʻu, and Kamehameha's successes in battle and unifying the islands are credited, at least in part, to his attentiveness to Kūkāʻilimoku.

—ᛒ—

PANINA (CONCLUSION)

Acting in unison for larger purposes and for the benefit of the wider community could help us to become more open-minded, idealistic, altruistic, and generous, and less self-absorbed and corrupt in the conduct of our public affairs than we are today. In an age when our societies are preoccupied with the pursuit of material wealth, when the rampant market economy brings out unquenchable greed and amorality in us, it is necessary for our institutions of learning to develop corrective mechanisms if we are to retain our sense of humanity and of community. (Hau'ofa 1998)

Over five years have passed since the arrests of kūpuna on the Ala Kūpuna in July 2019. Law enforcement presence and the potential for further arrests decreased with the arrival of winter weather in October and November 2019, when TMT developers indicated that it would not be feasible to begin construction. As the number of law enforcement officers dwindled, so did the number of kia'i. Kia'i maintained a minimal presence on the Ala Kūpuna until the arrival of the COVID-19 pandemic, when leadership decided it was in everyone's best interest to remove the structures on the Ala Kūpuna. Shortly after that, the state reopened the Maunakea Access Road.

The cessation of direct confrontations on Maunakea did not signal the end of the TMT consortium's ambitions, nor the ambitions of the state government. Nevertheless, TMT supporters continued their public relations campaign to garner support for constructing the telescope. One of these actions was the Hawai'i State Legislature passing House Resolution No. 33, H.D. 1 during the 2021 legislative session to establish the Mauna Kea Working Group. In addition to members of the State House of Representatives, the working group included kiaʻi Pualani Kanakaʻole Kanahele, Joshua Lanakila Mangauil, and Noe Noe Wong-Wilson. Also participating were representatives of the University of Hawaiʻi, the Office of Hawaiian Affairs, the State of Hawaiʻi Department of Natural Resources, and the astronomy industry. The working group's stated goal was to "develop recommendations, building on the Independent Evaluation of the Implementation of the Mauna Kea Comprehensive Management Plan, for a new governance and management structure for Mauna Kea that collaboratively engages with all stakeholders, particularly the Native Hawaiian community" (Hawaiʻi State House of Representatives 2022). On July 7, 2022, Governor David Ige signed a bill sent to him by the state legislature establishing the Mauna Kea Stewardship Oversight Authority (MKSOA) "to protect Mauna Kea for future generations and manage the lands contained therein for the purpose of fostering a mutual stewardship paradigm in which ecology, the environment, natural resources, cultural practices, education, and science are in balance and synergy" (Ige 2022). The board currently consists of Chair John Komeiji, Dawn Chang, Doug Adams, Gene Bal, Kamana Beamer, Paul Horner, Gary Kalehua Krug, Joshua Lanakila Mangauil, Noe Noe Wong-Wilson, Rich Matsuda, Pomai Bertelmann, and Bonnie Irwin.[1]

After decades of mismanaging Maunakea and ignoring their mandate to treat and afford it the highest protection possible worthy of its conservation status, the state and university admitted their failures while simultaneously claiming that they have done much better in recent years than has been reported in the media. However, there is a preponderance of evidence that they have not. Continued attempts by the state, the university, TMT consortium, and supporters to bolster backing for TMT's construction, which project the appearance of engaging with those opposed to its construction, are what Dylan Robinson (Stó:lō) has referred to as "inclusionary performance" (2020). He notes the similarities to the models of recognition and accommodation theorized by Glen Coulthard (Yellowknives Dene) and the shift in the relationship between Canada's First Peoples and the Canadian government after 1969 "from a more-or-less unconcealed and coercive structure of domination to one that is now reproduced through a more conciliatory set of languages and practices that emphasize the recognition and accommodation of Indigenous difference" (Robinson 2020). The actions of the State of Hawaiʻi, the University of Hawaiʻi, and the astronomy industry clearly give the appearance of implementing this model of recognition and accommodation, yet they continue to manipulate from behind the scenes to see that the astronomy industry in Hawaiʻi is prioritized over Kānaka ʻŌiwi and environmental concerns.

On October 8, 2019, the Canadian Astronomical Association (CASCA) included the following statement regarding astronomical construction and activities on Indigenous lands:

> We recommend that the Canadian astronomical community [e.g., ACURA, CASCA, and NRC-HAA] work together with Indigenous representatives and other relevant communities to develop and adopt a set of comprehensive guiding principles for the locations of astronomy facilities and associated infrastructure in which Canada participates. These principles should be centred on consent from the Indigenous Peoples and traditional title holders who would be affected by any astronomy project. In addition, *when such consent does not exist, the principles should recognize that the use or threat of force is an unacceptable avenue for developing or accessing an astronomical site* [my emphasis]. The principles should also acknowledge that ongoing consent from Indigenous Peoples and continuing consultation with all relevant local communities are both essential throughout a project's lifetime. (Canadian Astronomical Association 2021)

CASCA notes that while TMT and the state undertook a process of consultation with Native Hawaiian groups, consultation does not equal consent, adding that "the astronomy community does not have the privilege to define what consent is nor do we have the right to manufacture consent" (Canadian Astronomical Association 2021). Nor do the University or the State of Hawai'i, despite their attempts to do so.

On January 6, 2020, Native Hawaiian scientists and researchers submitted a white paper to the National Academy of Sciences for its Astronomy 2020 Decadal Review. In this document, the authors share their perspectives, based on Indigenous knowledge, on building telescopes on Maunakea. In a press release on its news website, the university framed this paper as an opportunity to "spark further discussions that will lead to more collaborative opportunities for the discipline and native peoples." This language distorts the authors' statement that "the recent developments on Maunakea, as well as the history of legal challenges to TMT and earlier endeavors (e.g., the Keck Outriggers), demonstrate that TMT currently lacks consent from the local Indigenous community" (Kahanamoku et al. 2020). The authors include a statement in the document's preface: "Our recommendations are *minimum* [my emphasis] first steps that can be undertaken to begin a process of building an iterative and equitable relationship with Native Hawaiians." The authors also put on the table an option that the state has never offered: that the TMT project not be built on

Maunakea. If the university and state genuinely intend to find a path forward, this option must be added to the discussion.

The state and university's inclusionary performance is no more evident than in the university's April 24, 2022, rerelease of an earlier report by the University of Hawai'i Economic Research Organization (UHERO). It contains the same figures as a report UHERO released on January 30, 2022, that touts the overall economic benefits of astronomy in Hawai'i, simply relabeling some figures as "spillover effects" (University of Hawai'i News 2022). The rerelease and rebranding of this information coincided with the state legislature considering HB (House Bill) 2024, which, among other things, would have stripped all responsibility for and authority over Maunakea from the University of Hawai'i and established a new Maunakea stewardship authority. As this bill proceeded through legislative committees and hearings, Governor Ige warned legislators that should the bill become law, "it does seem to be clear that it is intended to end astronomy on Mauna Kea and I do have a concern about that" (Richardson 2022). The state senate subsequently removed the language that strips UH of its responsibilities for and authority over Maunakea. However, conference committee members, including representatives of the House of Representatives and Senate, produced a compromise version of the bill that would leave UH in charge of lands on Maunakea used for astronomy for five years. After that time, authority for those lands would fall to the governing entity created by the bill.

HB 2024 contains a significant statement that exposes the state government's inability to comprehend and acknowledge the profound nature of Kānaka ʻŌiwi's genealogical connection to Maunakea. The first line of §-1 of HD 2024, "Findings and Purpose," reads, "The legislature finds that Mauna Kea serves as an important cultural and genealogical site to the people of Hawaii, particularly to Native Hawaiians." No one but Kānaka ʻŌiwi can claim genealogical ties to Maunakea, and regardless of how many generations an individual's settler ancestors have lived in Hawai'i, they cannot claim the same genealogical connection as Kānaka ʻŌiwi. In addition, it is more than a genealogical site—it is the piko, the umbilical connection to their origins. While specifically addressing the Asian American population, Candace Fujikane's observations of settlers' relationship to land apply to all non-Indigenous people residing on Indigenous lands: "Indigenous peoples are differentiated from settlers by their genealogical, familial relationship with specific land bases that are ancestors to them. One is either indigenous to a particular land base or one is not. Asian Americans are undeniably settlers in the United States because we cannot claim any genealogy to the land we occupy" (Fujikane 2005).

Buried further within this legislation is a passage that exemplifies the state's attempt to facilitate the development of additional observatories. In §-1 of HD 2024, "Findings and Purpose," the legislation states the intent to "commence the resolution of these issues to protect Mauna Kea and bring about a more harmonious coexistence of uses atop the mountain." In Section 8, "it is declared that the support of astronomy consistent with section -1 is a policy of the State." This point is reiterated at the end of the bill, which "declares astronomy as a state policy." The bill does not offer the possibility that further astronomical development on Maunakea will cease if the Kānaka ʻŌiwi community does not consent. Settler-colonial aspirations for Maunakea have been codified and prioritized over protecting the environment and Kānaka ʻŌiwi rights.

Once the TMT consortium determined that Maunakea was its preferred location to build its telescope, the state made every effort to see the telescope built. The myriad of community meetings, hearings, and other interventions were never intended to help decide whether TMT should be built. Instead, the state used these inclusionary performances to justify and facilitate its construction regardless of overwhelming resistance. It could now claim that "we have listened to the people and heard their concerns," only to privilege and amplify supportive voices and disregard those opposing yet another act of desecration on Maunakea. This attitude prevails today.

PUANA HOU ʻIA KE ALOHA ʻĀINA (LOVE FOR THE ĀINA IS EXPRESSED)

The genealogical connections between Kānaka ʻŌiwi and Maunakea and the kiaʻi's actions as they protected it inspired many to compose new mele. Performers and recording artists brought mele to life with their voices and further inspired kiaʻi and their supporters to remain kūpaʻa (steadfast) in kapu aloha. This cycle of inspiration, composition, performance, and listening, repeated many times on the mauna, continues today and will continue in the future.

As David Aiona Chang argues, "every day and every moment and every kiaʻi and every supporter up there is participating in the sacredness, which is not just ancient but is also contemporary" (2020). Every new mele composed for Maunakea and the kiaʻi reaffirms and reinforces genealogical connections and honors a beloved kupuna. Every recording and performance invites the audience and listeners to participate in the sacredness that Chang speaks of in a contemporary setting. In doing so, kiaʻi and their supporters perpetuate the musical activism of their kūpuna, such as the Aloha ʻĀina who supported Queen Liliʻuokalani before, during, and after the overthrow of the Hawaiian monarchy. Aloha ʻĀina also practiced musical activism during the Second Hawaiian Renaissance. Music documented and supported a social change in contexts such as the return of Kahoʻolawe to Hawaiian control and the eviction of Kānaka ʻŌiwi from native lands. The songs performed in these actions were ancient and new, as were the performance styles, instruments, technologies, and even participants' attire. The tradition of Hawaiian musical activism continues to evolve with each new generation of Aloha ʻĀina.

Unlike the ahu that the state deemed "not a traditional or customary right or practice," these compositions and recorded performances will be allowed to age. They will be heard by future generations and admired for the expressions of language within them and the aesthetics of musical performance. No action on behalf of the state can prevent that from occurring. They are a reminder of the challenges that Aloha ʻĀina have always faced. They inspire future generations to pick up pens (or type on their word processors) and compose new mele that will be embraced and utilized as those composed in Maunakea's defense.

Since kiaʻi, law enforcement, and construction equipment have left the mauna, its soundscape has returned to a modern normal. A visitor to the site of the Ala Kūpuna still experiences "the sounds of the Anthropocene" as motor vehicles race by the intersection of the Maunakea Access Road and the Daniel K. Inouye Highway. There are sounds made by occasional visitors and residents to the area, who have come to experience the site of previous confrontations and musicking. There are still brief periods of relative silence where one can hear the sounds of the winds, rains, and birds singing while observing the majesty of Maunakea, contemplating its history, and acknowledging its genealogical connections to Kānaka ʻŌiwi. I hope that this relative silence will no longer be threatened by convoys of vehicles hauling construction equipment, materials, and workers to begin new acts of desecration at the summit and spew the fumes of their fossil fuel-burning engines into the atmosphere. Likewise, I pray that we will not hear the reverberation of explosives necessary to dig the thirty-foot-deep hole at the summit of the mauna providing the foundation for the structure required by TMT. There is no such thing as respectful desecration, and should the construction of TMT commence, the desecration will not be conducted in silence.

During our conversation, I asked Pua Case whether she felt the music performed on and written in the months following the arrest of the kūpuna in 2019 accurately reflect the movement to protect the mauna and its commitment to kapu aloha.

> Yes, I do, because what they put into the music is exactly what they
> experienced firsthand on the ala and what they expressed when they were on

the microphone. Many of them said I've never been in a crowd like this. I was being so embraced with no alcohol, no drugs. Yeah, not like that. It's just pure spirit and pure positive, uplifting Hawaiian. That's the thing—everything is framed in Kānaka Maoli values and prayers and chants and dances. So even when we held concerts up there, and everybody performed up there is in a real live concert. This is something you've never experienced, and really it was the love and the discipline at the same time. And so, I think that the music is definitely straight out of there like true reflection. (2020)

Kānaka ʻŌiwi joined and arguably led a broader decolonial movement of Indigenous peoples who are not waiting for occupying or settler states to reform their colonial ways or return ancestral lands. They are actively creating individual and collective identities in the present to set the stage for future generations by engaging with and practicing moʻokūʻauhau consciousness. The acts of the state, university, and consortium advocating for the development of Maunakea further their attempts to buy, bully, cajole, and propagandize their way onto the mountain's summit. In doing so, they continue to "other" the Indigenous people of Hawaiʻi in their ancestral homeland. They attempt to define what it means to be Hawaiian by prioritizing their desires over Hawaiian values, the legitimacy and authenticity of which they dismiss, and using the settler-colonial structures and ideologies erected by their predecessors that gave them the power to overcome opposition. Their continued attempts to see that TMT is built demonstrate that their actions are examples of inclusionary performance intended to facilitate the ongoing desecration of Maunakea.

Emalani Case notes that "as Indigenous peoples, we know we take our ancestors with us wherever we go. We know we carry them in our bones and in our blood in the same way that our descendants will carry us" (2021). David Uahikea Maile has written about his efforts to "invert the colonial gaze" by observing and critiquing Canada's science and astronomy industries using the colonizer's methods and tools (2021). As a settler-ally, I cannot claim such a complete inversion. However, I have attempted to contribute to critically analyzing and dismantling foreign ideologies and practices that have harmed Indigenous communities and others that support those communities. As Case articulates, I intend to remain present for my children, grandchildren, and future descendants when I am gone. I will be carried in their bones and blood and hope that they will know of my efforts to assure that Hawaiʻi is a better place for them—one that honors Hawaiian genealogies, practices, epistemologies, and ontologies with more than just words. It is my kuleana to contribute to a future filled with aloha ʻāina for all lands, particularly sacred places like Maunakea.

I cling to radical hope that Hawaiʻi will achieve these loftly goals before I pass into the realm of the ancestors myself.

NOTE

1. Hawaiʻi Island senator Lorraine Rodero Inouye, an outspoken supporter of TMT and critic of kiaʻi during the confrontations, introduced SB81 SD2 during the spring 2023 legislative session. She claimed it was intended to clarify the previously enacted Act 255 and reestablish the BLNR as the ultimate authority on Maunakea. Her bill is, in fact, contrary to Act 255's language and the original intent of the legislation. According to MKSOA's chair, John Komeji, "My understanding is that we were an autonomous—supposed to be autonomous—group with full decision-making authority" (Angarone 2023). The House Judiciary and Hawaiian Affairs committee did not schedule a hearing on the bill during the spring 2023 legislative session. Its future remains unknown.

GLOSSARY OF HAWAIIAN AND OTHER INDIGENOUS TERMS

HAWAIIAN TERMS

'aha gathering.

'ai to eat (v), food (n).

'āina land, sometimes interpreted as "that which feeds."

akua god(s).

ali'i chief(s).

aloha 'āina love of the land, patriotism.

Aloha 'Āina one who embodies the precepts of aloha 'āina.

aloha 'āina 'oia'i'o true love for the land.

Aloha 'Āina 'Oia'i'o and individual who embodies and acts with true love for the land.

alu like working together, cooperating.

ao day, daylight, the emergence of light.

ea sovereignty, independence, breath.

'eha pain.

ehu kakahiaka the morning mist or dawn, also metaphorically used to describe youth.

'iewe umbilical cord and connection.

'ili'ili an idiophone made of small, smooth lava rock.

i mua progress (v), to move forward.

ipu gourds, an idiophone made from the shell of a gourd.

hā breath.

hae Hawai'i the Hawaiian flag.

haku mele Hawaiian poetry (n), the composer of Hawaiian poetry (n), to compose Hawaiian poetry (v).

hālau schools and the buildings where hula is taught.

hana hou encore, a call made requesting that the final verse or chorus be repeated.

Haole foreign, in modern use usually to describe white people.

haumāna student(s).

Hawaiʻi mokupuni Hawaiʻi Island, also known as Moku o Keawe.

Hawaiʻinuiākea great and broad Hawaiʻi.

hīmeni hymn(s)

hoʻokupu religious offering(s).

hoʻolohe to listen.

hoʻolono to listen deeply with other senses.

hoʻomau to continue, persevere.

hula the Indigenous dance form of Kānaka ʻŌiwi.

huliāmahi to rise and join in unity.

hulu kūpuna hulu means feather, and when preceding kupuna or kūpuna, refers to revered or cherished elders.

kāhili ceremonial standards, often made of feathers, that symbolize royalty.

kākoʻo to support, a support person.

kalāʻau a stick-like idiophone made of wood.

kalo taro—a food staple in Hawaiʻi.

kamaliʻi youngster(s).

ka naʻi aupuni the conquer of a nation, a nickname of Kamehameha I.

kanaka person, human being, also colloquially used for "Hawaiian" (singular).

kānaka people, human beings, also colloquially used for "Hawaiians" (plural).

Kanaka ʻŌiwi Native Hawaiian (singular).

Kānaka ʻŌiwi Native Hawaiians (plural).

kānaka ʻōlelo Hawaiʻi Hawaiian speakers.

kaona hidden or veiled meanings in Hawaiian poetry.

kapa/tapa a cloth most commonly made from the wauke (paper mulberry plant).

kapu aloha a commitment to nonviolent resistance, discipline, and aloha in the face of violence or other negative actions.

kaua war.

Ke Ala Kūpuna the path of the elders.

keiki child/children.

kiaʻi protector, guardian.

kīhei ceremonial shawl.

kīkā kī hōʻalu Hawaiian slack key guitar.

ko Hawaiʻi paeʻāina the Hawaiian archipelago.

koko blood.

kōnane an older Hawaiian game resembling checkers.

kūʻē to resist.

kuhi to point.

kūhōʻailona to stand as a sign or symbol. Metaphor.

kuleana responsibility, right, privilege.

kū like to stand together.

kumu teacher(s).

kumu hula master hula teacher.

kumu kōkua teacher's assistant.

kūpaʻa to remain steadfast.

kupuna elder (singular).

kūpuna elders (plural).

lāʻau lapaʻau traditional medicines and healing.

lāhui nation, a people.

lāʻī ti-leaf plant.

lanakila victory.

lei a garland or necklace made of flowers, nuts, other vegetation, or shells. Often used metaphorically to mean a beloved child.

leo kahea a call.

lōkahi unity.

lomiomi a Hawaiian form of massage.

māhele division (n), to divide (v).

maluhia peace, tranquility.

māmaka to bear or carry on the shoulders.

māmakakaua warriors, bearers of the weight of war.

mānaleo native speakers of Hawaiian.

mauli spiritual essence.

mauna mountain.

mele a poetic text in ʻōlelo Hawaiʻi intended to be recited, chanted, or sung.

mele aloha ʻāina a song or chant that expresses love for the land or patriotism.

mele Hawaiʻi a Hawaiian poetic text that features both a verse and chorus.

mele koʻihonua Hawaiian poetry documenting cosmogonic genealogies.

mele kūʻauhau Hawaiian poetry documenting kānaka genealogies.

mele oli Hawaiian poetry intended to be performed in a chanted style.

moku the largest subdivision of land in Hawaiʻi, also a shortened version of mokupuni (island) sometimes heard in spoken Hawaiian but more frequently in poetic Hawaiian.

mokupuni island.

moʻokūʻauhau genealogy.

moʻolelo stories.

naʻi conquerer.

nūpepa kahiko old Hawaiian language newspapers from the 1800s and early 1900s.

ʻohana family.

ʻohana waʻa canoe family.

ʻohu mist.

ʻohuʻohu to be adorned with a mist. Metaphorically used to describe the wearing of numerous flowers or lei.

ola to live, health.

'ōlelo language, to speak.

'ōlelo Hawai'i the Hawaiian language.

'ōlelo mele words of the song.

'ōlelo no'eau proverbial sayings.

oli the performance of a mele in a chanted style.

'onipa'a to remain firm, steadfast.

pahu drum(s).

paka the practice of giving a new mele to an experienced composer or highly proficient 'ōlelo Hawai'i speaker to review and offer suggestions, improve the composition, or remove unintended or potentially dangerous thoughts.

pīkake Indian jasmine.

pilikia problems.

pilina relationship

pō night, darkness.

pono that which is proper, commonly glossed as righteousness.

pua flower(s), sometimes used metaphorically to mean a child, lover, or spouse.

pū'ali koa soldiers or warriors.

pū'ili an idiophone made from a piece of bamboo with slots running part way up the length of the instrument.

pu'uhonua a place of refuge.

wa'a outrigger canoe.

wahi pana storied places.

wao akua the upper regions of Hawai'i's mountains, considered "the realm of the gods."

wiwo'ole fearlessness.

OTHER INDIGENOUS TERMS

iwi a tribe-like social unit (Māori).

kai food (Māori).

Pākehā citizens and residents of Aotearoa of predominantly European descent (Māori).

shxwelítemelh an adjective for a settler or white person's methods or things (Halq'eméylem).

tāngata whenua the Māori people (Māori).

te reo Māori the Māori language (Māori).

tino rangatiratanga absolute sovereignty (Māori).

tito waiata composer of Māori song (Māori).

xwélalà:m listening (Halq'eméylem).

BIBLIOGRAPHY

Akindes, Fay Yokomizo. 2001. "Sudden Rush: Na Mele Paleoleo (Hawaiian Rap) as Liberatory Discourse." *Discourse* 23 (1): 82–98.

Altonn, Helen. 2006. "Customary Release of Placentas Demanded." *Honolulu Star-Bulletin*, February 11, 2006.

Amer, Enas Subhi, Adhraa A. Naser, and Kamal Abdulmajeed Rufaidah. 2019. "Silence as a Tactic of Communication in Pragmatics, Novel, and Poetry." *AWEJ for Translation & Literary Studies* 3 (3): 51–67.

Andone, Dakin, Sarah Jorgensen, and Polo Sandoval. 2019. "'This Is Our Last Stand': Protesters on Mauna Kea Dig in Their Heels." *CNN Online*, July 22, 2019. https://www.cnn.com/2019/07/21/us/hawaii-mauna-kea-protests/index.html.

Angarone, Ben. 2023. "New Mauna Kea Authority Tussles with DLNR over Conservation Lands." *Civil Beat*, March 3, 2023. https://www.civilbeat.org/2023/03/new-mauna-kea-authority-tussles-with-dlnr-over-conservation-lands/.

Anthony, Alberta Pua. 1979. "Hawaiian Nonverbal Communication: Two Applications." Department of Indo-Pacific Languages, University of Hawaiʻi at Mānoa. Scanned copy of unpublished paper provided to the author by Hamilton Library, UH Mānoa on May 30, 2023.

Arista, Noelani. 2018. *The Kingdom and the Republic: Sovereign Hawaiʻi and the Early United States*. Philadelphia: University of Pennsylvania Press.

Barcarse, Kaimana. 2022. Interview with the author conducted on March 5, 2022.

Basham, J. J. Leilani. 2002. *He Puke Mele Lahui: Na Mele Kupaʻa, Na Mele Kuʻe A Me Na Mele Aloha O Na Kanaka Maoli*. MA thesis, University of Hawaiʻi at Mānoa.

Beamer, Kamanamaikalani. 2020. Interview with the author conducted on March 14, 2020.

Beckwith, Martha Warren. 1976. *Hawaiian Mythology.* Honolulu: University of Hawaiʻi Press.

Beniamina, Jean Ileialoha Keale. 2009. Interview with the author conducted on May 8, 2009.

Berger, Harris M. 2003. "The Politics and Aesthetics of Language Choice." In *Global Pop, Local Language,* edited by Harris M. Berger and Michael Thomas Carroll, IX. Jackson: University Press of Mississippi.

Big Island Video News. 2014. "TMT Opponents Halt Groundbreaking Ceremony." Video. https://www.youtube.com/watch?v=SZ4Gt35hs-s&t=953s.

Bishop Museum. 1997. *Nā Leo Hawaiʻi Kahiko.* Audio CD. Honolulu: Mountain Apple Company.

Bissen, Richard. 2022. Interview with the author conducted on March 15, 2022.

Black, Taroi. 2019. "NZ Artists Band Together with New Song 'Ka Mānu' for Ihumātao." *Te Ao Māori News.* https://www.teaomaori.news/nz-artists-band-together-new-song-ka-manu-ihumatao.

Brown, Marie Alohalani. 2016. *Facing the Spears of Change: The Life and Legacy of John Papa ʻĪʻī.* Indigenous Pacifics. Honolulu: University of Hawaiʻi Press.

Burlingame, Burl, and Kamohalu Kasher. 1978. *Da Kine Sound: Conversations with the People Who Create Hawaiian Music.* Kailua: Press Pacifica.

Canadian Astronomical Association. 2021. "The Canadian Astronomy Long Range Plan 2020–2030." May 2021. https://casca.ca/wp-content/uploads/2021/05/LRP2020_final_EN.pdf.

Carlson, Bronwyn. 2013. "The 'New Frontier': Emergent Indigenous Identities and Social Media." In *The Politics of Identity: Emerging Indigeneity,* edited by M. Harris, M. Nakata, & B. Carlson, Ultimo: UTS ePRESS. 147–68.

Case, Emalani. 2021. *Everything Ancient Was Once New: Indigenous Persistence from Hawaiʻi to Kahiki.* Indigenous Pacifics. Honolulu: University of Hawaiʻi Press.

Case, Pua. 2020. Interview with the author conducted on April 15, 2020.

Castillo, Isaac Maluhia. 2020. Interview with the author conducted on February 27, 2020.

Chang, David Aiona. 2020. Interview with the author conducted on March 17, 2020.

Chapin, Helen Geracimos. 1996. *Shaping History: The Role of Newspapers in Hawaiʻi.* Honolulu: University of Hawaiʻi Press.

Charlot, John. 2005. *Classical Hawaiian Education.* Lāʻie: Pacific Institute, Brigham Young University-Hawaiʻi.

———. 2007. "Helen Desha Beamer's Pānīʻau: Innovations in Hula." *Journal of Intercultural Studies* 34: 1–15.

Cord International. 1996. "The Music of George Helm, A True Hawaiian." Audio CD. Ventura: Cord International.

Coulthard, Glen S. 2014. *Red Skin, White Masks: Rejecting the Colonial Politics of Recognition.* Indigenous Americas. Minneapolis: University of Minnesota Press.

Cramer, Christopher. 2005. *Inequality and Conflict: A Review of an Age-Old Concern*. Geneva: United Nations Research Institute for Social Development.

Creative NZ. 2019. "Waiata Anthems Debuts at #1." *Creative NZ* (blog). October 2, 2019. https://www.creativenz.govt.nz/news/waiata-anthems-debuts-at-1.

Culler, Jonathan. 1997. *Literary Theory: A Very Short Introduction*. New York: Oxford University Press.

———. 2002. *Structuralist Poetics: Structuralism, Linguistics and the Study of Literature*. Classics Series. New York: Routledge.

Daughtry, J. Martin. 2003. "Russia's New Anthem and the Negotiation of National Identity." *Ethnomusicology* 47 (1): 42–67.

Dayton, Kevin, and Andrew Gomes. 2019. "Gov. David Ige Calls Mauna Kea Camp an 'Unsafe Situation.'" *Honolulu Star-Advertiser*, July 20, 2019, online edition. https://www.staradvertiser.com/2019/07/20/hawaii-news/gov-david-ige-calls-mauna-kea-camp-an-unsafe-situation/.

Department of Parks and Recreation, City and County of Honolulu. 1977. Hawaiian Song Composing Contest: First Annual, 1950-Twenty-Eight [Ie. Twenty-Eighth] Annual.

Diettrich, Brian. 2017. "Chanting Diplomacy: Music, Conflict, and Social Cohesion in Micronesia." In *A Distinctive Voice in the Antipodes: Essays in Honour of Stephen A. Wild*, 195–21. JSTOR Open Access Monographs. Australia: ANU Press.

Donaghy, Joseph Keola. 2010. "The Language Is the Music: Perceptions of Authority and Authenticity in Hawaiian Language Composition and Vocal Performance." PhD diss., University of Otago.

Edgeworth, Matt, et al. 2014. "Archaeology of the Anthropocene." *Journal of Contemporary Archaeology* 1 (1): 73–132.

Edith Kanaka'ole Foundation. 2017. "Nā Oli o Ka 'Āina o Kanaka'ole (The Chants for the Kanaka'ole Lands)." https://edithkanakaolefoundation.org/docs/NaOli NoKaAinaOKanakaole.pdf.

Elbert, Samuel H., and Noelani Māhoe. 1970. *Nā Mele o Hawai'i Nei*. Honolulu: University of Hawai'i Press.

Essman, Sandy. 2020. Interview with the author conducted on February 22, 2020.

Feld, Steven. 1991. *Voices of the Rainforest*. Digital Album. Smithsonian Folkways. https://folkways.si.edu/voices-of-the-rainforest/world/music/album /smithsonian.

Fellezs, Kevin. 2019. *Listen but Don't Ask Question: Hawaiian Slack Key Guitar Across the TransPacific*. Durham: Duke University Press.

Flavell, Te Ururoa. 2022. "Untitled Facebook Post." Facebook, October 18, 2022. https://www.facebook.com/teururoa.flavell.3/posts/2116349685191824.

Forman, David M. 2020. "Reoccurring Cultural Insensitivity: Confronting the Abdication of Core Judicial Functions." *University of Hawai'i Law Review* 43: 341.

Fox, Stephen. 2019. *Culture and Psychology.* Thousand Oaks: SAGE.

Frazer, Ryan, Bronwyn Carlson, and Terri Farrelly. 2022. "Indigenous Articulations of Social Media and Digital Assemblages of Care." *Digital Geography and Society* 3, 1.

Fujikane, Candace. 2005. "Foregrounding Native Nationalisms: A Critique of Antinationalist Sentiment in Asian American Studies." *Asian American Studies after Critical Mass* 73–97. Online book. https://onlinelibrary.wiley.com/doi /book/10.1002/9780470774892.

Gardiner, Wira. 1996. *Return to Sender: What Really Happened at the Fiscal Envelope Hui.* United Kingdom: Reed.

Garroutte, Eva Marie. 2003. *Real Indians: Identity and the Survival of Native America.* United Kingdom: University of California Press.

Gelo, Daniel J. 1999. "Powwow Patter: Indian Emcee Discourse on Power and Identity." *Journal of American Folklore* 112 (443): 40–57.

Gon, Sam 'Ohu. 2022. "Response to Untitled Post by the Author." Facebook. Accessed April 7, 2022. https://www.facebook.com/story.php?story_fbid=pfbido TyoswqItvanLJ9k4aEnCchusgs744wAA43k8D4PqsDLWxMiK3W816YRA7CXv EnS3l&id=543046807.

Gonsalves, Gerard. 2020. Interview with the author conducted on February 22, 2020.

Goodyear-Ka'ōpua, Noelani. 2017. "Protectors of the Future, Not Protestors of the Past: Indigenous Pacific Activism and Mauna a Wākea." *South Atlantic Quarterly* 116 (1): 184–94.

———. 2020. "On the Cattle Guard." *Biography* 43 (3): 527–29.

Griffin, Chris C. M. 2003. *Texts and Violence, Lies and Silence: Anthropologists and Islanders "Negotiate the Truth."* Suva: School of Social and Economic Development, University of the South Pacific.

Handy, E. S. Craighill, and Mary Kawena Pukui. 1958. *The Polynesian Family System in Ka'u, Hawai'i.* Wellington: Polynesian Society.

Hanlon, David. 2009. "The 'Sea of Little Islands': Examining Micronesia's Place in 'Our Sea of Islands.'" *The Contemporary Pacific* 21 (1): 91–110.

Hanson, Allan. 1991. "Reply to Langdon, Levine, and Linnekin." *American Anthropologist* 93 (2): 449–50.

Harris, Aroha. 2004. *Hīkoi: Forty Years of Māori Protest.* Wellington: Huia.

Haugen, Keith. 1977. "Requiem for George Helm." *Ha'ilono Mele,* June 1977.

Hau'ofa, Epeli. 1995. "Our Sea of Islands." *The Contemporary Pacific* 6 (1): 148–61.

———. 1998. "The Ocean in Us." *The Contemporary Pacific,* 10 (2): 392–410.

Hawai'i Academy of Recording Arts. 2022. "Hawai'i Academy of Recording Arts Website." http://harahawaii.com.

Hawaiian Kingdom. 2013. "The Hawaiian National Flag and Royal Flag." *Hawaiian Kingdom Blog* (blog). June 29, 2013. https://hawaiiankingdom.org/blog/the -hawaiian-national-flag-and-royal-flag/.

Hawaiʻinuiākea School of Hawaiian Knowledge. n.d. "About UH Mānoa Campus' Ahu." Hawaiʻinuiākea School of Hawaiian Knowledge. Accessed May 25, 2022. https://manoa.hawaii.edu/hshk/hawaiinuiakea/about-us/about -uh-manoa-campus-ahu/.

Hawaiʻi State House of Representatives. 2022. "Mauna Kea Working Group Final Report." January 25, 2022. https://www.capitol.hawaii.gov/CommitteeFiles /Special/MKWG/Document/MKWG%20Final%20Report%20.pdf.

Hawaiʻi State Judiciary. 2018. "In the Matter of Contested Case Hearing Re Conservation District Use Application (CDUA) HA-3568 for the Thirty Meter Telescope at the Mauna Kea Science Reserve, Kaʻohe Mauka, Hāmākua, Hawaiʻi, TMK (3) 404015:009 404015:009)." Retrieved from BYU Hawaiʻi website. https://www.courts.state.hi.us/wp-content/uploads/2018/11/SCOT-17 -0000777disam.pdf.

Hilder, Thomas R. 2017. "Music, Indigeneity, Digital Media: An Introduction." In *Music, Indigeneity, Digital Media*, edited by T. Hilder, H. Stobart, and S. Tan, 1–27. United Kingdom: University of Rochester Press.

HNN Staff. 2019. "UH Denounces Professor's 'Hurtful' Statements about Kamehameha Schools Students." *Hawaiʻi News Now*. https://www.hawaii newsnow.com/2019/09/19/uh-denounces-controversial-remarks-reportedly -made-by-uh-physics-professor/.

Hobsbawm, Eric J., and Terence O. Ranger. 1983. *The Invention of Tradition*. Past and Present Publications. New York: Cambridge University Press.

Holt, Hōkūlani. 2020. Interview with the author conducted on February 19, 2020.

Holt, Hōkūlani, and Pualani Kanahele. 2019. "Kapu Aloha: Remember Your Ancestors." Interview by Puʻuhonua o Puʻuhuluhulu, video. https://www .youtube.com/watch?v=adeqsmRgdyI.

Hoʻōla Lāhui Hawaiʻi. 2009. "Hoʻōla Lāhui Hawaiʻi." http://www.hoolalahui .org/.

hoʻomanawanui, kuʻualoha. 2005. "He Lei Hoʻoheno No Nā Kau a Kau: Language, Performance, and Form in Hawaiian Poetry." *The Contemporary Pacific* 17 (1): 29–81.

———. 2006. "From Ocean to O-shen: Reggae, Rap, and Hip Hop in Hawaiʻi." In *Crossing Waters, Crossing Worlds: The African Diaspora in Indian Country*, edited by Sharon Patricia Holland and Tiya Miles, 273–308. United Kingdom: Duke University Press.

———. 2014. *Voices of Fire: Reweaving the Literary Lei of Pele and Hiʻiaka*. First Peoples: New Directions in Indigenous Studies. Minneapolis: University of Minnesota Press.

———. 2017. "He Ahu Moʻolelo: E Hoʻokahua i Ka Paepae Moʻolelo Palapala Hawaiʻi/A Cairn of Stories: Establishing a Foundation of Hawaiian Literature." *Palapala* 1: 51–101.

———. 2019. "E Hoʻi I Ka Piko (Return to the Center)." In *The Past before Us: Moʻokūʻauhau as Methodology*, edited by Nālani Wilson-Hokowhitu, 50-68. Indigenous Pacifics. Honolulu: University of Hawaiʻi Press.

———. 2022. Email correspondence with the author on June 18, 2022.

———. 2023. Email correspondence with the author on June 1, 2023.

hoʻomanawanui, kuʻualoha, Candace Fujikane, Aurora Kagawa-Viviani, Kerry Kamakaokaʻilima Long and Kekailoa Perry. 2019. "Teaching for Maunakea: Kiaʻi Perspectives." *Amerasia Journal* 45 (2): 271–76.

Horowitz, S. S. 2012. *The Universal Sense: How Hearing Shapes the Mind*. New York: Bloomsbury.

Husband, Charles. 2009. "Between Listening and Understanding." *Continuum* 23 (4): 441–43.

Hviding, Edvard. 2003. "Opening Up? Reclaiming a Plurality of Knowledges." *The Contemporary Pacific* 15 (1): 43–73.

Ige, David. 2022. "Gov. Msg. No. 1358." July 7, 2022. https://www.capitol.hawaii.gov /sessions/session2022/bills/GM1358_.PDF.

Judd, Albert Francis. 1890. "Incidents in Hawaiian History." *Pacific Commercial Advertiser*, December 11, 1890.

Kaʻeo, Kaleikoa. 2019. "Kaleikoa Discusses Aloha Aina in Depth." December 5, 2019. Video. https://www.youtube.com/watch?v=VqjBkUijhcU&t=433s.

Kahanamoku, Sara, et al. 2020. "A Native Hawaiian-Led Summary of the Current Impact of Constructing the Thirty Meter Telescope on Maunakea." In *National Academy of Science Astro2020 Decadal Review: Maunakea Perspectives*. Online Collection. https://doi.org/10.6084/m9.figshare.c.4805619.

Kahaunaele, Donna Kainani. 2020a. Interview with the author conducted on April 4, 2020.

———. 2020b. "Mele and ʻŌlelo Hawaiʻi on the Mauna." *Biography* 43 (3): 541, 550.

Kaʻili, Tēvita, O. n.d. "Kāingalotu: Tonga Saints in the Diaspora." Accessed March 10, 2023. https://scholarsarchive.byu.edu/cgi/viewcontent.cgi?article=1221&con text=mphs.

Kalāhiki, Starr Kealaheleokalani. 2022. Interview with the author conducted on January 16, 2022.

Kalakaua, D., and R. M. Daggett. 1888. *The Legends and Myths of Hawaii: The Fables and Folk-Lore of a Strange People*. New York: C. L. Webster.

Kale, Sunaina Keonaona. 2017. *Localness and Indigeneity in Hawaiian Reggae*. PhD diss., University of California, Santa Barbara.

Kalima-Alvarez, Lehua. 2020. Interview with the author conducted on February 11, 2020.

Kam, Ralph Thomas. 2017. "The Gospel Roots of ʻHawaiʻi Aloha.'" *Hawaiian Journal of History* 51: 5–29.

Kamakau, S. M. 1867. "Ka Moolelo o Na Kamehameha, Helu 52." *Ka Nupepa Kuokoa*, 1867.

Kamanā, Kauanoe, and William H. Wilson. 1990. *Nā Kai ʻEwalu: Beginning Hawaiian Lessons*. Hilo: Hale Kuamoʻo, University of Hawaiʻi at Hilo.

Kameʻeleihiwa, Lilikalā. 1992. *Native Land and Foreign Desires*. Honolulu: Bishop Museum Press.

Kamohoaliʻi, Kumu Micah. 2020. Interview with the author conducted on June 15, 2020.

Kanahele, George S. 1982. *Hawaiian Renaissance*. Honolulu: Project WAIAHA.

———. 1992. *Kū Kanaka, Stand Tall: A Search for Hawaiian Values*. Honolulu: Kolowalu Books, University of Hawaiʻi Press.

Kanahele, Kekuhi. 1998. *Kekuhi*. Audio CD. Honolulu: Mountain Apple Company.

Ka Nupepa Kuokoa. 1861. "He Mele Hou no keʻLii o kakou!" *Ka Nupepa Kuokoa*, December 16, 1861, Buke 1, Helu 5 edition.

———. 1862. "He Mele Aupuni Hou." *Ka Nupepa Kuokoa*, February 9, 1862, Buke 1, Helu 11 edition.

Kauanui, J. Kehaulani. 2008. *Hawaiian Blood: Colonialism and the Politics of Sovereignty and Indigeneity*. Durham: Duke University Press.

Kaʻupu, Charles Jr. 2011. "Aloha From Hawaiʻi." In *Indian Voices : Listening to Native Americans*, edited by Alison Owings, 321–332. Piscataway: Rutgers University Press.

Keesing, Roger M. 1989. "Creating the Past: Custom and Identity in the Contemporary Pacific." *The Contemporary Pacific* 1 (1 & 2): 19–42.

———. 1991. "Reply to Trask." *The Contemporary Pacific* 3 (Spring): 168.

Kelman, Ari Y. 2010. "Rethinking the Soundscape: A Critical Genealogy of a Key Term in Sound Studies." *The Senses and Society* 5, no. 2 (2010): 212–34.

KHON2 News. 2019. "Costs for Mauna Kea Reach $12.2 Million." *KHON News*, December 19, 2019. https://www.khon2.com/local-news/costs-for-mauna-kea-reach-11-3-million/.

Kimura, Larry L. 2002. *Nā Mele Kau o Ka Māhele Mua o Ka Moʻolelo ʻo Hiʻiakaikapoliopele Na Joseph M. Poepoe: He Kālailaina Me Ke Kālele Ma Luna o Nā Kuʻinaiwi Kaulua*. MA thesis, University of Hawaiʻi at Hilo.

———. 2019. "The Beginning of Ka Leo Hawaiʻi." Hale Kuamoʻo, University of Hawaiʻi at Hilo. http://ulukau.org/kaniaina/?a=p&p=history&%20.

KITV 4 Web Staff. 2019. "Janet Jackson Stands in Solidarity with TMT Opponents." https://www.kitv.com/story/41357406/janet-jacket-stands-in-solidarity-with-tmt-opponents.

Kōmike Huaʻōlelo. 2003. *Māmaka Kaiao: A Modern Hawaiian Vocabulary*. Honolulu: University of Hawaiʻi Press.

Kuwada, Bryan Kamaoli, and Noʻu Revilla. 2020. "Introduction: Mana from the Mauna." *Biography* 43 (3): 515–26.

Lahr, John. 2013. "Songs of Angry Men." *New Yorker*, February 25, 2013. https://www.newyorker.com/magazine/2013/02/25/songs-of-angry-men.

Liliʻuokalani, L. 1964. *Hawaii's Story by Hawaii's Queen*. Rutland: Tuttle Publishing.

Linnekin, Jocelyn. 1983. "Defining Tradition: Variations on the Hawaiian Identity." *American Ethnologist* 10 (2): 241–52.

———. 1991. "Cultural Invention and the Dilemma of Authenticity." *American Anthropologist* 93 (2): 446–49.

Loughran, Maureen. 2008. "'But What If They Call the Police?' Applied Ethnomusicology and Urban Activism in the United States." *Musicological Annual* 44 (1): 51–68.

Lovell, Blaze. 2019. "UH Will Allow Students to Earn Credit While Protesting TMT." *Civil Beat*, August 6, 2019. https://www.civilbeat.org/2019/08/uh-will -allow-students-to-earn-credit-while-protesting-tmt/.

Lum, Zachary Alakaʻi. 2020. Interview with the author conducted on April 9, 2020.

MacKay, Gail. 2014. "'Learning to Listen to a Quiet Way of Telling': A Study of Cree Counselling Discourse Patterns in Maria Campbell's Halfbreed." In *Indigenous Poetics in Canada*, edited by Neal McLeod, 351–70. Ontario: Wilfrid Laurier University Press.

Maile, David Uahikeaikaleiʻohu. 2016. "On the Violence of the Thirty Meter Telescope and the Dakota Access Pipeline." *Hot Spots, Fieldsights*, December 22, (2016). https://culanth.org/fieldsights/on-the-violence-of-the -thirty-meter-telescope-and-the-dakota-access-pipeline.

———. 2021. "On Being Late: Cruising Mauna Kea and Unsettling Technoscientific Conquest in Hawaiʻi." *American Indian Culture and Research Journal* 45 (1): 95–122.

Makekau-Whittaker, Kalani. 2020. Interview with the author conducted on May 17, 2020.

———. 2023. Phone conversation with the author on March 26, 2023.

Makuakāne, Kenneth. 2020. Interview with the author conducted on April 24, 2020.

Maly, Kepa, and Onaona Maly. 2005. "Mauna Kea, Ka Piko Kaulana o Ka ʻĀina (Mauna Kea, the Famous Summit of the Land)." http://www.ulukau.org/elib /cgi-bin/library?a=p&p=redirect&d=D0&rurl=/elib/collect/mauna/index /assoc/D0.dir/book.pdf.

Martin, Liko. n.d. "Liko Martin." Accessed February 19, 2022. https://www .likomartin.org/page2.

Mauna Medic Healers. n.d. "The Mauna Medic Healers Facebook Page." Facebook. Accessed March 28, 2021. https://www.facebook.com/Mauna MedicHealersHui/.

Mayo-Harp, Maria Isabel. 1994. *National Anthems and Identities: The Role of National Anthems in the Formation Process of National Identities*. Ottawa: National Library of Canada, Bibliothèque nationale du Canada.

McLeod, Neal, ed. 2014. *Indigenous Poetics in Canada*. Indigenous Studies. Ontario: Wilfrid Laurier University Press.

Meyer, Manulani Aluli. 1998. *Native Hawaiian Epistemology: Contemporary Narratives.* EdD thesis, Harvard University.

———. 2001a. "Acultural Assumptions of Empiricism: A Native Hawaiian Critique." *Canadian Journal of Native Education* 25 (2): 188.

———. 2001b. "Our Own Liberation: Reflections on Hawaiian Epistemology." *The Contemporary Pacific* 13 (1): 124–48.

———. 2003. *Hoʻoulu: Our Time of Becoming: Collected Early Writings of Manulani Meyer.* Honolulu: ʻAi Pōhaku Press.

———. 2008. "Hawaiian Epistemology and the Triangulation of Meaning." In *Handbook of Critical and Indigenous Methodologies,* edited by N. K. Denzin, Y. S. Lincoln, and L. T. Smith, 148–164. New York: Routledge.

Moorfield, John C. 2003. *Te Aka Online Māori Dictionary.* Auckland: Te Ipukarea.

Myron B. Thompson School of Social Work. n.d. "Celebrating Our 80th Anniversary, Myron B. Thompson School of Social Work, University of Hawaiʻi at Mānoa." Accessed March 28, 2022. https://manoa.hawaii.edu /thompson/80th-anniversary-publication/.

Nogelmeier, Marvin Puakea. 2003. "Mai Paʻa i Ka Leo: Historical Voice in Hawaiian Primary Materials, Looking Forward and Listening Back." PhD diss., University of Hawaiʻi at Mānoa.

O'Connell, John Morgan. 2010. "An Ethnomusicological Approach to Music and Conflict." In *Music and Conflict,* edited by John Morgan O'Connell and Salwa El-Shawan Castelo-Branco, 4-14. Champaign: University of Illinois Press.

Office of the High Commissioner United Nations Human Rights. n.d. "About Human Rights Defenders." Accessed June 9, 2021. https://www.ohchr.org/EN /Issues/SRHRDefenders/Pages/Defender.aspx.

Oliveira, Katrina-Ann R. K. N. 2014. *Ancestral Places: Understanding Kanaka Geographies.* Corvalis: Oregon State University Press.

Oliveros, Pauline. 2005. *Deep Listening: A Composer's Sound Practice.* Lincoln, NE: Deep Listening Publications.

Osher, Wendy. 2019. "Hawaiʻi AG Addresses Concerns Surrounding LRAD 'Sound Cannon.'" *Maui Now* (blog). July 19, 2019. https://mauinow.com/2019/07/19 /hawaii-ag-addresses-concerns-surrounding-lrad-sound-cannon/.

Osorio, Jamaica Heolimeleikalani. 2020. Interview with the author conducted on April 20, 2020.

———. 2021. *Remembering Our Intimacies: Moʻolelo, Aloha ʻĀina, and Ea.* Minneapolis: University of Minnesota Press.

Osorio, Jonathan Kay Kamakawiwoʻole. 2002. *Dismembering Lahui: A History of the Hawaiian Nation to 1887.* Honolulu: University of Hawaiʻi Press.

———. 2016a. "Episode 2: The Meaning of Aloha ʻĀina with Professor Jon Osorio." Interview by Julia Steele. https://www.hawaiipublicradio.org/show /aloha-aina/2016-02-05/episode-2-the-meaning-of-aloha-aina-with-professor -jon-osorio.

———. 2016b. "Written Direct Testimony B.07a." https://dlnr.hawaii.gov/mk
/files/2016/10/B.07a-Osorio-WDT.pdf.

Parshall, Peter. 1999. "The Art of Memory and the Passion." *The Art Bulletin* 81 (3): 456–72.

Perea, Jessica Bissett, and Gabriel Solis. 2019. "Music, Indigeneity, and Colonialism in the Americas." *Journal of the Society for American Music* 13 (4): 401–10.

Perea, John-Carlos. 2014. *Intertribal Native American Music in the United States: Experiencing Music, Expressing Culture.* New York: Oxford University Press.

Perez, Andre. 2020. Interview with the author conducted on April 7, 2020.

———. 2022. Facebook Messenger conversation with the author on June 9, 2022.

———. 2023. Facebook Messenger conversation with the author on June 3, 2023.

Pettan, Svanibor. 2010. "Music in War, Music for Peace: Experiences in Applied Ethnomusicology." In *Music and Conflict*, edited by John Morgan O'Connell and Salwa El-Shawan Castelo-Branco, 177–192. New York: Oxford University Press.

Pignataro, Anthony. 2017. "Maui County Mayor Alan Arakawa Denounces Iao Valley Sacred Rocks." *MauiTime*, February 17, 2017.

Post, Elizabeth "Bam." 2022. Interview with the author conducted on March 2, 2022.

Pratt, Mary Louise. 2012. "Arts of the Contact Zone." In *Negotiating Academic Literacies: Teaching and Learning Across Languages and Cultures*, edited by Ruth Spack, Vivian Zamel, 171–186. New York: Routelege.

Protect Kahoʻolawe ʻOhana. n.d. "About Us." Protect Kahoʻolawe ʻOhana. Accessed June 17, 2020. http://www.protectkahoolaweohana.org/history.html.

Pukui, Mary Kawena. 1972. *Nānā i Ke Kumu*. Queen Liliʻuokalani Children's Center Publication. Honolulu: Hui Hānai.

———. 1983. *ʻŌlelo Noʻeau: Hawaiian Proverbs & Poetical Sayings*. Bernice P. Bishop Museum Special Publication, No. 71. Honolulu: Bishop Museum Press.

Pukui, Mary Kawena, and Samuel H. Elbert. 1986. *Hawaiian Dictionary: Hawaiian-English, English-Hawaiian*. Honolulu: University of Hawaiʻi Press.

Punahele. 2022. Interview with the author conducted on August 19, 2022.

Pūnua, Lee Ann Ānuenue. 2020. Interview with the author conducted on February 11, 2020.

———. 2021. Facebook Messenger conversation with the author on April 3, 2021.

———. 2023. Facebook Messenger conversation with the author on June 3, 2023.

Puuhonua o Puʻuhuluhulu. 2019. "Untitled Facebook Post." Facebook, July 26, 2019. https://www.facebook.com/puuhuluhulu/posts/2110662745903698.

Quiamzon, Courtney. 2020. "Keola Nakanishi//Mana Maoli." Podcast. https://open.spotify.com/episode/7xa7M8Rsv2q5636tIRexNb?si=BhBNP086RS28yI9xcWMXRQ.

Rice, Timothy. 2014. "Ethnomusicology in Times of Trouble." *Yearbook for Traditional Music* 46: 191–209.

Richardson, Māhealani. 2022. "Ige: Mauna Kea Stewardship Bill Would 'End Astronomy' on Hawaii Island." *Hawai'i News Now*, April 5, 2022. https://www.hawaiinewsnow.com/2022/04/06/ige-mauna-kea-stewardship-bill-it-is-intended-end-astronomy/.

Rios, Hāwane. 2020. Interview with the author conducted on May 15, 2020.

Roberts, Helen H. 1967. *Ancient Hawaiian Music*. New York: Dover.

Robinson, Dylan. 2020. *Hungry Listening: Resonant Theory for Indigenous Sound Studies*. Indigenous Americas. Minneapolis: University of Minnesota Press.

Rollmann, Rhea. 2016. "Protesters? Or Land Protectors?" *The Independent* (blog). October 28, 2016. https://theindependent.ca/to-each-their-own/protesters-or-land-protectors/.

Romaine, Suzanne. 2000. *Language in Society: An Introduction to Sociolinguistics*. 2nd ed. New York: Oxford University Press.

Said, Edward W. 2014. *Orientalism*. New York: Knopf Doubleday Publishing Group.

Sai-Dudoit, Kau'i, and Blaine Namahana Tolentino. 2022. "Aloha 'Āina: From the Historical Record." *Hawaiian Journal of Law & Politics* 4: 5–27.

Sheldon, John G. M., E. L. Like, and J. K. Prendergast. 1996. *Ka Puke Mo'olelo o Hon. Iosepa K. Nāwahī*. Hilo: Hale Kuamo'o, Ka Haka 'Ula o Ke'elikōlani.

Silva, Noenoe K. 2004. *Aloha Betrayed: Native Hawaiian Resistance to American Colonialism*. American Encounters/Global Interactions. Durham: Duke University Press.

———. 2014. "Hawaiian Literature in Hawaiian." In *The Oxford Handbook of Indigenous American Literature*, edited by James Howard Cox and Daniel Heath Justice, 102–117. New York: Oxford University Press.

———. 2016. "Mana Hawai'i: An Examination of Political Uses of the Word Mana in Hawaiian." In *New Mana: Transformations of a Classic Concept in Pacific Languages and Cultures*, edited by Matt Tomlinson and Ty P. Kāwika Tengan, 37–54. Canberra: ANU Press.

———. 2017. *The Power of the Steel-Tipped Pen: Reconstructing Native Hawaiian Intellectual History*. Durham: Duke University Press.

———. 2023. "He Mele Hānau no ka Lāhui." *'Ōiwi: A Native Hawaiian Journal* 5. In-press.

Small, Christopher. 2011. *Musicking: The Meanings of Performing and Listening*. Middleton: Wesleyan University Press.

Star-Advertiser Staff. 2022. "Gov. David Ige Makes First Visit to Mauna Kea since TMT Protests Began." *Honolulu Star-Advertiser*, July 23, 2022, online edition. https://www.staradvertiser.com/2019/07/23/breaking-news/gov-ige-asks-mayor-kim-to-lead-effort-for-peaceful-resolution-on-mauna-kea/.

Stillman, Amy Ku'uleialoha. 1999. "Aloha Aina: New Perspectives on 'Kaulana Na Pua.'" *Hawaiian Journal of History* 33: 83–99.

———. 2005. "Textualizing Hawaiian Music." *American Music* 23 (1): 69–94.

————. 2020. Interview with the author conducted on March 26, 2020.

Takatsugi, Chad. 2020. Interview with the author conducted on February 17, 2020.

————. 2022. "Question About Kūhaʻo Maunakea." Email reply to the author on May 28, 2022.

Tatar, Elizabeth. 1982. *Nineteenth Century Hawaiian Chant. Vol. 33. Pacific Anthropological Records*. Honolulu: Department of Anthropology, Bernice P. Bishop Museum.

Tatofi, Josh. 2020. Interview with the author conducted on February 25, 2020.

Teaiwa, Katarina. 2014. *Consuming Ocean Island: Stories of People and Phosphate from Banaba*. Tracking Globalization. Bloomington: Indiana University Press

Teaiwa, Teresia. 2014. "The Ancestors We Get to Choose: White Influences." In *Theorizing Native Studies*, edited by Audra Simpson and Andrea Smith, 43–55. Durham: Duke University Press.

Te Huia, Awanui. 2016. "Pākehā Learners of Māori Language Responding to Racism Directed toward Māori." *Journal of Cross-Cultural Psychology* 47 (5): 734–50.

Testa, Francisco Jose. 2003. *Buke Mele Lahui*. Honolulu: Hawaiian Historical Society.

Teves, Stephanie Nohelani. 2018. *Defiant Indigeneity: The Politics of Hawaiian Performance*. Critical Indigeneities. Chapel Hill: University of North Carolina Press.

Thomas, Allan. 2007. "'Pokarekare': An Overlooked New Zealand Folksong?" *Journal of Folklore Research* 44 (2): 227–37.

Thornton, Russell. 1997. "Tribal Membership Requirements and the Demography of 'Old' and 'New' Native Americans." *Population Research and Policy Review* 16(1): 33–42.

Titon, Jeff Todd. 2015. "Applied Ethnomusicology: A Descriptive and Historical Account." In *The Oxford Handbook of Applied Ethnomusicology*, edited by Svanibor Pettan and Jeff Todd Titon, 4–29. New York: Oxford University Press.

Trask, Haunani Kay. 1991. "Natives and Anthropologists: The Colonial Struggle." *The Contemporary Pacific* 3 (Spring): 159–67.

————. 1999. "Decolonizing Hawaiian Literature." In *Inside Out: Literature, Cultural Politics, and Identity in the New Pacific*, edited by Vilsoni Hereniko and Rob Wilson, 167–182. Oxford: Littlefield Publishers.

Treaty Times. 1995. "Return to Sender! The Fiscal Envelope Policy: Divide and Rule for the '90s." *Treaty Times*, February 1995.

Truax, Barry. 2001. *Acoustic Communication*. New York: Ablex Publishing Corporation.

Turner, Kimo. 1976. "Profile Artists, George Helm." *Haʻilono Mele*, 1976. http://ulukau.org/gsdl2.80/collect/hailono/cgi-bin/hailono?a=pdf&d=DHMN00200 6.1.3&dl=1&sim=Screen2Image.

Uechi, Colleen. 2017. "40 Years after Men's Disappearance at Sea, Their Vision for Kahoolawe Has Become a Reality." *Maui News*, March 5, 2017.

University of Hawaiʻi News. 2022. "Astronomy Impact on Hawaiʻi Even Greater with 'Spillover' Effects." https://www.hawaii.edu/news/2022/04/24/uhero-astronomy-economy-spillover-effects/.

Vaughan, Palani. 1977. "Iā ʻOe E Ka Lā - Vol. Three." Mountain Apple Company. https://www.mountainapplecompany.com/palani-vaughan-ioe-e-ka-l/volume-three.

Wall Jr., James A., and Ronda Roberts Callister. 1995. "Conflict and Its Management." *Journal of Management* 21 (3): 515–58.

Weinstein, Deena. 2000. *Heavy Metal: The Music and Its Culture*. Boston: Da Capo Press.

Weintraub, Andrew N. 1998. "Jawaiian Music and Local Cultural Identity in Hawaiʻi." In *Sound Alliances: Indigenous Peoples, Cultural Politics and Popular Music in the Pacific*, edited by Philip Hayward, 79. Washington, DC: Cassell.

Wendt, Albert. 1982. "Towards a New Oceania." In *Writers in East-West Encounter*, edited by Guy Amirthanayagam, 202–15. London: The MacMillan Press.

Williams, Ronald Jr. 2010. "Freedom Fighter." *Hana Hou!* May 2010.

Wilson, Alex, Bronwyn Lee Carlson, Acushla Sciascia, et al. 2017. "Reterritorialising Social Media: Indigenous People Rise Up." *Australasian Journal of Information Systems* 21:1–4.

Wilson-Hokowhitu, Nālani. 2019. *The Past Before Us: Moʻokūʻauhau as Methodology*. Indigenous Pacifics. Honolulu: University of Hawaiʻi Press.

Wong, Laiana. 1999. "Authenticity and the Revitalization of Hawaiian." *Anthropology & Education Quarterly* 30 (1): 94–115.

Wong-Kalu, Hinaleimoana. 2014. "Kumu Hina." https://kumuhina.com.

———. 2016. "Mele Kū Haʻaheo e Kuʻu Hawaiʻi." Kamakakoi. March 6, 2016. https://www.kamakakoi.com/mele.

———. 2020. Interview with the author conducted on April 4, 2020.

———. 2021. "Meet Native Hawaiian Māhū Activist Hinaleimoana Kwai Kong Wong-Kalu." Interview by Alexis Cheung. https://atmos.earth/kapaemahu-hinaleimoana-kwai-kong-wong-kalu-film-interview.

Wong-Wilson, Noe Noe. 2022. Interview with the author conducted on April 4, 2020.

Yglesias, Jaz Kaiwikoʻo, and Yuki Kaʻea Lyons. 2020. Interview with the author conducted on March 2, 2020.

Younging, Gregory. 2018. *Elements of Indigenous Style: A Guide for Writing by and about Indigenous Peoples*. Edmonton: Brush Education.

Yuen, Leilehua. 2022. Personal correspondence with the author on April 8, 2022.

INDEX

JOSEPH KEOLA DONAGHY is Associate Professor of Music and Faculty Coordinator of Music Studies and the Institute of Hawaiian Music at the University of Hawai'i Maui College. He is a Nā Hōkū Hanohano Award-winning composer, performer, and producer of Hawaiian music.

For Indiana University Press

Tony Brewer, Artist and Book Designer

Allison Chaplin, Acquisitions Editor

Sophia Hebert, Assistant Acquisitions Editor

Samantha Heffner, Marketing and Publicity Manager

Brenna Hosman, Production Coordinator

Katie Huggins, Production Manager

David Miller, Lead Project Manager/Editor

Dan Pyle, Online Publishing Manager

Jennifer Witzke, Senior Artist and Book Designer